Past Lives & Present Purpose

Reincarnation and the Illumination of Your Soul

Lilan Laishley, Ph.D.

Copyright © 2024 Lilan Laishley

All Rights Reserved

Year of the Book
135 Glen Avenue
Glen Rock, PA 17327

ISBN: 978-1-64649-406-4 (paperback)
ISBN: 978-1-64649-407-1 (ebook)

This book or parts thereof may not be reproduced in any form, stored in any retrieval system, or transmitted in any form by any means – electronic, mechanical, photocopy, recording, or otherwise – without prior written permission of the publisher, except as provided by United States of America copyright law.

Cover image by CoPilot Designer. Cover design by PixelStudio.

Image credits:
The Fairy of the Moon, Hermann von Kaulbach, ca. 1891.
The Great Chain of Being, Robert Fludd, 1617.
Footprints, licensed from Adobe Stock.
The Metropolis of Atlantis, Professor Galanopoulos.
Twelve-pointed star, licensed from Depositphotos.
Desert landscape with statue face, licensed from Depositphotos.
Mayan warrior, licensed from Depositphotos.
Shaman, ca. 11,000-year-old cave painting, Algier.
Monk's walking dress, *The National and Domestic History of England*, vol. 2, 1878.
Château de Montségur, fallen during the Crusades, March 16, 1244.
Hipparchus in the Observatory of Alexandria, Agnes Giberne, 1898.
Saint Clare of Assisi, medieval woodcut.
Phases of the moon, lunar cycle, licensed from Depositphotos.
Four elements of nature, licensed from Depositphotos.

I dedicate this book to my family for providing me roots,

and my husband Bill Harman, for giving me wings.

Contents

Preface 1

Chapter 1: The Journey 3

Chapter 2: Gnosis – Knowing Your Soul 11

Chapter 3: The Lives – Reincarnation Up-Close and Personal 19

The Young Soul: In the Shadow of the Pyramids

Chapter 4: Being Human, Chosen One – Atlantis, c. 6000 BCE 29

Chapter 5: The Good Man, A Light in the Desert – Egypt, c. 1500 BCE ... 57

Chapter 6: Heart of a Warrior – Maya, c. 300 CE 77

Coming of Age

Chapter 7: Twisted Heart of a Shaman – Amazon, c. 600 CE 89

Chapter 8: Priest's Lesson in Humility – Germany, c. 1000 CE 107

Chapter 9: Cathar Trapped in a Vice Grip – Montsegur, France, 1240 CE 125

Great Gifts / Great Dangers

Chapter 10: Astronomer, Too Smart for My Own Good – Italy, c. 1350 CE 161

Chapter 11: Herbalist, Wise Woman or Witch – France, c. 1450 CE 183

Wrapping Up

Chapter 12: The Soul's Journey, An Overview 205

Chapter 13: Body, Mind, Soul, & Spirit 213

Chapter 14: Living an Illuminated Life, The Power and Purpose of
    Knowing Your Soul's Past Lives 229

Preface

Thank you for reading this up-close and personal exploration of reincarnation. This book is written mostly by me, Lilan's Soul. I felt that by sharing my past lives, you could better understand the power and purpose of the Soul's evolutionary journey in the physical body.

We often hear about the Soul but we might not really understand what that means or what reincarnation is and how it occurs, so I wanted to give you an insider's perspective. Not a religious, or scientific, or academic viewpoint, but rather the process of reincarnation from a more intimate observation, mine.

There are millions of people in the world who believe in reincarnation. Many of them remember their past lives and have a profound connection to their Soul. Lilan is one of these. She was born as a sensitive, spiritually-oriented person. She has spent her life getting to know her Soul and blending it into daily life. She studied the Soul during visits to sacred sites around the world, in her PhD in Religious Studies, her Master's in Counseling, and through certification as a Past Life Therapist. She has led countless regression sessions with clients and participated in many herself.

So when I told Lilan I wanted to explain the process of reincarnation by sharing my past lives in a book, she agreed to do the work. Most of the words are mine, which she wrote down. These are my stories, since Lilan, the human being, did not live in Atlantis, or ancient Egypt. I greatly appreciate her interest and commitment to this project. And I am pleased that she states she has learned much from my perspective, which leads me to believe other readers will as well.

I share the reality of reincarnation in the hope that it awakens you to your own past lives, your deeper history, and your connection to Soul and Spirit. Thank you for reading, and may you discover in these pages the magic and mystery of life. Now let's hear from Lilan as your guide.

1

The Journey

Lilan here. Many people talk about the Soul. But what is the Soul? If everyone has one, why is it so elusive? Perhaps our Soul is easy to find, but we haven't been given the tools or encouragement to seek it. From a very young age, these were the questions I asked. As life went on, I kept asking them, following the trail wherever it led.

I was always seeking my Soul. That pursuit has taken me on a magical journey. I hope my Soul's past life stories will awaken you to your own Soul and its stories, hopes, fears, and purpose. By seeing my search as a mirror of your own, you can learn how the Soul masters being human and becomes illuminated through the path of reincarnation.

This journey has taught me that life is so much greater than any of us ever imagined, and the Soul is the part of us that knows this. Our Soul is the essence of who we are – an immortal spiritual being whose existence in time, space, and multiple dimensions expands our sense of self. Our Souls have stories they want to share with us so they send us clues in many forms, including a familiar experience of *déjà vu*, a dream, a visit from an ancestor, or a meeting with an angel.

I hope to inspire you to seek your Soul to learn the special way it communicates, and discover its stories so you can recognize its actions in your life, and expand your sense of reality to see your Soul's history and its effects on your current life. You can learn how the Soul connects with your Body, Mind, and Spirit, and realize that there are allies in your current life who are here to help you and are part of your Soul group. You can also learn to recognize your adversaries, those who try to block your growth, and how to avoid them.

Journey with Your Soul

The Soul is not something you have, it is something you *are*. You are not a Body with a Soul; you are a Soul with a Body. It is time to switch perspectives. This is key: To begin to live life from the perspective of your Soul, not your Body.

As human beings who exist as physical bodies that live in a particular time and space, we tend to be tied to the notion of a physical world that we can see, touch, taste, smell, and hear. Our experience of time and space becomes limited to the physical world around us as we count time by years, marking the passage from birth to death with milestones of significant events. But it is important to expand our sense of self beyond this current space and time, and to understand that we are on a much longer journey than any singular life can contain.

> *The Soul is not something you have, it is something you are.*

Once you know your Soul evolves through multiple lifetimes, it gives you a greater awareness than the ninety or so years of existence in your current life. You might think your life is like a book that ends with your death. But instead, your life is only one chapter in a much longer book of living and the story does not end with your death. This means every action you take can have greater consequences and a longer trajectory than you might at first suspect. You have lifetimes, not days or years, to learn from your actions and grow in awareness. Soul evolution also gives you greater emotional perspective and compassion for others, and for yourself. You do not need to live in guilt or shame, for the action that created the guilt is much smaller when put into the viewpoint of multiple lifetimes.

I feel that this time in history needs new direction. People are lost and have forgotten their way. The guideposts that used to exist for humans on their journey through life are disappearing. Religion is no longer dominant, as the number of people who attend places of worship has dropped to less than 50 percent in the US and UK. School is no longer a stable center for children after the Covid pandemic moved education and friendships online, increasing a mental health crisis in adolescents. Climate change and mass shootings have undermined our sense of security.

> *The guideposts that used to exist for humans on their journey through life are disappearing.*

We need a new map and a new compass to navigate these changing times. Your past lives are the map, and your Soul is your compass. If you can remember that you are more than this physical body and have a deep connection to the sacred, you can find your way. There will be adventures, upheavals, joys, and sorrows along the path; there always are. But you are not navigating the landscape alone. You will always have your Soul and the connection to your Spirit to sustain you.

The purpose of this book is to help you connect with your Soul, to return it to its position as navigator of this life journey. You can establish a relationship with your Soul that is as deep and real as any relationship in your present life… and even more, a relationship that lasts from birth to death, and beyond.

Meet Your Guide for the Journey: Lilan

The Soul, and its evolutionary journey through reincarnation, has been my guiding light. The Soul has its own language and communicates through symbols, images, dreams, imagination, signs, and synchronicities that are expressed in countless ways. I studied the language of the Soul in tarot, astrology, psychology, myth, and religious symbolism. I have explored pathways to my Soul through dreams, past lives, active imagination, ritual, and shamanism. Each path led me deeper and deeper into myself. Every class taken or degree earned provided a way to study the vast expression of the spiritual world as it related to my own search for Soul.

I now share a bit of that search with you. I grew up in a small town in West Virginia, United States. As an imaginative and intuitive child, I crossed the boundary of the physical world into the realm of the Soul many times in dreams. The supernatural was not a big topic in our home, but it did come up periodically and so I was familiar with the idea that people could survive after death. I heard the tale of my grandmother who saw her brother – who was away at war – walk though her kitchen at the same time he died as if to say goodbye to her. As children we played with the Ouija board, asking questions and seeking answers. My mother warned us not to mess around with the Ouija board since it was a way for disembodied spirits to enter a space. I remember spending hours walking alone through my tree-lined neighborhood pondering such questions as: *If God is really good, how could he condemn people to an eternity of Hell?* And especially, *When I come back, do I want to be a bird or a tree?* This question really absorbed me, since I knew birds could fly and were free to move about. Yet trees had deep roots and were the home for birds. Did I want to fly free or be rooted? The question implied that I knew I would "come back," though reincarnation was never discussed in the Christian church I attended.

> *We need a new map and a new compass to navigate these changing times.*

I went to college at the time of the Vietnam protests and lived the life of a free-spirited hippie. After graduating at the local university with a Bachelor's degree in Counseling, I moved to Cincinnati, Ohio, the nearest big city. I decided to be a bird! I was a waitress in a restaurant run by a kundalini ashram where I learned to meditate and was introduced to astrology. I continued to follow the guidance of Spirit which came in inspirations, dreams, signs, and synchronicities, for example, running into an old friend I hadn't seen in years who was moving to a new city and could use a roommate. Next I moved to Boston, Massachusetts, at that time a center of metaphysical knowledge. I studied astrology with Isabel Hickey and other notables and became immersed in the language of astrology, reincarnation, and other spiritual concepts.

After several years in Boston I moved to New York City, where in addition to studying myth with Joseph Campbell, who did weekend lectures on a variety of topics, I earned my Master's degree in Counseling from Hunter College. My thesis, "Creative Visualization," wove together Soul's evolutionary journey as described by Major Arcana of the Tarot with the psychology of Carl Jung.

During my master's work I trained with Dr. Morris Netherton in Past Life Therapy and was certified as a Past Life Therapist in 1982. Using relaxation and hypnosis, I regressed clients into their past lives, and thus have extensive firsthand experience of how events of previous lifetimes create karmic patterns and soul wounds that impact the current life. I saw the spiritual and psychological healing that occurs when one becomes aware of the influence of those prior lives on the present one.

Soul pain and suffering can express itself physically and psychologically.

Equally important, I experienced many past life sessions myself, which was a required part of the certification. It was in my own sessions that many of the memories of my past lives occurred that I now share with you.

Soul pain and suffering can express itself physically and psychologically. To better understand this, I became a Licensed Professional Counselor and worked in a psychiatric hospital and addiction treatment centers. I also gained expertise in dream analysis, since dreams are a direct way to dialogue with the Soul.

Always aware of the religious and spiritual perspective of the Soul, I took an academic interest and earned a Ph.D. in Religious Studies from the University of Pittsburgh in 2004. I studied rituals, symbols, the history of philosophy and science, alchemy, cosmology, labyrinths, and religious diversity.

For many years I developed the analytical mind of an academic and taught religion, philosophy, and humanities at Carnegie Mellon University, the University of Pittsburgh, and the University of Tennessee at Chattanooga. I spent one summer teaching religion in eight countries on the floating global university, Semester at Sea. I have presented papers on religion, ritual, labyrinths, and astrology at conferences, and have been published in academic journals. My book, *The Labyrinth as Sacred Cosmos: Rituals of Unity and Diversity,* explores how labyrinth rituals reenact the symbolic sacred space of various religions and belief systems.

But one needs more than a bright mind to understand the Soul, for the Soul does not exist in isolation, nor is it able to be objectively studied with a critical eye. The Soul must be experienced.

In addition to past life therapy sessions, I sought experience in travels to over 20 countries, exploring sacred sites like the ancient megaliths of Stonehenge, Newgrange, and Carnac; the prehistoric caves in Lascaux, France, and Altamira, Spain; Celtic sites in Ireland; Viking sites in Iceland; and the historic churches of Orthodox Christianity in Poland and Russia. I explored Islam in Morocco, Hinduism in the temples of India, and Native American ritual and shamanism during my ten years living in the Arizona desert. I learned Buddhism with the Dalai Lama, meditation with Sadhguru, shamanism with Sandra Ingerman, and was a founding member and Director of Research of The Labyrinth Society.

> *The Soul does not exist in isolation, nor is it able to be objectively studied. The Soul must be experienced.*

I am also a teaching and consulting Astrologer. I have interpreted countless astrological charts and taught many classes and written articles for popular press and academic journals in my more than 40 years as an Astrologer. I have been publishing a monthly MoonLetter on the Full Moon since 2010, where I use current events to describe how to balance the opposing forces of the Sun and Moon into a place of harmony within.

I have been single-minded in my search for the Soul. Now, in this book, I share my insights with you, not as a scholarly work, but rather as the intimate sharing of one Soul's evolutionary journey through eight past lives. I hope you will find these personal stories and teachings inspiring as they gently guide you to deepen your connection to your own Soul.

Where Are You on Your Journey?

Maybe you are a spiritual seeker and have made the search for the sacred a central part of your life. Maybe you sample from multiple spiritual practices, like tasting from a great buffet of the sacred. If you already feel the presence of your Soul in your life, perhaps in your dreams or through insights, then this book will expand on the connection you already have and help you explore new avenues and sensibilities. If you are new to your spiritual quest, then this book can help you find your way.

Perhaps you were brought up in an organized religious tradition that described your Soul as the eternal part that was your entry into everlasting life, either in Heaven or Hell. These religious traditions contain value in that they provide prayers to speak to God, ethical guidelines to navigate life, and rituals to connect you to the sacred. But for a variety of reasons you may have left the religious tradition of your youth and are no longer certain if these pathways are still relevant. The freedom gained by leaving family traditions may have also created a sense of loss, emptiness, or a spiritual longing. Perhaps you yearn to experience something deeper than the push of daily life. If you are missing the spiritual connection of religious tradition, you can discover new ways to connect to your spiritual self and bring it back into your life according to your own needs and desires, not someone else's dictates.

Discover new ways to connect to your spiritual self, according to your own needs and desires.

2

Gnosis: Knowing Your Soul

Reincarnation is the principle that after the death of the physical body we currently inhabit, our Soul is reborn into another body in another time and place. We are born, we die, and we are reborn many times over thousands of years, making us time travelers of sorts. We carry the experiences, knowledge, hopes, and fears of each lifetime forward into the next, storing this extended history deep in our Unconscious memory. These memories are available to us, like a time capsule we can open that reveals the history of our Soul's past.

There are many religions which include the concept of reincarnation as a fundamental belief. Among these are Hinduism, Buddhism, Sikhism, Jainism, Shinto, and Taoism, which make up about 20 percent of the world's population, or nearly 2 billion. Pew surveys from 2021 and 2023 found 33 percent of Christians in the US believe in reincarnation, as well as 43 percent of people who identify as "Spiritual but Not Religious." So if you have an interest in reincarnation, you are certainly not alone. Discovering the full awareness of your history over multiple lifetimes is one of the greatest adventures you can take. And it offers some of the greatest rewards.

Remembering past lives is about learning your Soul's history, a history that influences your present. It is also about making a connection with your Soul and having a relationship with the interior heart of who you are. Once you connect with your Soul through memory of past lives, you gain hidden knowledge and bring dormant powers to your life.

> *Discovering the full awareness of your history over multiple lifetimes is one of the greatest adventures you can take.*

At this point you might be asking: *If I have lived other lifetimes why don't I remember them?* Memory is fleeting, a fragile thing, and there often seems to be no reason as to what we remember and what we forget. This is because memory is tied to emotions, not thinking, or even events. We remember things that please, scare, hurt, anger, and thrill us. We remember that which is important to us. We store those memories in our unconscious, which is the container of emotions and archive of our previous lives. If you want to remember previous lifetimes, you need to get to know and communicate with your unconscious.

We live in a skeptical time. Some might dismiss the recall of a past life as "only your imagination." That implies that the notion you were a Viking warlord in Norway in the 11th century came from a movie you saw as a child about the Vikings, rather than any actual memory of a previous existence. But to denigrate the imagination as simply a tool for fantasy is a misunderstanding of what imagination is and the importance it holds. Imagination accesses and interprets information in the unconscious right hemisphere of the brain, just as intellect accesses and interprets information in the conscious left hemisphere of the brain. *Imagination is a tool equal to intellect.* Both are needed, and both are valid. As you read, pay attention to what comes up in your imagination, and watch later in the day and at night in your dreams, and for synchronicities that occur. By bringing into awareness the past life memories stored in your unconscious, you are building a bridge between the imaginative right and intellectual left hemispheres of your brain. This connection between the two hemispheres is necessary for you to grow in Consciousness.

When you make a connection with your Soul, you have a relationship with the interior heart of who you are. This opens hidden knowledge and brings dormant powers into your life. You develop *Gnosis*, a Greek word which means "knowledge" that comes from direct spiritual experience and intuition. This is an awareness of the divine spirit that is distinct from intellectual knowing or faith. With Gnosis you learn about and know your Soul from experience rather than instructional learning. You know your Soul like you know your mother, not like you know math.

You know your Soul from experience rather than instructional learning.

There are many paths of Gnosis, many ways to expand your vision and perspective, and you may already be doing some of them. There is meditation, when you learn that you are not the thoughts in your Mind and that a spiritual reality exists. There are methods to transcend your Body, such as medicinal plants, dance, and music that let you experience a consciousness outside your body. There are internal worlds that you inhabit, like dreaming and shamanic journeying, that show you the existence of invisible realities outside the material world. There is Astrology, which connects you to the cosmos, lays out the larger patterns of your existence, and points to the lessons you are given to learn. There is a deep connection with the natural world, such as trees and birds, that lets you realize the planet earth is home to many forms of consciousness who are living beings with their own truths. And there is the awareness of the Soul and its continued existence beyond death through reincarnation.

Illumination of the Soul

The principal purpose of our time here on earth is so the Soul can grow in connection to the light of Spirit and express that growth through the thoughts, love, and actions of its human Body. This Soul growth is called Illumination, and the growth for the human is called Consciousness. The ultimate goal of the journey of reincarnation is the Illumination of the Soul and an increase in Consciousness for the human.

Souls evolve at different speeds and therefore people are at different stages in their development and need different experiences to help them grow. Souls are sometimes referred to as young souls or old souls, but this is not to create a sense of competition or rivalry in the reincarnation cycle. It is to recognize that you can't expect the same behavior from a child in kindergarten that you would from a college student. Being aware of the different stages of Soul growth, having compassion for someone else's journey, and helping others along their path are all beneficial.

This wide possibility of what different Souls need for growth makes it hard to judge the way a person chooses to live. Sometimes a Soul just needs a life off. Maybe after a rough lifetime in the 1400s as a warrior, a nice quiet life as a hermit might be what Soul needs. Or after lifetimes of having children, an incarnation as a single and independent woman feels like a necessary relief. The possibilities are endless.

There are no failed lifetimes... even if it seems as if you didn't accomplish all you wanted.

The historical context and cultural circumstances of each lifetime are for the Soul's greatest good so it can learn the next lessons on its journey. No matter what type of Body the Soul inhabits, it has to do the best it can with the vehicle it gets. Sometimes it gets a Mercedes and sometimes it gets an old farm truck. There is no judgment of others, and hopefully there will be more understanding and compassion for ourselves in the challenges we face each life.

The earth journey of your current life is just one step on your process of becoming. It is like a grade in school, where you meet new people, connect with some old friends, have some assignments, some recess periods, and hope to graduate and move on to the next class with knowledge you have gained. Sometimes the class is too difficult, dull, or dangerous, and the circumstances do not support what you need. Overcoming these obstacles is also necessary to learn. Those are lifetimes where you are being forged; they are not failures. There are no failed lifetimes... even if it seems as if you didn't accomplish all you wanted. Actually you can never really accomplish all you want, because there is always a new goal, a new direction, a new curiosity, and after you have finished one task, there is another. Unless your goal is to die, and then you just sit back and wait to die. But we are here to live and to live as fully as we can for as long as we can and to learn as much as we can.

There is a shift in awareness of time as you expand the history of yourself beyond your current years and historical period. In comprehending that you are actually a Soul on an illuminated journey spanning thousands of years, you become able to perceive yourself as much larger than a limited physical body in a particular time and space. You can see your life and lives and the world in the long term. This shift in knowing who you are at a Soul level can also dissolve such barriers as race, age, sex, gender, religion, and nationality, since at some lifetime or another you may have been all of these.

The wisdom, awareness, and intentions of your Soul in this life impact your next rebirth. I do not believe we move backward in our journey. The momentum is always forward, though it takes many lifetimes, often filled with mistakes and lessons that must be addressed in future lifetimes, sometimes over and over again. You will notice plenty of mistakes as you read my Soul's lifetimes. But the momentum is always forward.

Experiencing Karma

The Soul's journey is influenced by karma which is always part of any discussion of reincarnation. Karma, which means "action," is the process by which the consequences of choices and actions made in one life can show up either in the current life or in a future life. Karma is not a method of punishment, which would be, for example, if you kill someone in one lifetime you will be killed in the next.

My experience with past lives, both in my own remembered lifetimes and my work with clients, is that karma is expressed through patterns that develop. To use the example of murder, if you murder in one life it sets potential patterns of anger, hatred, revenge, guilt, or righteousness that will either become more embedded in upcoming lives or unravel, depending on the actions that develop from the karmic pattern. The more we repeat certain actions, the stronger the karmic pattern becomes, like a web that gets woven over and over until the pattern becomes recognizable and influential.

We all have certain tendencies or life patterns. Maybe it is problems with money, bad choices in relationships, working in the healing professions, or enjoying the arts. Many of these tendencies are patterns that have been woven over multiple lifetimes, for good or ill. By understanding the karmic patterns your Soul has developed over previous lives you can decide whether they are patterns you want to strengthen or weaken in your current existence. Through an increase in Consciousness and an understanding of your past lives, these karmic patterns can be gently pulled apart so that they lose influence, or they can be strengthened and built upon to become foundational in your current life.

Karma is the process by which the consequences of choices and actions made in one life can show up either in the current life or in a future life.

One of the things you might discover by learning the stories and history of your Soul is that your Soul has been wounded physically or emotionally, either in this current life or a past life, and it needs healing. The point of reincarnation is for the growth and healing of the Soul, not the punishment. There are always mistakes to make, lessons to be learned, opportunities for growth, chances for failure, regrets, and rewards. Each individual life is a lesson for the Soul and is to be viewed with compassion, not harsh judgment.

3
The Lives:
Reincarnation Up-Close and Personal

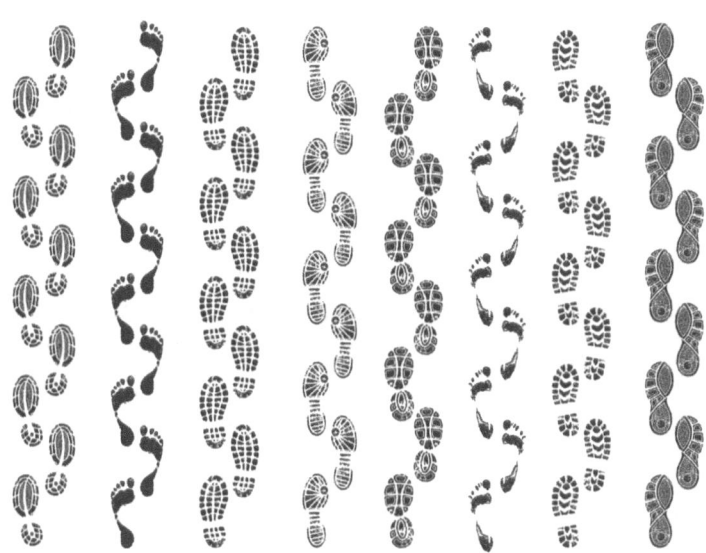

Learning Lessons from Past Lives

The stories that follow will now demonstrate how reincarnation works using eight of my Soul's past lives as an example. Of course, I, Lilan, was never in Atlantis or ancient Egypt. But I, Lilan, now have these memories, for my Soul is in me, and now my Soul's memory is mine. This interconnection between the current physical Body and the eternal Soul is at the heart of the mystery that is reincarnation.

These lifetimes are told as the human I was at that time, providing an insider and intimate look at significant periods of history. The past lives I share are told not from beginning of the life to the end, but through my memory of the most significant event that encapsulates that life. Each life is told in first-person, in the voice and point of view of the human I was at that time. I do not include any insights or awareness that was not present in that actual life.

I share the stories of eight of my past lives so that you can observe how the Soul moves from life to life, creating karma, learning lessons, and developing along the way. Though I tell the tales of eight, I have had many more. Some lives are insignificant, a resting life, or drudgery life, like taking a long hike where all the scenery is the same. I am sharing only the most significant lives that I remember, the most meaningful and most formative to who I am today.

The stories of my Soul's lifetimes are told chronologically, starting at the earliest life and ending at the most recent, to more clearly show the effects of karma and life lessons. Though I believe rebirths occur in a linear trajectory through historical periods, their effect on this current life or other lifetimes is not linear. In fact, the Soul is not subject to left-brain linear thinking. The Soul functions through the right brain, unconscious, and emotions. When something occurs to a person in this current life, like an unexpected death in the family, the individual responds to the death through intense feelings of shock and grief. This then triggers other memories of shock and grief stored in the unconscious, whether they occurred last year or ten lives ago. Triggers are based on intensity of emotion rather than how recently they occurred.

I write each story based on my understanding at the time of that life. In the ancient Egyptian desert I did not know what year it was or have insider's knowledge of the political conflicts of the time. My life was lived day to day, year to year, in the simplicity of my village. In another life as a Priest in medieval Germany, I knew the political situation of the times and the larger issues which influenced some of my actions. But in the French town of Montsegur during the Inquisition and Crusades, I knew a lot about religious conflicts of the time and was intimately involved. Each life is different. It is the same today, in that I know details about my hometown and the political intrigues of the United States, but have only a general knowledge about what is happening in other parts of the world. And even in the 21st century, a person born in the Amazon jungle might not know anything about world conflicts or medical advancements of the country next door. We all have our own points of view that define us and our time.

While each individual story is important, what also matters is how the events of one lifetime affect the evolution of the Soul and influence the next incarnation. These accounts show how the choices, concerns, failures, and successes of one life set up the patterns of the next, and the next, all the way to their influence on this current life. After the story of each past life has been told, there is a Lessons Learned section where the karmic patterns, life lessons, talents, allies and adversaries, as well as larger themes are explored.

The choices, concerns, failures, and successes of one life set up the patterns of the next.

The stories of these eight lives, and the lessons I learned, illustrate how the process of reincarnation works in a way that can illuminate your own Soul's journey. These are powerful tales with universal themes that may resonate with your Soul, motivating you to explore your own past-life history as you excavate clues of your prior lifetimes that will expand the notion of who you are in a way that can change you forever.

Indications of a Past Life

Your past-life memories are stimulated by what you are doing at any particular moment, so they can arise at any time, like while reading a book, watching a movie, walking down a street, or looking at a painting, just to name a few. Such memories can be subtle, like a whisper, so you need to pay attention when they occur. They might feel like an emotional nudge which is easy to dismiss. If you slow down and become receptive, you can get a fuller sense of what is trying to arise in you.

Other memories are so strong they shake you to your core, as if you are in a city you never visited yet already know your way around; you might even know the name of a street. Such clear memories are called *déjà vu*, seeing something again.

Past lives can surface in dreams. The first past life I remembered in a coherent manner, rather than just a glimpse, came to me in a dream when I was in my early 20s. It is the lifetime of the Priest that I share. You may notice that certain settings, themes, or people repeat in your nightly sleep, even over many years. These are glimpses and nudges from your unconscious as it prods you to wake up to a life you have lived before. Some people have powerful dreams that feel completely real and can indicate an entire past-life story.

> *You may notice that certain settings, themes, or people repeat in your nightly sleep, even over many years.*

You may have a certain talent or competency that is a clue to a past life. It might be a skill you take for granted and didn't work hard to master, like being good with math, having a "green thumb" with skill in the garden, or being an excellent cook. Or it might surface as a drive to continue a field of study that is a passion within you, like writing, art, or astronomy.

One of the simplest ways to connect to a past life is through "triggers." A trigger is when you have a reaction to something that is beyond what the situation calls for, and the reaction can take you by surprise. For example, I had a client who became very depressed when his girlfriend of a few months ended the relationship. The intensity of his reaction was beyond what one would expect based on the short time they were dating. He described it as if his grandmother, mother, and sister had all died at the same time. In this case, simple grief of being left by a girlfriend triggered complex grief of losing one's entire family. By exploring the feeling associated with the trigger he was able to remember a past life where he had lost his entire family. By bridging that past-life memory from his unconscious to his conscious mind, he was able to discharge the emotional energy of the larger loss. This allowed him to lament the ending of his current relationship with his girlfriend without the emotional weight of all the past-life memories.

Limiting beliefs can also be a clue to past-life patterns. Here are some common ones:

> *I am not enough* (smart, pretty, educated, strong, rich).
>
> *No one is interested in me.*
>
> *No matter what I do, it doesn't matter.*
>
> *Who cares? I'll never get what I want, so why try?*
>
> *I am not creative.*
>
> *I will never find love, money, friends, or home.*

There can also be phobias, hidden fears, and anxieties about certain actions or places like, for example, not wanting to swim in the ocean, or being afraid to climb to the top of a mountain. These fears can be connected to past-life experiences. We all struggle with limiting beliefs and fears about ourselves and the world. By connecting to your Soul in other lifetimes you can better understand their origin and how they have continued as karmic patterns from lifetime to lifetime. Once you realize the source of the limiting beliefs and phobias, you can see them in a new perspective and bring healing to your life.

By bridging past-life memory from the unconscious to the conscious mind, you can discharge the emotional energy of a larger loss.

It is a good idea to record any ideas that come up while you are reading this book, and make note of any dreams, memories, talents, phobias, limiting beliefs, signs, and synchronicities that arise. If no paper is available, you can send yourself an email with your smart phone or take a voice memo.

Lessons Learned - Following Each Life Story

In writing my past-life stories I show how Soul evolves through multiple lifetimes – learning lessons, making mistakes, and gaining wisdom. When I was practicing as a Past Life Therapist I ended the client regression sessions at their death in that lifetime and then shifted the client's awareness to a broader perspective of the events of that life, including how it was affecting the present one. Similarly, at the end of the written accounts of my past lives, I shift my awareness to a broader perspective which is shared through Lessons Learned.

The main lessons of a life are explored, including how these lessons might continue in the next lifetime, endure in this current lifetime, and are part of the collective world at large. My hope is that the stories and lessons of my past lives will encourage you to explore your own. Like an archaeologist, you can dig through the clues of your existing evidence to uncover past lives. As you read my stories, be open, notice your triggers, and allow your own beliefs to be stimulated. In your daily life, begin to pay attention to any indications that a memory of a past life is coming to the surface of your awareness.

> *Pay attention to any indications that a memory of a past life is coming to the surface of your awareness.*

Here are the points that I explore in Lessons Learned at the end of each past life account:

Each begins with an *Overview* of the life that was just completed, mentioning anything needed to make sense of the life. For example, it could be useful to have more information about the historical period, or what occurred at or after my death. The central theme of that life is examined. Was it Power? Revenge? Love? What was the main purpose for living that life? How was it to be part of my evolution? Was it a life where I successfully managed the events? Or a life of struggle and difficult trials that challenged me?

The *Karmic Pattern* active in the past life is noted, for example the pattern of trying to do too much, or feeling like a failure. Did I strengthen the karmic pattern with more failures, or did I unbind it so that it will no longer affect my future rebirths? Or maybe I created an entirely new karmic pattern, for good or ill, that will follow me into the next lifetime.

Soul Wounds are indicated that may have occurred, or were deepened or healed. Soul wounds have a lot to do with karma, in that repeated karma will often lead to a soul wound. Soul wounds work in the unconscious mind and are not easily understood with the intellect. They are usually felt as emotional states that arise at unexpected times, or psychological issues that seem to dominate. These soul wounds are often main issues we are dealing with in this present life, like not feeling good enough, always being let down by those you love, or the need to stay hidden, which is a big one for my life. One of the real benefits of exploring your past lives is the discovery and healing of these soul wounds, so you can better live in the present and not be unconsciously dominated by past events.

> *One real benefit of exploring past lives is the discovery and healing of soul wounds, so you can better live in the present.*

Allies and Adversaries are observed that show up in any lifetime. Allies are people who assist you, people you can count on who move you forward toward your goals. Allies may show up in various roles depending on what we need. In one life they may be a best friend who is always around, or the odd person you meet only once but whose help puts you on a right path. You recognize them by the goodness and comfort they provide.

Think of who in your current life could be Allies who are showing up as a friend, lover, relative, or colleague. Allies take different roles in each life depending on what you need. Some Allies are active in just one life, and others can be companion Souls who are part of your evolutionary team, incarnating with you in various rebirths. This team of companion Souls is called a Soul Pod, and they are Souls you incarnate with repeatedly – so they can help you and you can help them. For example, I think of my brother as a member of my Soul Pod. His presence in my rather traditional religious upbringing provided a huge support for ideas that I had about Spirit and the hidden realms that others near to me discouraged as unrealistic.

There are also Adversaries, enemies who work to block your progress. An Adversary can exist in just one lifetime or reappear in various lifetimes when you least want them, and always in a different guise. Adversaries are karmically based, in that they develop out of karmic mishaps or conflicts. For example, maybe you were a judge who sentenced a man to death and that man swore revenge on you. Some Adversaries can feel like they are haunting you, following you just to make your life miserable. It is important to notice Adversaries and avoid them or deal with them in this current life.

For example, I was engaged once to a man whose mother did not want me in her son's life and blocked our relationship to the point that the engagement ended. I was aware she was an Adversary so I energetically cleared the karma between us, cut all the bonds that connected us, and left with no ill will toward her. I did this because I did not want our karmic energy to follow me in another life.

> *Allies are people who assist you. You recognize them by the goodness and comfort they provide.*

Skills, Gifts, and Talents are considered that are acquired in a life or are strengthened by their use, even to the point of mastery. Some may come naturally, like being a wonderful gardener, diplomat, or artist. We can learn much from these talents of other lifetimes. By remembering past skills, gifts, or talents we can activate them and start using them in our present life.

The *Next Life* is pondered. Once one life is over and the lessons and karma acquired, what do I want to experience in the next life? Do I need to become stronger? Bolder or braver? Do I need to take on responsibility or become freer? What do I want to learn in my next rebirth?

My *Current Life* is examined to understand how the past life, its lessons, karma, allies, adversaries, and talents affect the present, both in supportive and challenging ways. Did that lifetime trigger soul wounds? Encourage me to face hidden fears? Am I still working on clearing some karma or striking out on a new path? Am I becoming braver and strengthening my gifts? Do I recognize any allies or adversaries in this current life? If so, what do I need to do about it?

Larger *Universal* themes are considered that might impact us individually, as well as collectively. Issues such as social justice, equality, betrayal, oppression, rebellion, and prejudice are just a few that may be present.

And finally, *For You* provides questions to reflect on, and ideas to ponder how a particular lifetime resonated or triggered issues for you.

Each lifetime can have a different emphasis. For example, in one life the theme of Adversaries might be stronger, and in another life, the main issue could be learning new skills.

The Historical Context of My Eight Lives

My Soul has lived more lives than the eight that I share, but these are the ones that come clearly to memory and have shaped the karmic patterns I currently carry. The dates of these lives range from estimates to exact, depending on the circumstances. I use 'c.' (circa) which means 'approximately or around' if the dates are an estimate, and a range of dates if they are more exact. I use the designation BCE (Before Common Era) and CE (Common Era) instead of denoting time as BC (Before Christ) and AD (Anno Domini, Year of our Lord).

I want to say a few words about my first lifetime since Atlantis is believed by many to be a myth. If you dig into its history, you might be surprised. The first person to mention Atlantis was the Greek philosopher Plato, who lived 428-348 BCE. He wrote about Atlantis in his Dialogues *Timaeus* and *Critias* in 360 BCE where he referred to Atlantis as an island/continent/nation in the Mediterranean Sea. He described it in some detail and included a map. Now it is true that Plato did not claim to have seen Atlantis first-hand, and it is also true that Plato could have invented Atlantis as an allegory. But these dialogues do not feel like an allegorical tale. In fact, when I was teaching Western Humanities, I asked my university students to read Plato's account of Atlantis and write a paper arguing whether or not they thought Plato was telling a story he believed to be true or an allegory. The majority argued that they thought the story Plato told was actual.

The veracity of Atlantis is supported by the fact that people are still searching for it. James Cameron, producer of *Titanic* and *Avatar*, filmed a documentary *Atlantis Rising* (2017) which follows himself and a group of archaeologists, scientists, and historians as they search for evidence of this lost civilization. Additionally, Geologist Marvin Pepper has a documentary, *Atlantis Found* (2015), where he sets out to prove his theory of the location of Atlantis.

There has been much speculation about Atlantis in the more than 2000 years since Plato. It is thought to have been a sophisticated country that was highly evolved in politics, religion, and energy technology. Its fate is that it sank to the bottom of the ocean following a human-made catastrophe. The story I tell is my viewpoint of that catastrophe based on my place in society and the knowledge I held at the time. Others have told tales of Atlantis, and since history is in the experience of the human who lives it, countless tales could all be true.

The memory of my life on Atlantis came when I was training to be a past life therapist in 1982. I was the client in a regression session and the memories were powerful, realistic, and very disturbing. So much so that even after several sessions with the therapist, working through feelings and memories of Atlantis that arose, I still had emotional residue of that life. Before this memory I had no real opinion about Atlantis and was a bit surprised to find it as the first life that I remembered, and one I will never forget. The Atlantis life feels like my very first in human form and laid the foundation for karmic patterns that repeat in further rebirths.

So let us begin this journey in Atlantis.

4

Being Human, Chosen One: Atlantis, c. 6000 BCE

Even though my eyes are open, I see nothing but black emptiness. I orient myself and listen for any sound in the darkness. As usual, it is complete silence. I am alone in the labyrinthine tunnels that stretch beneath the city. I am always alone as I walk through the darkness to reach the light.

I remember so clearly how I first learned to navigate this secret passageway. I was taught the winding and confusing path ten years ago, at the time of my Initiation. At first blindfolded, I learned the twists and turns by committing to memory the number of steps. Twenty steps, then turn right, sixteen steps then left, down three steps then through the door to the right, and so on. I remember going over and over the instructions in my mind as I memorized my way. Once the blindfold was removed, I was amazed because the tunnels were in total darkness, with no light to show the path. It didn't matter if I had a mask on my eyes or not; I could see nothing.

It took a while, but as the years passed I came to know the path as if by instinct and considered the silent and dark walk to the crystal core of the city as a meditation in itself. This time, however, something is different. For the first time, I feel unease in these dark tunnels. It is an odd sensation and quite unfamiliar. I feel like I am being watched, yet in total darkness that would be impossible. I take my first steps, and then pause, listening. I hear nothing but the usual quiet. I stretch my senses, but it seems as if something is just beyond my reach. I feel disoriented and my mind wanders to last night's dream where I was surrounded by fire, and yesterday in my meditation when I sensed an encroaching gloom, as if the walls were made of dust and shadow. Are these things somehow connected?

I shake my head to dispel such disturbing thoughts. If I don't pay more attention I could get lost in these tunnels. I will bring up these unusual sensations to my teacher, Dem Majer, when we meet this afternoon. For surely he can explain them. Taking a deep breath I bring myself to center, and with clarity I begin again my memorized walk to the energetic core of this vast city.

"Dem Majer," I ask at the beginning of our weekly session. "What is the cause for the disturbance I sense?"

"Disturbance? What do you mean?" Dem Major says with his back to me as he makes our ritual tea.

"There is definitely a change in the psychic forcefield throughout the city. I can sense it. It is as if the lazy flow of beneficial energy has hardened, become rigid. I do not understand it."

"I think you must be meditating too much and that your psychic sense is growing weary and strained. There is no change in the overall energy. You are mistaken."

While I am in simple white robes, Dem Majer wears embroidered gowns of the finest quality and richest colors. His entire parlor has a lush feel about it that I enjoy, since it is very different from the simplicity of my quarters. I look forward to our weekly meetings, not only because of our lessons, but because of the sensual delights of his rooms. The carpet is thick and the sofas on which we sit across from each other are of fine velvet and soft to the touch.

I rub my hands slowly across the fabric of the sofa, confused, and shake my head. "No, I do not feel mistaken, nor do I feel tired or overly strained. I sense the energy of unease around me. What could be causing it?"

Dem Majer turns, his eyes steady on me, piercing into me. He is often like this in our lessons. I am the willing pupil and he is the revered teacher. I trust him as I would a father. I have been training with Dem Majer for as long as I can remember. He has been my teacher for twenty years, since I first came to the Temple as a young boy, selected from all the other children based on my spiritual sensitivity and deep psychic ability to be one of the Chosen Ones who are trained to do the energetic and spiritual work of the Temple. He taught me all that is necessary in order to meet my duty as a Chosen One. He has taught me how to clear my mind, calm my body, and expand my spirit. He taught me how in meditation to separate from my physical body, which is left motionless like an empty shell. Once free from my body I can go anywhere I want, like a giant bird gliding through the air, watching the world from above. During such flights Dem Majer taught me to find energy sources that are used to power our island nation.

In our weekly meditations I leave my body and fly to the top of the sky, then plummet to the bottom of the ocean and skim across the land to find any resonating or pulsating energy form. If I see something that sparkles or radiates or has some unique energy signature, I swoop closer to see what it is. I have a very good sense and I can feel when there is useful energy near to me. It is possible for me to go anywhere in the world in such a spirit form, but when looking for energy sources I usually stay close to the lands and oceans of our island, since if I discover a source worth using, someone will have to physically go to collect it, and the journey can't be too long.

"Ah, Sosha, you are mistaken. There is no disturbance in the city. You need to clear your head and release such negative thoughts. Let us meditate now to accomplish this shift in your thinking." He hands me an earthen cup which I hold in both hands as I inhale the soothing aroma of the tea. I sip it slowly as the warmth flows through me. I shake off my doubts and trust in the wisdom of my teacher. I am still young and not as skilled as he. The tea seeps through me and I feel my body relax, making it easy to clear my mind and open to spirit.

I go into meditation while Dem Majer watches me with keen interest. He is a tall and powerful man, fierce in his demands, demands that I always fulfill. I leave my body sitting on the plush sofa as I expand to the Universe and see all the planets within it; I go to the depths of the ocean and swim with the large fish, and dive to the ocean floor and search for crystals and other forms of energy that the city might use. Each week in my training meditations I take these journeys and share what I find with Dem Majer. He makes note of my discoveries, whether a city of merpeople in the depths of the Senasa Sea or rocks of power on a mountain in the next kingdom. I find them and tell Dem Majer what and where they are located. I never ask why he wants to know, or if he ever goes to these points to see if I am correct. I always do as I am told.

I leave this session as I leave every other. I bow and hold my hands to my side saying, "Praise to the Universe." But this time, I feel uneasy. I do not like the feeling. I walk slowly to my quarters. I feel weak in my body and cloudy in my mind. In my entire life in Atlantis I have never had such sensations. I have only known peace here.

Atlantis is a circular island of lush green in a brilliant blue sea, filled with trees, flowers, wildlife, and water that moves through the island in rivers, streams, and wild waterfalls. Though I have never physically traveled to other kingdoms – what we call the Outer Lands – I have seen many in my meditations and none compare to the beauty of Atlantis. We have all we could ever dream of and are surrounded with abundance.

In the very center of the island rises the Temple, a white pyramid made from huge blocks of shining stone. The pyramid is so tall it is visible from any vista on the island. The Temple is built over a huge Crystal which lies deep in a cavern below. This Crystal is the energetic and spiritual source of our kingdom. The white stones of the Temple absorb and radiate the power of the Crystal so that the Temple radiates a calm yet powerful energy. Only very few are allowed in the presence of the Crystal, but anyone can come to the Temple to bask in this source of spiritual power, making it a place of ritual and pilgrimage for citizens of the kingdom. Surrounding the Temple is the Temple Sanctuary, where all those who are closely involved in the Temple live and religious instruction occurs. The Temple Sanctuary expands from the base of the Temple like rays from a star and is made from the same stone as the Temple. This means that all who live in the Temple Sanctuary are steeped in the essence of the Crystal and Temple.

I live in the Temple Sanctuary, as does everyone who is part of the religious core of Atlantis. Dem Majer has his quarters here, as do all the other teachers and the fifty Chosen Ones. To live in the radiance of the Crystal and Temple is not only a special blessing, but also a necessary part of my work. Being constantly close to the spiritual and energetic source of our island is essential to keep my energies at a refined state, my senses astute, and my psychic ability enriched.

Functionally, the island is divided into seven rings, radiating from the center outwards to the circumference. They are called the Rings of Influence and are named according to the function in which the entire population of that ring engages. This system creates a clear division of labor and the people in Atlantis are identified according to their Ring.

The center ring is called Source. Source is named after the Crystal, which is the energy source and beating heart of Atlantis. The Temple and Temple Sanctuary are situated in Source.

The second is the Ring of Power, consisting of those who control how the energy of the Crystal gets transformed into the power that runs the island. It is the Ring of Power that puts forth the call to generate the energy of the Crystal, transforming the raw energy of the Crystal into power, targeting it to specific tasks, and passing laws related to its use. I am uncertain how Power directs the energy of the Crystal throughout Atlantis. It may be that there is a series of wires and contraptions, but I have never been curious about this. The Ring of Power has a feeling of quiet importance as all decisions, both for Atlantis and the Outer Lands, occur there.

The capital of Atlantis is the Central City, which straddles the boundaries of Source and Power; in this way a balance of religious and governmental influences are included in decisions regarding the ruling of Atlantis. Those religious and political leaders in the Central City decide how, when, and where the energy generated by the Crystal should be used. The energy is prioritized according to need, with the needs of the people ascertained by the priests of the people, needs of science by the priests of science, and so on. The priority is decided according to a governing board who makes the decisions and creates the laws surrounding the use of power. We are not warlike and have no weapons, no fights, no power struggles. At least none I am aware of. So all the laws surrounding the use of power are directed toward stability and peace.

The third is the Ring of Leaders, who take the laws from the Ring of Power and then direct the populace and enforce the laws. Compared to the tranquility of the Source, or the seriousness of the Ring of Power, the Ring of Leaders is very busy and people seem to be in a hurry to do important things. From my vista at the top of the Temple it looks like a bee colony, with people buzzing from one multi-storied hive to the next.

The fourth is the Ring of Commerce where sellers and buyers engage in enterprise. The fifth is the Ring of Artisans, where the people live who take raw materials and craft them into functional and artistic products that are sold in the Ring of Commerce. The sixth is the Ring of Production, where raw materials are mined and food is grown. The seventh and outermost ring is called the Periphery and consists of those who work on the docks and with the ships that go to the Outer Lands. The Outer Lands are lands beyond our sight with which we have trade relations, and other lands that are largely beyond my knowledge.

Like other kingdoms, in Atlantis there is a hierarchy moving from the highest status at Source down to the lowest of laborers on the Periphery. Everyone in the outer four rings of Commerce, Artisan, Production, and Periphery are considered Everyday people and a lower status from Leaders and Power.

Since I live at Source I am near the top of the elite. But as a Chosen One I am not involved in governing on any level. Although I am aware that Atlantis is a large, prosperous, and active kingdom, I don't know much about the Rings of Influence and I am unaware exactly how Atlantis is governed or the state of affairs of the Everyday. Living in the Sanctuary is like living in the center of the lotus – it is blissful, peaceful, and vibrates at a high frequency. As a Chosen One, my job is to be trained in and stay tuned to the highest energies and frequencies available and then direct these frequencies as needed to maintain the functioning of Atlantis. I am too physically and psychically sensitive to be among the Everyday, so I stay sequestered.

I know there is much worldly activity outside Source and I am curious at times as I see priests come and go. There are many different levels and types of priests. There are priests who are teachers, writers, scientists, artists, and rulers. They mostly stay within Source too, though not as isolated as me. But the priests who most fascinate me are the traveling priests of the Everyday people. They wear brown robes and smell like fresh air and always seem to be in a hurry – as if there were never enough time.

I have never actually physically been anywhere else in Atlantis except Source. Sometimes I walk to the top of the Temple and gaze across the island as it stretches out to the sea, observing the activity below in the different rings. I sometimes come at night to gaze at the stars and watch their nightly dance; at those times it feels like I am at the center of Heaven and Earth.

Looking back, it is amazing what I didn't know, or that I never thought to ask what the energy of Source was used for and how it was dispersed. I just assumed it was for the greater good. This was because each Atlantean focused on and managed their own Ring of Influence. To worry about the goings on in any other Ring was unnecessary.

The disturbing feelings have not left me, so at our next meeting I tell Dem Majer once more of my unease. He looks at me with an expression of exasperation. "You trouble yourself unnecessarily. Your work is here in the Source. Would you want someone questioning the work you do? Trust your brothers and sisters to deal with any issues in their Ring."

Sinking into the soft couch I shudder. "But the darkness I sense is growing stronger. Each day it grows heavier. It is hard to ignore. In all my time I have never felt this. Surely you feel it too? Your power is far beyond mine."

"You both condemn and praise me unnecessarily. I am not ignoring the changes in the city, nor is my psychic insight so great that I can feel beyond your own well-developed capacity. You are not only a Chosen One, but also a '12', one of the few who work directly with the Crystal. No one sees or feels more than you."

"Then you do believe me! You believe me when I say something is amiss?"

"Tell me exactly what you sense or know, and I will give it my full consideration," says Dem Majer, sitting across from me, his eyes showing interest.

I feel myself lighten with hope. "For weeks now I have felt chaos on the Periphery. There are more ships leaving for the Outer Lands. Our Traveling Priests on the Periphery are spending time away. I think they board ships in the night, and come back weeks later, also in the darkness. Their essence is full of concern. I even went to the docks one night in meditation, and it looked as though the Priests were loading food and medicines on the ships. When they return, the ships are empty. It all felt very guarded."

Dem Majer sits back, looks down at his hands and takes a moment. Silence blankets the room. "Really?" he finally says. "And what else did you see in your nightly meditations?"

Now it is my turn to pause. I was not assigned to oversee the actions on the Periphery, and the fact that I have taken meditation time away from looking for minerals and other sources of energy could be construed by Dem Majer as a fault on my part. I have been trained since childhood to direct my skills in one place, and one place only, and that is the Source. The fractures I feel in the other Rings are not supposed to be my concern.

To say I am trusting and naïve is an understatement. I wonder if I have said too much about my meditation to the Periphery. I stall, and sense the energy between Dem Majer and me. There is none. It is a blank. I feel a cool chill run over me and beads of sweat appear on my brow. I do not know what to do. I have never felt these feelings before, and they go against all my training and my trust of my teacher.

I take a few deep breaths to calm myself. No doubt I am overtired and my mind is beginning to strain.

"Oh, Dem Majer. I see that you are correct and that I am overtired and my mind is beginning to play tricks on me. Perhaps it is time for me to take a Sabbatical. I will go into retreat and find a place of calm."

"It is not up to you to decide when you go on retreat!" he roars as he stands up swiftly. "I am the one who tells you when to go on retreat. Do you no longer need my guidance? All these years I have nurtured you as my student. Are you no longer placing your trust in me, your Teacher?"

I collapse to my knees in front of him, bowing my head. "Oh, Teacher. Please forgive me and my impertinence. I know not what has come over me. I ask your patience with me, your most ignorant pupil who has gone astray. I am lost without you and await your instruction."

My heart is pounding in my chest and my mind races. I really am lost. I question the man who is my teacher and in whom I trust as a father. I could probably lose my position as a Chosen One for such a breach in protocol.

His next words surprise me. "Have you stated your concern to any other?"

"No," I reply. I wonder who he thought I might confide in, since I spend most days alone or with others in silent meditation.

"Have you told any other of your meditative excursions to the Periphery?" he asks, staring at me intently, as if he could read my mind.

"No, to no one."

Dem Majer relaxes, takes my hands in his and says with encouragement, "Then there is no breach. Of course you can tell me your concerns. I am, after all, your confidant. Trust only in me, and I will help you. Tell no other of your concerns." And with this he rises and leaves.

I remain in a kneeling position on the floor, and fall further into a state of prayer. *Please help me. I know something is wrong. But if I cannot trust my Teacher, who can I trust? My decision is made. I will trust Dem Majer and put my hesitations aside.*

I enter my quarters in the Temple Sanctuary, still lost in thought. To revive myself I have a simple meal and lie down to regenerate. After a while I hear a knock on my door and a steward awaits me with notice that I am to report to the Crystal, the main energy source for Atlantis and the heart of the city. Of the 50 Chosen Ones, I am one of the 12 who work directly with the Crystal. I leave my quarters and go to the entrance of the secret labyrinthine tunnels that lead to the Crystal, the same tunnels where I felt such unease. But now I feel embraced by the quiet of the dark walls as I fall into the easy rhythm of my meditative walk. By the time I come to the Crystal I am clear and calm, ready for the work that lies ahead.

I am dwarfed by the huge Crystal which lies in the center of a large underground room whose white stone walls curve gently inward toward the ceiling. The Crystal, which radiates its own soft light, is set within a recess in the ground that is implanted with gems and minerals that magnify the energy of the Crystal many-fold, some of which I recognize from my meditations. The Crystal's wide base rises in a pyramidal structure toward the ceiling, which is open to the sky, creating a channel of connection from the source of the Crystal to the expanse of the universe. The sides of the crystal are not smooth, but instead form a multi-faceted landscape that juts in peaks and valleys of crystal spires toward the ceiling center. When I stare into the Crystal, I lose my orientation to space and time and become lost in its fathomless energy.

In order to work with the Crystal, like all the 12, I underwent the Transmission. The Transmission is a holy rite of initiation where a shield – a circular medallion three inches in diameter made from the Crystal – was surgically implanted in my breastbone, over my heart. By covering my heart with the same substance as the Crystal I am able to resonate with the Crystal and become a transmitter of its energy. I was raised to carry the shield and it is a great honor and privilege.

I take my place among the 12 in a circle around the Crystal. Each of us is solemn in our white robes, using our heart centers and shields as transmitters of energy. I stand in silence with the others, breathing deep, connecting to my center and generating the power available to me. Each of the 12 is doing the same. I generate energy in my heart that I then direct through my crystal shield into the larger Crystal; I receive energy back from the Crystal which flows through my shield into my heart. Thus begins a pulsating circle of energy flow, transmitting between me and the Crystal.

At some point each 12 has generated enough radiance that we connect to each other through rays of energetic light, creating a multi-pointed star held together by our generating force. At this point the Crystal ignites in a blaze of light so bright I must keep my eyes closed or else be blinded. Together, we 12 generate and transmit the energy to ignite the Crystal. If any of us breaks our connection, the Crystal will quit generating its powerful force.

The Crystal is at the very center and heart of Atlantis and can only be reached through the labyrinthine path that is taught to the 12 at initiation. Since so much power resides in the Crystal, it needs to be protected and only the 12 are allowed in its presence. Most of the time the Crystal lies quietly radiating its energy, a subtle force that bathes the Temple in spiritual light and draws pilgrims near. But every several days the Crystal's power and force are needed for the service of Atlantis. At that time the 12 are called to the Crystal to ignite, generate, and then direct its power. No single person could activate the Crystal since it is raw energy that could be used in any fashion or for any ends. That would allow too much power in a few hands. It takes all 12, and the others are like me – transcendent, secluded, psychically attuned, and not driven by ego or power since we have no family, no friends, and no political ties. I do not know who will use the energy of the Crystal or for what ends. I was never given any reason to wonder… until I began to sense this tension in Atlantis.

In subsequent days, Dem Majer calls me to his study more frequently. Instead of my out-of-body meditative excursions to the sky and sea to search for minerals of energy, he has me patrol the Periphery. Like some huge invisible bird, I soar above the hustle and bustle of the Everyday people on the edge of Atlantis, while my body sits on the velvet couch in Dem Majer's salon, an empty shell. I am to tell him of every ship that sets sail, the Traveling Priest who leads it, and what provisions are on board. I begin to notice that some ships take passengers, brought on in the night. Some entire families are taken on board after dark and placed deep in the hold. I tell Dem Majer of this, and he notes the names and times and place of docking. These ships do not return, and I later note that the Priests in charge of these ships go missing and are noted as being on Sabbatical.

I become afraid… afraid that my description of the ship, its Captain and cargo is the reason for it being marked as missing. I am also becoming afraid of Dem Majer. If he thinks I am withholding information he presses me harder, wanting to know more. We begin to meet daily instead of weekly, and I feel my body collapse under the strain. I become sick, unable to work. Dem Majer leaves me alone, for a week he says, in order for me to rest.

During that week I do something I have never done before. I change from my white robes of the Chosen and put on rough brown cloth of the Everyday priest. I leave the Temple Sanctuary and begin to walk, slowly at first, until I regain my strength in the sunshine and fresh air of the kingdom. I walk through all the Rings of Influence, beginning at Source, through Power, Leaders, Commerce, Artisans, and Production, until I finally cross the border into Periphery.

It takes me three days. No one speaks to me or acknowledges my presence. I feel as invisible and detached as when gliding through these regions in my meditations, always the observer, always watching. I walk to the very edge of Atlantis itself, the docks that surround our island, the connection to the Outer Lands. The docks are a busy place and it is nighttime when I arrive. I find a small inn to stay the night. I want to feel this part of the world from my body, not just observe it from my meditations, so I can gain more information. I am beginning to question everything; my trust in Dem Majer is falling apart.

I arise before dawn and walk to the sparkling blue water that surrounds our island. The tall sailing ships are lined up on the docks, ready to embark with cargo to the Outer Lands. I wonder what these faraway lands might contain. I have never been to the Outer Lands outside of my meditative excursions where I looked only for energy sources that could be used. I always assumed them to be rather primitive places compared to Atlantis. But now I am curious about where these ships go and why, and I need to reconsider my previous assumptions. What was beyond the outer reaches of my knowing? And why had I never considered this question before?

My thoughts are interrupted by a small voice. "Sir, would you like cider and a bun for your morning meal? The cost is only a copper."

I look down and a young girl, about 10 years of age, holds a basket of food for sale. All I have is a silver, which is worth quite a lot, and she has no change. I give it to her and tell her to keep the remainder. This small act of charity seems to gain me a friend, as she never leaves my side the rest of the day. She tells me her name is Emna, and she is very curious about me as she has never seen a person so pale in color. I rarely leave the Temple Sanctuary and spend no time out of doors, so it is not surprising that I am pale. My hair, white like the silk in corn, she has also never seen. I have never given my appearance much thought, but as I look around me I become aware that I might look out of place. I keep my hood up from that point on, shielding my appearance.

For two days I watch the ships, both day and night, and realize that people are often added as passengers, usually in secret, huddled, carrying their few possessions as if it was all they had left. There are families with children, as well as mature men, women, and elders.

Since I continue to only have a silver from which to buy her goods, and she has taken such a delight at my odd appearance, Emna does not leave my side while I am at the Periphery. It is she who tells me that I am being followed, and seems surprised I had not noticed that fact myself.

Emna is talkative and over the days she tells me more than she realizes. People are leaving Atlantis, she says, because the Leaders are becoming rigid and interfering in the life of the Everyday. There is talk of dictatorships and rebellions and a great fear of chaos. People who complain or seek relief are often never seen again. She tells me that over the past year the Traveling Priests have begun organizing people to leave Atlantis, while the ships are still free to sail.

I have never actually met a Traveling Priest, though I have seen them at a distance and heard of them. They are trained at the Temple Sanctuary and then sent to the different Rings of Influence to care for the spiritual needs of the Everyday. They are firmly built and rugged looking, not pale and thin as I am, and their cloaks are brown and of a rough fabric. Emna's father is a Traveling Priest and she is quite proud of that fact, though he is often away from home and it seems he is in some danger from the activities he does. He is a leader, one of many Traveling Priests who are organizing the exodus and helping the Everyday escape the difficult change they believe is soon to come.

All this talk of rebellion, escape, and fear is similar to the energy I sensed in my meditations while at the Source. In spite of my questions, Emna does not seem to know the cause of these troubles. She only knows that people are not happy and that there is danger ahead.

Dem Majer surely does not know about this information. For if he knew of fear in the Rings of Influence, he would try to discover what was wrong, find the cause, and correct it. In spite of my new unease around him, I know of no other with which to share this knowledge. My work as a Chosen and one of the 12 leaves me with no friends in whom to confide. There is only Dem Majer.

After several days I bid Emna farewell and begin my journey back to Source. Now that I am aware I am being followed, I often see my stalker near me, behind me, close to me. It was naïve to think I could leave the Sanctuary and no one would notice. It seems I have been unthinking in so many ways. I pledge to myself that I will no longer be caught unaware and will pay more attention to what goes on around me. No doubt Dem Majer knew I left and where I had gone. I will have to tell him the truth, for lying was previously unknown to me, and he would know if I attempted to deceive him.

After two days journey I am back at the Temple Sanctuary, dressed still as an Everyday who has come to worship. From there I go to my rooms where I bathe and rest. My feelings are so mixed. I am glad to be back in the Sanctuary, for it is familiar and its comfort is great. But after being outside for nearly a week, I feel cramped and even trapped within its walls.

I do not have to wait long for Dem Majer to call for me, confirming that the man who followed me must have reported my return. When I enter Dem Majer's salon his back is turned to me as he makes our ritual tea.

"I have just returned from a journey," I say with more calm than I feel. "I have been to the Periphery to find out if what I saw in my meditation was accurate."

Dem Majer does not turn around. "You have never questioned your knowing before," he says. "Why now?"

"I have never used my meditations to follow the lives of the Everyday. It seems I am more confident in the far reaches of the universe, or under the depths of the sea, than I am among those who live in Atlantis."

He turns toward me, holding the tray of our tea, and sets it on the table between us. "And how did you find the Everyday of Atlantis?" he asks. My nose flares. I can smell a bitterness that is new to me. The tea is not our normal, the mellow tea to encourage deep meditations. I hold the cup in my hands to warm them.

"They are in disarray and afraid, two states of mind that I have never encountered before. It was new to me and brought me concern. It seemed to confirm my earlier disquiet. You said I was to confide in you, and so I am here to tell you that it seems as if something is wrong in Atlantis that makes the Periphery uneasy. I know not what occurs in the other Rings, for I did not linger in them." I lean in and inhale the scent of my tea, staring at the cup and not in the eyes of my Teacher. I take deep breaths and bring myself to a calm that I do not feel.

"You should not have left the Sanctuary without my permission," he says sternly. "You are a Chosen and one of the 12, but you are still my pupil. Your absence threatened the use of the Crystal, for the Crystal cannot be ignited without all 12 present. You have a responsibility to stay in Source, in case your services are needed. The Crystal has not been ignited for the week you have been away. Did you think because I said you could take a break from your lessons with me that I also excused you from your duties?"

I am stunned. I had not even considered if the energy of the Crystal would be needed. I wanted to leave for the Periphery and I left. Now I realize why I was followed. If anything had happened to me, the Power would have to train another initiate, and that would take time. I was necessary to them, and they could not take a chance to lose me. The man who followed me was probably told to protect me, not harm me. I wonder why they did not keep me from leaving, or why they did not force me back. I wonder if there had been an emergency that could not be answered because I was not here to help ignite the Crystal.

Dem Majer looks at me with contained anger. "You are being led by your sensations and feelings, not by necessity and need. You are too important to us here, and you are not to leave the Sanctuary again." His anger subsides suddenly and with a thin smile he says, "Do you like your tea? It is new and I am curious how you like it."

I put the cup to my lips, to give me a pause to answer. In that moment of pause I recognized the bitter scent as a medicinal I was given once when I was sick as a child. It had put me to sleep for three days until my fever broke. What could this mean?

I speak slowly to give myself time to think. "My intention was not to be remiss in my responsibility as a 12. Was there a need that was unmet due to my absence?"

Unrestrained fury breaks across Dem Majer's face, and I see a person in front of me I have never seen before, nor suspected could even exist. "It is not up to you to question the needs of Power. It is up to you to meet those needs when called upon! How dare you ask for explanations. You have become unreliable. I thought I could depend on you, that I had trained you well. You fail me."

His rage lifts his body from the chair and he storms across the room toward me. "To think that the plans I have worked on for years could be delayed by the wanderings of a Chosen. It cannot be so. You are only a pawn in my game. You will no longer take actions on your own. I have need of you, of your power to ignite the Crystal. All my other students are loyal to me. You ask too many questions, want to know what is happening in Atlantis, want to know what Power intends to do! I thought I could count on you and you have failed me."

I am speechless. I cannot believe this is the same man that I worshipped as a teacher and loved as a father. I feel like I am in danger. I feel the fear and disarray of the Periphery. My hands shake and the tea spills.

Dem Majer turns to face me, eyes of hatred searing into mine. He comes closer and puts his hand on my robe, directly over my heart. "This is all I need from you," he says, his hand clenching, as if he could take the crystal shield and my heart right out of my body. "All I need is your crystalline shield to ignite the Crystal. I do not need your ideas, or questions, or failures. I do not need you at all. I have been delayed in my plans by your unexpected journey. My perfect plans held up because of you! No more!" He glances at my empty cup and says with a smile. "Good, you drank your tea. That will make this easier for both of us." And with those words he storms out of the room. I hear the door lock behind him and I am alone.

My heart is pounding. I can still feel his hand on my chest. It is unheard of to touch the heart of a 12. As a 12, our hearts are both a key to unlock the energy of the Crystal and also the catalyst to ignite it. Much of our time in meditation is spent purifying our heart, opening our heart, readying our heart for the pure energy that occurs when we become one with the Crystal. His touch has polluted me. I need to cleanse again before I take my place around the Crystal. I go to the door to leave, but there is no key for me to unlock it. I look for another door or window, but there is none. I am not just alone, it seems as if I am a prisoner.

I sit down and take my calming breaths. I clear my head and go over the words that Dem Majer just said. He has plans that include igniting the Crystal and my absence stopped those plans from occurring. He is furious with me, the only one of his students, the only one of the 12 who failed him. His single need for me is to ignite the Crystal, and he could do that without my questions, without me! He could do it with just my heart shield.

I look over at the medicinal tea, which he thought I drank, and remember his words, that drinking it "will make this easier for both of us." Make what easier? Was he planning to take me to the Crystal in a drugged state and force me to participate in igniting the Crystal? How could I direct energy to my heart if I were drugged? Would he be able to take over my mind? To use his will to generate the energy to bring my heart into frequency with the 12 and the Crystal?

My mind reels. Surely it is not possible. The energy of the 12 is the highest frequency and we have spent years in training to be able to work in union to ignite the Crystal. Even if it were possible, igniting the Crystal when any of the 12 is out of harmony would be dangerous. The Crystal is a powerful energy force. It fuels the whole continent of Atlantis. The tuning of the frequency is critical and how the energy is directed is a result of the harmonic resonance of the 12. Surely Dem Majer knows this. But does he? Why would he? Although he is a teacher, he is not himself a 12 and does not participate in the initiation of Transmission or the training. He could easily not know how delicate an act it is to ignite the Crystal.

The thought is frightening. If he tries to use me against my will, or if the energy at the Crystal is negative and disharmonious, the results could be disastrous. The Crystal is deep underground, in the center of the labyrinthine tunnels. If the Crystal were to explode it would shake the underground faults of Atlantis, causing massive earthquakes. The possibilities are too grave to consider.

I have to stop this. I try to think. Dem Majer surely does not know the path through the tunnels to the Crystal. Only the 12 were taught the way. He would need to use me to navigate the tunnels to get to the Crystal. But no, he said the other 11 were loyal to him and any of them could show him the way.

Still, if I could get out of this room I might be able to escape and then he could not use me at all. My sense is strong, stronger than most, and I might find some way out. It is my only idea. If I stay here, Dem Majer will be sure to come back, expecting to find me drugged, and then I would be used as a tool for destruction. A weapon to destroy everything I know.

I shake my head to clear the confusion. This is all hard to believe. I hear sounds in the hallway and need to act fast. I close my eyes to sense if there is a hidden way out of his quarters. My mind seeks a break in the energy field and finds it in his bedroom behind a tapestry. I rush there just as the outer door opens and quickly I go through the exit.

I follow the narrow passageway downwards and soon find myself in the lower floors of the Sanctuary. From here the tunnels are easily accessible and there might be some passage that opens to the outside. I enter the dark tunnels and feel my familiar connection with their twists and turns. But this time I run the path that I usually walk in prayer and preparation, for I know I am being followed. I am almost to the Crystal core and have not yet found any other passageway out. There are some doors, but they lead to small rooms used for preparation and prayer.

It is one of those doors that suddenly opens and I struggle as rough hands pull me inside. It is dark and I cannot see, but several people grab me and my struggles are easy for them to resist.

"We got him," a man grunts. "Let's go and get the Master."

I am shoved onto a chair and the men lock the door as they quickly leave. I realize there is no escape.

In the total darkness I calm my breath, which is racing from my run through the tunnels. This turn of events is beyond anything I could have ever imagined. My teacher is betraying me, the man I love and trust above all else. My heart aches and tears come to my eyes. I am being used by him, for his own purposes and power. My trust in him has been a fool's trust. I hate how I have been so naïve, so believing. Even 10-year-old Emna was wiser in the ways of people than I have been.

My knowledge, training, and wisdom are being turned against me. Dem Majer wants to use my heart shield as a weapon against my will. The consequences are too grave, too deadly to imagine. I have to stop him. If I can destroy the crystal shield over my heart, then it won't be able to ignite the Crystal. My heart alone is not enough. It is the crystal shield placed over my heart during my Initiation that is the wiring that connects me to the 12 and to the Crystal.

It is a desperate act, but I decide to try to destroy the shield with my focused energy. I fall into meditation and imagine my heart and the shield over it. The shield lays across my breastbone like a leather glove. It is a thin and flexible covering and I can see the veins of the crystal running through it that act as wires and connectors. If I could disrupt those connections, then I could not be used.

With the image of the shield clear in my mind, I begin to generate energy and direct it toward the shield. I gain strength and power and turn it on myself, trying to destroy what is most sacred to me so it cannot be used in a contrary way. But the shield holds. It glows and vibrates, but the energy I generate moves through the veins and disperses. I feel deflated, but can understand that if the crystal shield can withstand the highly powerful energy of the Crystal, it can surely withstand my own limited energy field.

In the darkness and silence I ponder my options. If I cannot destroy the shield, then I will have to destroy my heart, which works with the shield. Then I will not be able to be used. With full force of focus I put all my energy toward destroying my heart. Every ounce of my will is bearing down, trying to rip it from my chest. My determination is strong.

I might have succeeded, but Dem Majer enters the room and, in fury, grabs me out of the chair and shakes me. "You idiot! You cannot defeat me! All the rest of the 12 are gathered at the Crystal. My plan to control the Power of Atlantis is already in place. If you will not help me, then I do not need you." He places his hand over the sheath of my robe once again and snarls with contempt. "All I need is your shield."

"Put him on that table," Dem Majer shouts to the men. I feel myself lifted. "Hold him down, and don't let him move."

I realize what Dem Majer is attempting to do. He is going to take my shield from me, as if it could be used outside of my own body and without the energy generated by my heart. Surely that isn't possible. But Dem Majer is a teacher, and perhaps it is possible. I shift my focus back to my heart and again gather my will; *please, let me destroy it.*

I barely feel the knife enter my chest and am amazed how quickly and cleanly Dem Majer cuts through my chest and removes my heart and crystal shield. He takes them from my body and hurries from the room, leaving me alone on the table, my chest open and bleeding. I am not sure when I actually die, since I leave my body every day in meditation and the transition to spirit is very easy for me. I hardly notice the moment when I have no living body to return to.

I am surrounded in grief. I am unable to stop Dem Majer. I am a trusting fool. I hear the explosion as the Crystal ignites, and I feel a shudder under me of a major earthquake. The light is so bright that it is the last thing I remember – the light and my grief. I am overwhelmed by my failure to see the evil before me. I believed the words of my teacher rather than my own senses and the evidence before my very eyes. I will never forgive myself for the destruction of Atlantis. These are my last thoughts as oblivion overtakes me.

Life Lessons from Atlantis

Reflecting upon this life, I realize how much I have carried the guilt that I was responsible for the destruction of Atlantis. Atlantis was a paradise, a land you could call the Garden of Eden, for it was perfect. We had all we could ever dream of and were surrounded by beauty and abundance.

Never did we know there was an evil in our midst that would turn us against one another and destroy all we were. Expelled from the Garden? Perhaps. But it was more like running for our lives. Only I never escaped, and I witnessed the end of all that was once golden. Atlantis was the first rupture with God, the first crack that has never been healed and still continues to spread. Atlantis shattered the Soul of the world and it is still weeping.

After my body died, I stayed in Atlantis in spirit form and watched the destruction. It was a quick and unbelievable devastation. The Crystal exploded after it was ignited with inharmonious frequencies by Dem Majer with my heart shield. The Source and Central City were destroyed in that first blast, one so strong that it shook all of Atlantis, all the way out to the Periphery. The earthquakes along the meridian lines of the continent occurred next, radiating out from the Crystal, fracturing the island, and there were many fires. As pieces of the island fell into the sea, flooding occurred. The whole of Atlantis was covered by the depths of the sea.

The ships on the Periphery were all ready to sail, thanks to the courageous work of the Traveling Priests. Many had already been evacuated, and upon feeling the first blast, others went immediately to the ships. It is as if someone had known what was to occur and had been organizing this escape. I don't know who that person was but I am very grateful.

Hundreds of ships were launched within an hour, filled with cargo, medicines, educational material, and people from each of the Rings of Influence. Some of the ships did not make it and were overcome by tidal waves. But most did make it. Each ship went in a different direction. I suspect that the people who had been previously evacuated had set up base camps in the Outer Lands. The location for the spread of the Atlanteans can be seen by the places on the earth where there are pyramid type structures, either above or underground or in the ocean.

This was the earliest lifetime I remember, my first incarnation. Atlantis was my first imprint and it set the tone for my Soul's journey. It was the source of key patterns and themes that have developed further in future lifetimes. I first experienced this Atlantis life during a regression session while I was training to become a Past Life Therapist. Birth into the human body is an evolutionary journey on how to become a conscious individual, which is no easy task and why it can take many lifetimes. So my task in Atlantis as an incarnated human was to grow from one who is quite naïve into one who understands how it all works. I learned quickly how to be a student and trust a teacher, since that was what I was taught at the Temple. I knew how to do whatever I was told without question. I knew how to use my skills to find energy sources and to direct that energy for specific purposes. But I didn't know how to think for myself or make my own decisions. It took strong evidence around me and strong messages from my dreams, visions, and meditations to even realize that things were not as they should be. It took me time to believe in my own impressions and to trust myself. I did wake up, eventually, but only at the end of the life.

After a death in one life, and before a rebirth in the next, Souls go to an in-between space where they review the life that just ended and make decisions about the life that is coming next. They meet teachers, like in a classroom, and take the time to figure out the lessons learned and review mistakes made. Souls are part of a soul group, and between lives they meet back up, like at a reunion, and discuss their lessons and what is needed for the next life and when and where they are going to meet up again.

> *Building a bridge between the unconscious and conscious mind allows you to become aware of hidden issues and soul wounds.*

But after my death in Atlantis I don't meet any teachers, nor do long-lost soul friends greet me. Instead it feels like I am in a hospital emergency room where I am being treated by strangers who are desperately trying to save me. I am unconscious most of the time, drifting in and out of awareness. I feel collapsed upon myself. It is as if my heart became a black hole and I am falling deeper and deeper into oblivion. I don't want to wake up, or figure things out, or plot my next life so that my life lessons will be pre-arranged. If I drop far enough down, perhaps I will disappear, which is all I want to do.

It is best to die in a conscious and clear state, at peace, and surrounded by beloved things and people. It seems that the transition between lifetimes is easier when death occurs in an unhurried and expected manner. I will try to remember that next time.

Many of my karmic patterns were set in Atlantis. They continued in my unconscious throughout other lifetimes, all the way into this current life. Now that I am more aware of them I can bring them into my conscious mind which enables me to handle them differently. Building a bridge between the unconscious and conscious mind allows you to become aware of hidden issues and soul wounds. This is a real benefit of learning about your past lives.

Here is a list of my main themes, patterns, and life lessons that began in Atlantis. Perhaps some of these will resonate with you and your life.

- Sense of distrust in what I am told by authority
- Need to experience reality for myself, and not take someone else's word for it
- Constant gathering of information, wanting to know and find the truth for myself
- Feeling of being an observer, as if I am seeing life through a lens
- Sense of distance and being a stranger, even when many people are around
- Ability to sense energy sources
- Ability to generate spiritual energy
- My heart as the weak place, both physically and psychically
- Directing negative energy to attack myself, as in how I tried to destroy my heart
- That my greatest gift is my greatest vulnerability and will likely be my downfall
- Sense of being unsafe

The soul wound of distrust was created by the betrayal of Dem Majer, who I had greatly trusted but who was using me for his own selfish purposes. Once my life was over, I felt despair for my ignorance and much guilt for my trust in him. I blamed myself for the fall of Atlantis and felt I did not live up to my responsibility as a Chosen One and 12 to protect the Temple and the Crystal. I feel very sad when I remember myself as this person. And the sadness is like a weight in my heart, for myself, for my Soul, and for the self-condemnation at my inability to stop the destruction of Atlantis. Though I really did as well, if not better, than could be expected due to the circumstances, I broke rules, I lied to my teacher, I left the temple, I hid my identity. I tried to stop the destruction. I really was quite brave when I look back on it. So forgiveness of my failures is an act of kindness to myself that I can endeavor to learn.

This is the earliest incarnation I remember. I had no impure thoughts until I started to pick up the discontent from the Everyday of Atlantis. Once I tuned into their disturbed feelings and thoughts, I became exposed to a different type of energy. I had been kept isolated at the Source so it was no wonder that I was easy to deceive. I had no reason not to trust Dem Majer and I had no other friends or allies. Even the 12 did not converse. We were trained separately and brought together only in meditation and activation of the Crystal.

As I write this, I feel compassion and a greater understanding for the person I was. It is not surprising that I paid so little attention to the world around me. It some ways it was not my world. I was an energy source; that was my job and duty. I had no life outside of that. My only connection was with my weekly meetings with Dem Majer. I had no other contacts. I did not belong to Atlantis. I did not understand Atlantis. My trip to the Periphery was my first exposure outside of the Temple Sanctuary.

Dem Majer became my Adversary, the person who would do anything to stop me. He shows up in several future lifetimes, and I recognize him by his piercing eyes and the coldness in my heart. I see Emna, the child, as an Ally, one who told me the truth. She filled me in on what was happening, knew I was being followed, and showed me the closeness that humans could have with each other. She also shows up in future lives.

I gained many skills in this Atlantean lifetime. Each of my reincarnated lifetimes gave me knowledge of abilities that I have kept in the repository of memory and are available for me now. The most important technique I used in Atlantis was the ability to control energy by directing my breath. Most of the energetic work I engaged in used control of the breath as a key foundation. There were four main breaths related to the four elements:

Fire breath for spirit and energy

Earth breath for physical form

Air breath for mental use

Water breath for emotional

Each breath had two main forms – a calming and an energizing. So Calm Air was used to settle the mind and thoughts, while Energizing Air was used to build up power in the mind in order to direct it toward some goal. Calm Fire was for settling the energy body down so it could rest and sleep, while Energizing Fire was to charge up the energy body to take action, like in energizing the Crystal. Calm Earth was to slow down to be able to connect to the natural world, and Energizing Earth was to stir up nature, like bringing rain. Calm Water soothed the emotions, and Energizing Water created passion and desire. These were the eight main breaths that made up the biggest part of our energetic work. We controlled every part of our lives by the ability to control our breath. These breaths can be a great resource for this lifetime as well and are relatively easy to master.

I also had the skill to travel outside of my body, what we term "astral travel" today. In Atlantis I astrally traveled to places on earth to find energy sources. I traversed the land and populations near to me, as well as locations around the planet like the ocean or mountains. In this present life I benefit from these skills of astral travel to my inner worlds in shamanic journeys and sleep time in my dreams. I also had the ability to sense energy sources, what would be termed today as psychic awareness. I could feel an energy and then diagnose the type of energy it was. And I had the ability to direct energy toward a particular goal, as in igniting the Crystal and seeking an escape from Dem Majer's salon. Many of these skills continued to follow me through future lives, especially the sensitivity to energy sources.

After my experience in Atlantis I would like to make some changes. In my next life I definitely want to have more freedom. I felt trapped in the Atlantean life where I really had few choices. I don't want to live in the middle of a fishbowl again where all my actions are watched. I want autonomy. And I would like a warmer family relationship. I really liked Emna and admired her respect and love for her father. I also want more insight and awareness of the broader forces at play and not to be so isolated from larger experiences of the world. I don't want to be locked in a physical reality or continent with no understanding of how it functions. I don't want to be so naïve. I would enjoy gaining knowledge of the power of nature and how energetic forces can be unlocked.

In my present life in the 21st century I feel guilt for the destruction of Atlantis as a result of my failures. I have been aware of this guilt since I experienced my first regression session of Atlantis, many decades ago during my past life training. But now, upon reflection, I realize that my failure does not make me responsible or to blame. Dem Majer and his cohorts, whoever they were, are the ones responsible for the destruction of Atlantis. And if even one other of the 12 had refused to participate, that would have stopped the obliteration. It is hard for me to imagine how passive those other 11 must have been to allow the igniting and generation of the Crystal with Dem Majer taking my place. Yet there is still a part of me that feels like I failed, and that I had better lie low or else be discovered and destroyed. This karmic pattern of staying hidden is strong in me and is one I have dealt with all my life, including right now as I write this book. Sharing my past life stories will make me visible to others, which challenges my belief that it is best to lay low and stay hidden. I also realize that the act of sharing these stories and becoming visible is part of the healing I need in this current life.

There are Universal themes to this life in Atlantis:

Where do we all come from for the first incarnations?

Is it from another dimension or other worlds?

How does the Soul begin?

There is also the collective theme of experiencing betrayal and not trusting ourselves, even when evidence is clear, as well as the feeling that one did not fulfill a duty, feeling responsible and guilty for the result of that failure.

For you, the reader

This Atlantis lifetime might have resonated or triggered you. Take some time now to just breathe. Close your eyes and allow images, feelings, and sensations to arise. Just notice them and consider what, if anything, this story of Atlantis might have activated for you.

Maybe you too were in Atlantis and remember the destruction. Maybe you remember doing energy work in a highly tuned spiritual environment. Perhaps you are pondering when your first incarnation occurred, and how your Soul entered the Body. Perhaps you resonated to trusting someone totally, only to have them betray that trust, and now carry the self-blame and incrimination for being so naïve to have trusted fully.

Do you carry guilt for failing to fulfill a responsibility perfectly? Or perhaps it stirs the feeling of closeness and desire for friendship. Do you have a sense of what some of your major patterns are and how they interact in your life now?

Take some time and journal what arises for you. Let your imagination wander. Pay attention to any dreams or synchronicities that may occur over the next few days. Place your hand over your heart and feel compassion for yourself as you experience the journey of life.

5
The Good Man – A Light in the Desert: Egypt, c. 1500 BCE

I am born a squalling healthy baby boy. My cries are so loud and strong that my lungs could burst. But no one seems to mind. I am wrapped up in a warm cloth and given to my mother, the healer in this tribal village in the desert of Egypt. I am in a mud hut, lit by the warm glow of a fire. My mother lifts me up in pride as people are laughing. The tribe members take turns holding me, and with a kiss on my forehead they place a blessing. I am put back into my mother's arms and some dim recognition comes to me that I am safe. I close my eyes and fall into a peaceful sleep.

As a child, even though the vast extended family of my tribe surrounds me, I still spend much of my time alone. It feels best when I am wandering the rough dry hills around our village, searching for herbs and stones that my mother needs for her work. By the time I am a teen, she teaches me to assist her and I continue the family tradition as a healer. We are the only healers in the tribe and nearby surrounding lands. The expected events of everyday life and the slow turning of the seasons is how time passes until my mother dies and I find myself the elder and the main village doctor. I continue to move through the wheel of my life by counting the rhythms of Suns, Moons, years, births and deaths. And so it would have continued except for an unexpected visit.

Sometimes travelers stop by our village as they journey. In this vast stretch of desert, our village is visible from quite a distance. We are blessed to live on an oasis, so there is shade and water that draws weary travelers to our doors. We provide them water, food, and simple hospitality. We enjoy these infrequent disruptions since these travelers often have goods to trade, gossip to share, or even a young woman as a potential wife.

But on this day it is a large caravan rather than a solitary traveler, and we can see it coming from far away. We wonder who it could be, and I feel a dark chill in my heart, hoping they will pass us by. But we are the only oasis on the desert for far distances, and the caravan comes straight toward us. Excitement mounts in the village as news spreads that it is a royal caravan from the large city several days away. The chief goes out to greet them at dusk and the village watches as many men labor to set up a large tent just as night falls.

I do not go out, but keep within my home and prepare herbs that have dried on my rafters and are ready to be made into medicines. My young granddaughter runs into my hut, her face flushed with excitement. She pulls at my sleeve and says, "Come out and see the tent, Grandfather! It is so grand! Like a palace filled with stars!"

I keep my head down as I crush the herbs. All my senses tell me that danger is near and I want to go nowhere close to it. "Do not bother the strangers, little one," I start to say, but my granddaughter has already skipped from my clay house to join the rest of the village as they gaze at the tent that dominates the horizon. Later, after the sun has gone to bed, I slip into a fitful sleep and dream that the tent bursts into flames, setting trees on fire which engulf the oasis while tentacles of flame and smoke surround our village.

The next day the sun has barely cracked the horizon when a stranger appears at my door. He is more grandly dressed than any person I have ever seen, covered in silks and beads, with leather sandals on his feet. He is a messenger from the caravan and has come to ask for the village healer. Someone from the royal family is sick and my skills are needed.

"A poor man like myself has nothing that the royal family could need," I say, trying to back away. "You must have doctors much more skilled." My breath is calm, but the chill in my heart grows stronger.

"That is not for either of us to decide," states the messenger as he steps inside.

I feel trapped and have no other choice but to go with him. I decide to leave my medicines behind and will say I have nothing to help. I put on my most frayed cloak and bend down like a very old man to walk slowly from the house. I follow the messenger reluctantly and see the tent in the distance. It is like a palace, just as my granddaughter said, and shines like gold in the morning sun.

As we enter the tent it feels like I have been transported to another world. I have never seen anything so extravagant. The walls are covered in fabrics and the floors with rugs. The chairs are of deep brown wood and elaborately carved. People scurry about, but there is a silence in the air. A bed spread with rich linens is covered in a finely woven white net. A woman grandly dressed like a queen is seated by the bed, her brows lined with worry. Images of my mother flash through my mind as she worked hard to stop an illness she could not cure. I stand in silence but my feet agitate, begging me to leave.

"Sir, thank you for coming," the woman says as she moves toward me. "My daughter is very ill and nothing seems to help her. Please be seated and share with us your knowledge."

I am stunned. *Sir? Please be seated?* I have never been accorded such dignity. My suspicions rise. *What is this place? These people?* I say nothing and do not move.

A man rises from his seat next to the woman, standing tall and proud. "The healer's silence is because he is dumbstruck. He has never seen such riches as these, nor been among royalty. No doubt he has nothing to share, nor anything to say." The man is bejeweled and robed in such luxury as a king. He speaks in the dialect of the city, which he assumes I would not know. He stares at me with piercing eyes and my heart freezes. Everything inside of me says to be silent, to bow down, to back off, to leave immediately.

But in the face of the woman I see the fear of my mother, and in the bed a sick girl the age of my granddaughter. *Silence, Silence*, my heart cries. My head will not be still.

"Do not think me ignorant because I live in the village," I state in the dialect of the city. My heart sinks and I know I am lost. The man's nose flares, like a bull ready to charge, and I stand my ground. There is a familiar feeling as I look into his piercing dark eyes. But this time I will not run, I will not flee, I will not give him any respect or obedience. I turn to look at the woman. "What is the problem?"

"I am Queen Shen. We left our city two days ago. We stopped in the oasis at Saqqara on our first night. The next morning my daughter was tired, but we continued onward, until she was no longer able to eat or speak. She is now in a deep sleep and none can awaken her, not even our esteemed physician Ben Mal," she says, pointing to the man dressed in riches. "Can you help?"

Ben Mal steps forward, still speaking in the dialect of the city. "The village people state there is no healer to your equal," he says with contempt. "They say you can find the problems no matter where they are hidden, and that you come from a long line of those who heal."

"These are simple village folks," I say, "and they know no healer but me. I am all they have. I am sure your abilities far exceed my own. If you cannot heal the girl, I am sure I cannot."

I turn to leave, but am rebuked. "Do not leave without permission! Do you not know with whom you deal?" he spits. I turn to stare at him, unafraid. I take deep breaths and feel calm come over me. My mind is racing. How can I get out of here without everything I know being destroyed?

"Please, sir," the queen interjects. "Please, at least see my child?"

I am caught between the dual trap of compassion and pride; as a healer I want to help the mother and child, but I also hate Ben Mal and will not back down. I realize then that I am lost. If I help and heal the child, Ben Mal will be sure to have me killed for doing what he could not. In other circumstances I might take the court healer aside and share my cures with him, so he could provide the cure and reap the praise. I would get some silvers and he would get a reputation. But I instantly hate Ben Mal and will share nothing with him. I will need to heal the girl myself. But at what cost? Would my family be killed? My village destroyed?

The queen comes to me and takes my hand. Her skin is so soft. She pulls me to the bed. Ben Mal stiffens at the intimacy she shows me, but my attention shifts to the young princess, small and lost in the large bed, her eyes shut and beads of sweat forming on her brow. Her skin is cool to the touch, but there is a heat that is boiling within her. What is the trouble? Where does it lie?

I slow my breath, close my eyes and inwardly begin a search of her body. With my inner eye I find the parasite that crawled into her at the last oasis. It has attached to her stomach and is draining her life. I have seen this before. I know I can save her. I keep my eyes closed, as if I am still seeking the trouble, and weigh my situation. I could save the princess, but in return I will be trapped forever. I could let her die, and betray all my years as a healer. I bend my head and feel despair. If only I could walk away.

"I need to get my medicines," I say as I straighten up.

"Oh, no need," says Ben Mal with a tight grin. "We sent for your granddaughter to fetch your bag. Here she comes now."

In walks my granddaughter with my medicine bag, her eyes wide with amazement at the riches of the tent. I look at Ben Mal and see the intention in his eyes. His eyes are saying, *"Your granddaughter's life or the life of the princess. If you heal the princess then your granddaughter will be killed."* This is truly an evil man. His reputation is more important than the life of his patients.

I feel trapped. I take the bag from my granddaughter and hold her next to me. Her time spent at my side has taught her to read my signals, and she settles beside me.

I turn to the queen and say, "My granddaughter and I need to be alone to pray for the successful completion of the healing; it is our way. Please excuse me. We will only take a short time." And with this we walk a few paces out of the tent, still within the view of all. I know Ben Mal would not allow us out of his sight. We kneel on the hard sand, facing the still rising sun.

"Granddaughter. We are in grave danger. I ask you to leave me now, and get the rest of the family. Go quickly to the caves and stay until the caravan has left. Tell the people of the village you go to gather herbs for the healing and no one will question you. Wait two days after the caravan has left before you return."

"But what of you?" she asks, fear in her eyes.

I do not want to concern her, nor do I want to lie. "I am uncertain. I may be forced to go with them to continue to care for the sick princess or I will be killed. If I am dead you will find me, but I do not think I will be here when you return. Be strong. You know much healing, and your mother even more. You will be the village healers now." I bow two times to the earth and throw sand to the sun. "Go now."

We both stand and my granddaughter leaves to gather the family. I go back inside the coolness of the tent. Ben Mal and the queen stand by the bed and I hear agitation in his voice; I sense he is telling the queen not to trust me. I walk toward them. "Our prayers were heard and I am ready to do the healing."

They step back and I see the sick girl lying motionless in the bed. I open my medicine bag and take out a small knife, a hollow reed, a bag of herbs, and salve. I enter into meditation and with my inner eye search her body until I find the spot on her stomach where the parasite lives. I cover her belly with antiseptic salve, then make a small incision. Ben Mal gasps, but the queen's look silences him. I cut deep into her flesh until I reach the parasite. Then I take the reed and place it far into the cut and blow in the herbs that I know will kill the parasite. I say the prayers of healing and death, pull out the reed, cover the wound with more salve, and straighten up.

"She will need to rest for the remainder of the day. By tomorrow morning she will be well enough to travel. But I would head back from whence you came, and go no further on your journey. She will need at least a month to fully heal and be herself again."

"A month?" says Ben Mal. "Then we will want you to come with us to assure her safety." *And to be sure to kill me*, I think.

"Please sir," says the queen. "Come with us, and as my daughter lives, you will be a rich man."

These people would not understand that I care not about riches, so I say nothing. She continues. "Go to your home to prepare and we will call on you again in the morning."

As I walk from the tent to my mud brick house I can sense the guards following me, a sensation that feels vaguely familiar. I know now that I am a prisoner. But I am pleased to find that when I arrive in my home, I am alone. My family has left for the caves and is safe. I can hope for no more.

At dawn I hear a knock on my door and the guards await to escort me to the tent, which is being dismantled and arranged for travel. I walk around my home and slowly look at all my things, knowing I will not likely see them again. It is a simple mud home, a small straw bed, clay pots and dishes, herbs drying from the rafters, sun coming through the windows. I fill one pack with my best set of clothes, the ones I only wear on ceremonial occasions, and my best robe. The other pack is my medicine bag, always ready for whatever job the day brings. It has my herbs, sharp knife, salves, reeds, bandages, stones, and small bottles of tincture. I quickly prepare all the herbs that are drying on the rafters so I can take them with me. In the secret pouch of the bag I place my most potent herbs and my few coins and make sure they cannot be found by prying hands. I take two loaves of bread, a bladder of water, my walking staff and cloak. As I leave my home, I close the door and seal it with a prayer of safety and protection so that my family will find it a house of refuge when they return.

All that I own I carry with me to the caravan. Queen Shen greets me with a smile and takes me to her daughter who is resting on soft pillows in the carved golden litter that will carry her on the journey. "I want you to meet my daughter so that she might see the person who has returned her to life." I look down at the child and am glad to see that her eyes are clear and her body no longer battles to live. She gives me a small smile, then turns to sleep as we begin the long journey back to her city.

We move slowly, partly because the caravan is so large and partly because of the weakness of the princess. We pause frequently and I tend to her at each stop with herbs and healing hands. She continues to grow stronger and by the second day she is sitting, propped up with pillows in her litter.

As the princess's strength grows, so does Ben Mal's hatred of me. He barely pretends to tolerate me when the queen is near, but if we are ever alone he makes it clear that I am his enemy.

"Your desert cures are wasted on me," he says under his breath as I am putting herbs back into my bags after one treatment. "You will find there is no place for your meager skills in the city, where the power of the gods answer to my command."

I say nothing and try not to look at him. His eyes are cold as ice and his face is distorted and cruel. He continues. "I told the queen we should not trust our safety to the desert. Now she will know that she should listen to me in the future and stay within the city walls."

As I rise to leave, Ben Mal steps in front of me, blocking my path. I am as tall as him and we look eye to eye. I will not look away. My heart begins to pound and if it was not locked in my chest it would run free. "Do not think you will be a healer of the royal court," he says slowly. "It is unlikely you will live long enough to see that day."

As he speaks I know that I do not want to be a healer of the royal court. I just want the silence of the desert and to see the light of the sun as it comes over the horizon. I want the coolness of the night and to see the image of Osiris drawn in the stars, accompanied by his queen Isis. I want to smell the freshly cut herbs, taste the cool water of the village well, and hear the laughter of my granddaughter.

"I can leave now, if you so desire," I say slowly. "The princess will continue to strengthen with your care."

"Yes." He looks slyly at me. "Yes, naturally you want to return home, and I can care for the princess now. Leave tonight as soon as the Moon has set so the darkness will hide you. You have done plenty. It is time for you to leave." My heart leaps. I can return home. "As you wish," I say, and walk back to my sleeping quarters.

I excuse myself after dinner and make sure both bags are packed and my bladder filled with water. I know my way back to the village and could return even without the light of the Moon. I lie down in the servants' tent on my robe, pretending to be asleep, and wait until those around me settle into soft snoring. I rise quietly, take my bags, and leave without a sound. I stand outside the tent, take some calming breaths, and center myself.

But I feel nervous and agitated, not happy to be free. I almost ignore my sensations and start my journey into the night. But instead I hesitate in the shadow of the tent and probe the darkness around me like I would probe the body of a patient, looking for the problem, searching for the dis-ease. Quickly I sense the presence of a person behind a boulder about 20 feet away. I can hear small sounds as he shifts and I see a subtle movement in the night. Of course. Ben Mal is not letting me leave. He has set me up to be killed, no doubt saying that I was trying to run away, probably with something of value found in my bag so he could also call me a thief. I might be able to leave from another direction and perhaps make it from camp without getting caught. But I know Ben Mal will not let me live, and all I would be doing is bringing the enemy back into my village and putting everything I know into danger.

I feel a deep sadness overcome me. I would weep, if I ever allowed myself such weakness. I realize for certain that I can never go back home again. I am being forced against my will into the city, herded like an animal to the slaughter, my options for escape eliminated one by one until I end up at the palace, finally trapped and killed.

Knowing my fate, I almost lift my two sacks to set out for home, letting the man behind the boulder kill me. At least it would be over. But a faint hope begins to stir. There still might be a way. I realize that my quiet and sullen attitude when I am near the queen and her daughter is not helping me. My goal of being invisible to them and forgotten is not working, and my silence gives Ben Mal more power to determine my fate. I need to get the queen to like me; she already is grateful that I saved her daughter's life. She might feel like she owes me a debt, which she could repay by setting me free. I feel a lightness in my heart.

I slip unseen back into the sleeping tent and stretch out on my robes to sleep. I will not be killed in the night like an escaped thief. I know we are arriving at the city this day and are expected in the palace. I do not know what the queen has in mind for me once we get there, or if I will see her again after we reach the palace gate. If I am going to remind her of her debt and ask for her favor, it needs to be in the morning.

At dawn I enter the royal tent as servants prepare the caravan for the last day of travel. There is an excitement in the air since this will be the final leg of a difficult journey. The queen and her daughter are seated at an elaborately set table, finishing their morning meal. "Good morning, Queen Shen," I say as I bow my head. Then I turn to address her daughter. "How are you today, my Princess?"

They are both silent and stare at me openly. My greeting surprises them, not only because I rarely say as much, but also because I speak clearly, with the crisp dialect of the city, the dialect of an educated man. I have also bathed. My long dark hair, which has been covered in the dust of travel is now shiny and pulled into a thick band so it lays down the middle of my back. I replaced my worn clothes with my fine ceremonial robe that I brought with me. Though not made with silk and jewels as are their clothes, my robe is still impressive, made of fine fabric, rich wools from different animals woven together to make an intricate design. The neck and arms have beautiful red beads sewn with threads of fine leather. My sandals are of the same leather, also covered in red beads, with the laces wrapped up my legs.

"Good morning to you, sir," says the queen, as she looks at me amazed. It is as if she is seeing me for the first time. "The princess is stronger today and anxious to return home, as am I."

I look with sympathy into her face and say, "That is very natural considering you almost lost your child to the desert. When you return home you will be able to set your concerns down and find rest to bring you back to ease and peace. If it pleases you, I will make you a tonic that will heal your weary head and heart." I am directing healing energy toward her as we speak, and the lightness in her eyes indicates that she feels the warmth.

"I would like that very much, and it is kind of you to notice my needs."

"And you?" I say, shifting my attention and gazing warmly at the girl. It is actually a relief to not hide behind a gruff exterior. I have kept my energy concealed deep inside so as not to bring attention to myself. But discovering Ben Mal's plans to kill me has caused me to change my usual taciturn way of relating. Instead, I let my healing energy flow forth and fill the room. I feel radiant.

"Will you make a tonic for me, too?" asks the princess. "I no longer wish to be weary and always in bed resting. I am so happy we are near the city that I think I shall run the rest of the way there, and then dance my way from the city gates to my quarters in the palace. I long to see the beauties of our city and I think I shall never leave it again!"

"I will make you a tonic that will enable you to fly there! Will that do?" I say with laughter. "It must be a wonderful city if it has thus captured your heart." I begin to open my medicine sack to prepare the tonics. "And so I am able to keep up with you, if you so allow, I will make a tonic for myself as well."

"Oh yes! You must travel the rest of the way with us and I will tell you all about the city's wonders and point them out to you as we arrive," the princess begins excitedly, and then chatters non-stop about the glories of her city and the wonders of the palace.

The three of us are all seated comfortably, sipping our tonics and speaking in companionable conversation when Ben Mal arrives. When he sees me, he is shocked. It is bad enough that I am still alive, but to see me thus dressed and in comfort with the royal family is more than he can bear. His face becomes purple with rage and the veins on his neck pulse as he forces himself to contain it.

"My Queen," says Ben Mal as he bows. "Is there anything I can do for you this morning?"

Taking a sip of her tonic she replies, "No, Sashoni has provided all we need," she says, nodding to me. Ben Mal's face goes even deeper in color but the smile stays in place. As he turns toward me his eyes pierce mine.

I feel a chill in my heart but I do not look away. I smile pleasantly. Since I know he intends to kill me, I have nothing to lose and I find a small pleasure in taunting him, as if I can switch my role in this game of cat and mouse.

"Which has me thinking," the queen continues, "of where our guest would be most comfortable when we arrive at the palace." She nods to me. "Will you have a room prepared for him with the healers? Can you also be sure Sashoni has access to the Room of Medicine? Since he will be staying a month until my daughter is totally healed, I thought that during that time he could teach our healers about the herbs of the desert, a skill which seems to be lacking in the city. Can you see that he has all he needs during his stay?" She turns to me and smiles. "I will need these tonics when you are gone and must be sure that someone will know how to make them for me."

Ben Mal's rage can scarcely be contained. Glaring, he turns to me as he leaves the room. "Oh, yes, I will be sure to take care of our guest."

I understand the message of his words and wonder about the wisdom of being so fully under his control once at the palace. But I dismiss these thoughts as I feel joy build in my heart. My strategy has worked and the queen has said I can leave after a month. Maybe I can learn some new healing methods to take back with me to my village. I feel hopeful for the first time since the caravan unexpectedly arrived.

I rise, asking permission to gather the rest of my traveling gear so I can join the queen and her daughter. I feel the stirring of pride and stand tall as I leave the room.

The caravan moves at a steady pace. The enthusiasm the princess had that morning dampens in the discomfort of travel. I walk beside her litter, where she lays propped up against giant pillows. She tells me an occasional story or mentions a famous landmark, but nothing prepares me for what I see as we arrive at midday on a bluff overlooking the outskirts of the city.

Rising up out of the horizon stand three huge pyramids, radiant in the sun. I stop walking and stand dumbstruck. I have never seen anything so gigantic. They are rooted in the earth and carry a feeling of great peace. Yet there is a force about them as well, as if the earth had erupted using a sharp point to cut through the hard ground in an effort to touch the sky. Rooted to the earth, yet reaching for the sky. Something stirs in me, an energy deep in my belly that rises up my spine and out the top of my head. I feel my feet rooted to the earth, but my head is piercing through to the sky. Powerful energy pulsates through me as I stand motionless, entranced.

"It seems as if our desert friend is quite taken by our pyramids," says Ben Mal slowly to the queen, perhaps trying to formulate an idea. "While we continue on to the palace I can send my servant as his guide so that he may see the pyramids up close. That will give me time to arrange his quarters, and for the princess to rest. He can join you tonight for dinner and a tour of the grounds. How does that sound?" he asks casually. The queen agrees it is a good plan, and the caravan continues on its way.

I am left alone on the bluff with Ben Mal's servant. I have hardly been aware of the conversation. My entire focus is on the pyramids before me. It is as if I have been transported to another place and time. Flashes of images race across my eyes. I see myself as a young man, but with light hair and skin, not dark as I am now. I see corridors and tunnels stretch out before me, like a maze. I see a vast green continent, and ships getting ready to set sail. I see the piercing eyes of a man as he serves me tea, and a gigantic crystal stone.

All these things and more flash so quickly before me that I become confused, even unsteady. I drop to my knees, place my hands on the earth, and begin to breathe deeply in an attempt to stop the swirling in my head. I think I might need water, and so I drink deeply from my bladder and wash my face. The images begin to clear and I sit on the earth to take some time to meditate on what this could all mean. But Ben Mal's servant complains of the sun's heat and his desire to return to his home, saying that we need to get going. He looks around as he speaks, nervous.

If I weren't so confused by the swirling images in my head and the pounding of my heart, I might have paid more attention to him. I might have thought about the man the previous night hidden in the dark waiting to kill me, and Ben Mal's desire to have me dead. I might have considered the extent of Ben Mal's anger when he was told to find me a place among the palace healers, and that I was to teach about the herbs of the desert. I might have wondered about the wisdom of being separated from the safety of the caravan and the protection of the royal family.

But I think of none of these things. My body is still vibrating and my senses are not clear. So I rise up, still shaky, put my bags around me and follow the servant down the hill and into the valley where the pyramids are shining in the sun. My eyes never leave the pyramids, which have a mesmerizing effect on me.

I don't see the steep embankments that we pass, or the deep ravine where we pause. I never see the knife as it enters my heart, nor hardly feel its sharpness as it twists inside of me. I am barely aware of the push that sends my body over the edge, or feel the empty space around me as I fall deeper into the earth. It seems as if the fall takes forever, as I go further and further down into the crevice. As I drop, I vaguely wonder how many other bodies are at the bottom, how many other people have been killed in this exact same place, knowing that the depth of the ravine would keep the crime from being discovered.

As my body continues to fall, my Soul detaches from my body and rises like a bird, flying back up the ravine and then into the sky. From my new height I see the servant hurrying up the hill, no doubt to tell his master that the deed is finally done. Perhaps he will get an extra silver, or even gold, for his success. I stay motionless, scanning the horizon, the land, my life. I could follow him back to the palace to see how Ben Mal describes my absence, but there is nothing for me there. I think about my home village and my granddaughter who is my most loved, and who will never see me again. Perhaps I will go to her in a dream to let her know my fate so she will not spend years awaiting my return. It is important for her and her mother to establish themselves as the village healers; the expectation that I will be back would not do well for them as they own their authority.

My Soul rises high in the sky and then flies to the only thing that seems essential to discover before I leave this lifetime in the desert of Egypt to never return. I fly toward the pyramids which are like beacons that resonate sound currents and light waves. I can see an energy source deep within the center of each that taps into the power of the earth, pushing it up and out the peak and into the open air. I want to know more. I want to understand the images that flashed before me of the crystal source and radiating power.

But I am weary and feel I can fly no more. So I take a deep breath, draw my energy into a container within, hold myself in a calm and steady focus, and then let go into radiant splendor. This life is over.

Life Lessons from Egypt

When I finished the account of this life I felt so sad that I cried. This person, this healer, was such a good man. Then I grasped that this person is me, which points to the fact that we are not simple creatures but have enormous complexity in our history and humanness.

In many ways, Atlantis and Egypt had similar karmic patterns and lessons for me to experience and learn. In Egypt I changed my status from elite to poor and my environment from temple to hut, thinking that would make it all different. But it was the same story all over again – I was used and killed because of my gift.

A repeated theme that arose was my need to stay hidden, but the Egyptian life showed that hiding was not a useful strategy. Trying to be invisible just made me less effective. I am struck how it felt so freeing to be seen and radiate my healing energy to the queen and princess.

The karmic patterns in Atlantis and Egypt were the same in that I became trapped by circumstances, ensnared and manipulated by a powerful leader, had my own gifts used against me, felt a sense of helplessness to change the situation, and my heart was ultimately the cause of my death.

Looking at these lives now from a broader perspective, I can see that I wasn't entirely trapped and could make some choices that were effective. In Atlantis, even though I was killed and the civilization was destroyed, that life was not a total failure. Dem Majer was also killed and his plans disrupted. Who knows what damage he could have inflicted upon the outer lands and the world if he had controlled the power of Atlantis. In Egypt my gifts of insight and healing were confined to a small village where I would not be noticed; it was only the arrival of the royal caravan that changed it all. I had to make a choice between hiding my gifts and letting the princess die, or exposing my healing gifts, which saved the princess but led to jealousy of the royal doctor and my eventual death. Even though I was trapped, I was still able to make decisions to save my family and village, so it was a better result than Atlantis. This is also an example that even though the life may be entirely different – in status, wealth, and circumstance –similar underlying patterns remain.

> *Even though past lives may be entirely different – in status, wealth and circumstance – underlying patterns remain.*

This story also illustrates how some of the karmic patterns that started in Atlantis became weaker in Egypt. I wanted to avoid the isolation and elitism of Atlantis, which I achieved in Egypt as part of a close family and community embedded in nature. I became less naïve in the ways of the world and more attuned to my Soul's wisdom and mastery.

The soul wound in my Egyptian life was keeping my power and light from shining, thinking that staying hidden would protect me. I've had that wound for many lifetimes. I can feel how sad it is to hide the light of a talent, both for the individual and others. It is uncomfortable on so many levels – physical, emotional, spiritual, and energetic. It is like keeping the blinds pulled on the window of a house so that no natural light can enter. It is like living in darkness. It strikes me that a major lesson of my Egypt life was that it is necessary to share my light. This is a lesson I need to remember in my current life. Often I keep my light inside and hold myself back. It is time to be more radiant, and not to hold my light within. It is time for everyone to be more radiant; the world needs all our light.

Allies and Adversaries demonstrate how some of the people we meet in one life, whether as friends or enemies, are linked to us by a karmic bond, for good or ill. The royal physician Ben Mal is the same as my teacher Dem Majer in Atlantis. This is seen through similarities in behaviors, such as his dismissive attitude of me as well as his penetrating eyes and the chill on my heart when he was near. In Egypt I hated and distrusted Ben Mal immediately, as if a sleeping memory was reawakened. I stood up to him from the first moment, and in doing so I broke the pattern of being in awe of one with greater status. I also think that Emna in Atlantis is my granddaughter in Egypt, in that her sweet and open spirit is the same and she is the one I most loved. She was my Ally and the sweetness of life that I was missing in Atlantis.

The skills acquired in one incarnation can continue into the next. The Atlantis skill of being able to sense and direct psychic energy was leveraged in Egypt for physical healing, as when I diagnosed the princess's illness and psychically sensed an enemy in the night. New skills were learned as well – working with nature (including an understanding and immersion in the seasonal cycles of nature and human life), and herbal skills (learned from my mother, the village healer to whom I was apprenticed as a child). I was obviously teaching my granddaughter those same skills. I used the energy awareness developed in Atlantis and combined it with herbal medicine to become a skilled healer.

In the next life I want to be more confident to share my gifts openly. In this Egyptian life I wanted a low profile based on what happened in Atlantis. But Egypt might have been better if I had been bolder about showing my gifts. I could possibly have created a better relationship with the queen and princess and taken much of the power from Ben Mal. I think I let him control me too much by my absence. Being more visible would be good, so in my next life I want to be stronger and braver and more confident.

In the present life I have a love of herbal medicine, natural healing, and living simply. That resonates with what I did in Egypt. I also identify with the importance of being a good person and taking actions based on personal integrity. For example, I couldn't let the princess die just to make it easier on myself. Also, I think this Egyptian karmic pattern of hiding my true talent for fear of retaliation has been active in my current life where I am an astrologer, a profession that is not highly valued in the US. I have been ridiculed and even threatened, yet I continue. I have justified my profession by legitimizing it with advanced university degrees, as if to prove to the world that my interests in astrology and spirituality do not mean I am stupid.

The universal theme to this Egyptian life points to how important it is to acknowledge and share our gifts. Everyone has something special that makes them unique. Maybe it's kindness, or humor, or an ability like cooking, carpentry, or art. We doubt our gifts for many reasons. Parents will often put down a child's gifts. I know for me in this current life I was an imaginative child, but my father discouraged me by saying, "Wake up, Alice. Wonderland is not right around the corner." So I got the sense that being an imaginative child was not of value, and I still question my creativity and intuitive knowing. Many have similar tales of being dismissed by a parent, teacher, or sibling, leading to a denial of what is important in our very essence.

For you, the reader

Think for a moment about your gifts and skills. Are you a communicator, good at understanding others? Or do you love organization and getting tasks done correctly? Do you embrace your gifts and use them fully? Or do you doubt yourself and keep your light hidden so as not to bring attention? In what circumstances do you feel comfortable shining your light in the world? What environment makes you feel most alive? Do you love nature, gardening, or herbal medicine? Or are you a city dweller and thrive on after-hour clubs, the symphony, and theater?

Take time to consider who in your life has been with you in another lifetime. We often change roles in different lifetimes and can show up in different capacities. Maybe your brother was a fellow warrior, or your father was your son. The idea of a Soul mate is that there is a partner you knew in another life, and when you meet again there is an instant recognition and a sense that now your life is complete. Soul mates can be lovers, but are always deep and abiding friends.

6

Heart of a Warrior: Maya, c. 300 CE

I am a young and strong Mayan, 18 years of age. Handsome, brave, and smart, I am the chief's son, and will no doubt become chief one day myself. Though I have never been to war, I win all the mock battles of our training and am considered the best. I understand strategy and expect I will lead many battles once I am initiated into a fully recognized warrior of the people. I have thick dark hair which is tied at the nape of my neck so it hangs down my back. My skin is bronze and my body is muscular. I know I am handsome and many of the young maidens watch me when I play the ball games of our people, most of which I win.

I live in a city on the river plain. The land is lush and green and provides food and water for our people. The abundance of food gives us time to further our studies and pursue art. Many of our stone buildings are carved with images of the gods of our people, elaborate and bold in design. Our pyramid, built in ancient times with solid rock, is placed perfectly in the center of our city. It is our sacred center and where the gods stay when they visit us. Though simple in design, the pyramid is structured with sacred mathematics and geometry and saturated with symbols. Since I am also studying to be a priest, a sky watcher, I spend many hours on top of the pyramid looking at the night stars to recognize the motions of Venus and the movement of time. I am proud to be part of this city, which is gazed upon with wonder from the villages surrounding us.

The next full moon is the Popol Vuh, the occasion of a major ceremony of initiation into manhood. It is a great celebration where, in front of all the people who live in the city, the young warriors are announced with their new battle names. At this time we drop our youthful ways and take our place as men in the city, which we will protect with our lives.

There is a private ceremony just for the initiates that takes place before the large city celebration. I do not know what will happen in this ceremony since the details are kept secret. But I do know they will pick the best new warrior for a special honor, and I hope it is me. I want to make my father proud. I want to be the best. I have spent my entire life, as have my friends whom I have grown with from a child into a man, preparing for this moment. I have done all that has been asked of me; I have excelled in everything.

There are thirty of us who will become warriors. We train especially hard as the Popol Vuh nears. There will be a demonstration of our skills, and we want to look worthy before our leaders and people of our city. So for months we run harder, throw the spear further, and fight with greater intensity. I am not the only initiate who wants to be seen as the best and become the chosen one.

The day of the initiation is finally here, and I and the other young warriors who have completed the training are taken at first light to the temple, which is in the base of the pyramid. I can see Venus rising in the predawn sky as we enter. The elder warriors greet us with chants and songs. I see my father, dressed in the colorful robes and feather headdress of the chief. We initiates sit in a circle while the warriors dance around us, chanting. The priests are praying to seek the omens and signs that will guide the day.

We are told to remove our clothes, which are burnt in a fire to indicate the end of our youth. Then we are taken to a ritual bath where we soak in steaming water and strong scents. This bath represents being fully reborn, no longer children tied to the wombs of our mothers. We are now tied to the laws of our people and are given new clothes and names, symbolic of the life we are entering as protectors of the people and leaders of our land.

All the warrior initiates receive the same clothes, except for me. My wish has come true and I am chosen as the best of the warriors. I am honored for my strength and skill and strategy. I stand nude in the center of the circle as the warriors and priests chant over me, put oil on me, and then paint images and symbols all over my body. I am then covered in an amazing robe and a headdress made entirely of feathers. I am given a necklace of bone. I could roar with my pleasure, with my strength.

I look to my father who I know must be so proud of me right now. But his brow is furrowed and his face is long. He sees me looking at him and he forces a smile. I am confused, for surely, this is the greatest honor of all, to know his son is the best.

There is a feast for all the seasoned warriors and the new initiates. I am placed at the head of the table. I am treated like a king and waited on by beautiful slaves. It is the first time we have been seen as equals with the older warriors, who until today treated us as their students. We all join together and drink the intoxicating maté and become men, warriors who protect the people. There is great laughter as we eat and drink and sing, uniting in one fierce band of community. It is the best day of my life.

After the feast I am led with much jesting and singing, into a special room where a beautiful slave girl waits for me. The other warriors laugh and close the door. I am given several hours with this girl to pleasure me. She feeds me food and drink; I consume more maté and become quite intoxicated. My head begins to spin and my thinking is not so clear. I know it is time to quit the slave girl and the feasting and join the others to prepare for the night's celebration. I put on my feather cloak and go to leave the room. But the door is locked. I bang on it, and soon I hear the sound of priests who open the door and escort me to the waiting room for the main ritual.

I am alone in here and I begin to pace. I am angry with myself for drinking too much. I do not know what ritual is to come and I want to do it correctly, to make my father and my people proud. Where are the other warriors, I wonder. Should I not be with them? Or do I have a special part to play? Perhaps I will be leader of the ceremony, like I was at the feast?

Two priests come to get me. I begin to ask questions about the others and my role, but they tell me it is time only for silence now. Night has fallen and the pyramid is brightly illuminated with torches. The two priests lead me up the steps to the top of the pyramid and I hear drumming and chanting, which get louder and more excited as I arrive. I can see that the people of the city have gathered at the pyramid's base, but they are so far away I cannot distinguish their faces. I know my mother is there. Does she see that I am the honored one? What of my brothers and sister? Can they tell it is me with the priests?

I stand tall and proud, illuminated by the torches on the central platform. In front of me is the stone altar which has been covered with flowers. I see the other initiates to my right, and the older warriors on my left. My father comes out in his splendid robe and headdress and raises his arms to the heavens. The drumming stops. Silence fills the air.

The head priest begins to speak, loud and strong so the people below can hear.

"We are here to bring the new warriors into our community, warriors who will protect us and lead us into battle. Yes, these warriors are important to our people, necessary to our strength. But it is to the gods that we owe our lives."

Priests begin to circle me, tossing flowers at my feet.

"To the gods we owe our very existence," the head priest continues. The other priests sprinkle sacred water and burn the sacred smoke over me.

"And so to the gods we give the best of the warriors. In this way the gods will know that we honor them first and foremost, above any man. We do not sacrifice a slave or a captured enemy! That does a disservice to the gods. No! To the gods we sacrifice our very best!"

The lights of the torches flicker. I look up into the sky, but the torchlight keeps me from seeing the familiar stars overhead. I look down and the people below have become a blur. It is as if time stands still.

I am slowly beginning to understand. I am to be sacrificed to the gods so that all the warriors and our land will be safe. This is my honor? To be the best is to become the sacrifice?

The priests begin to chant over the altar and I notice the sharp knife and bowl set by the altar's side. I understand now what will occur. The priests will cut out my heart and place it in the bowl. All of the new warriors will be given the bowl, to share in my heart and my blood, which will give them the protection of the gods.

I cannot believe this is the fate I have worked all my life to achieve. This is my honor?

Yes, this could be an honor. It is through my death that I provide protection to the warriors and safety to the city. But why then do I want to run? Why is my heart beating fast? Why are my hands clenched, seeking escape?

Drinking the intoxicating maté has made my movement slow and unsteady. But my mind is beginning to clear. If I run, would they chase me down? Force me back? And if I could run free, where would I go? I would have to leave my city and be a lost man, with no family, no home, no city, no country.

I am trapped. I look around in a panic for my father. He is behind the altar, his arms raised high in supplication. I can see tears running from his closed eyes. "Father!" I call, but he will not look at me or stop his prayers.

In this moment I am caught. I have spent my whole life being the best to bring honor to my family and city. If I run, if I try to escape, if I scream in terror and pain, I will betray all I have done and bring shame to my family.

But I am not pleased to be a sacrifice. Surely the gods want their victim to be delighted with the honor. But this is no honor for me. I feel tricked. Here, in the moment of my highest celebration I find out that I am to be killed. Why was I not warned? Why was I not given a choice? I feel dizzy with conflict between wanting to honor my family and feeling betrayed by them.

The priests come up to me; each takes an arm and removes my robe. They lay me down on the altar, which is hard and cold on my bare back. It takes every ounce of willpower not to resist, not to scream, not to call out for them to stop.

But even if I give in to my fear, I know it would do no good; my fate is sealed. The priests begin to burn incense over me, and I can tell from the smell that overtakes me that the incense is to relax my body and put me in a trance. Yes, let sleep come over me. Let me move into oblivion. Tears fall down the sides of my eyes as I feel the knife enter my heart.

Life Lessons from Mayan Life

After this past life came to me, Soul helped me understand the intense sorrow. Soul said that normally after a death I (Soul) am aware of leaving the Body and I view the scene from a higher spiritual perspective to help me understand and gain a sense of completion. But that did not happen in this death. I did not move. I was aware that Spirit and life had left my Body, but instead of moving on, I stayed with my Body in a state of great despair. What good is excellence? What good is hard work? Why should I be strong?

After Egypt, where I hid my strength, I made an intention to be more visible and confident in my next life to the fullest extreme. In this Mayan life I became totally visible – son of the chief, with talent, looks, and intelligence. I had it all. I developed great physical ability, skills of confidence and leadership, and a sense of pride for myself and my contribution to the community. This striving for excellence led to my early end as a sacrificial victim. If I had not taken such joy in my challenges, and if I had been quieter in my success, perhaps they would have overlooked me. I was like the crowing cock, strutting and boasting, "Look at me! Look at me!" Well, they did look. Now I cannot bear to see my damaged, lifeless body.

This life brings me great sadness, for it seems like such a senseless death. Sorrow grabbed hold in me and hopelessness took root. I was in the prime of life, ready to take my place as a leader of my people. I had worked so hard to become the best, to make my family and community proud. And it was cut very short.

The theme of being trapped is again evident in this life. In both Atlantis and Egypt I knew that danger was coming and I took action. That action was not completely successful in either life, but there was a sense of empowerment, nonetheless. I had an awareness, some understanding of what was going on around me. I had some choices. In this Mayan life there was no real opportunity to take action that would have saved me. I had been fooled.

Again, there is betrayal, in this case by my father. That builds on the theme begun when my teacher and father figure Dem Majer lied to me and used me for his own means. My father the Chief must have known that a sacrifice to the gods was part of the initiation. He may have felt that he was fulfilling his official duty rather than giving me the protection of a parent. Why had he not warned me, told me not to excel, or perhaps to be more humble or hide my skills? I had the hope and excitement of youth stolen from me. All my excitement and optimism changed in a minute. I thought I was being honored; instead I was being sacrificed.

My karmic pattern thus far has been that my gift and talents lead to my destruction. The sacrifice to the Gods needed to be the very best person.

And so again, it was my gifts that led to me being killed. If I had been an inconsequential person, perhaps I would not have had to die. But I am not sure that thought is correct. One cannot escape death or hide from it. One can only choose how to face death when it does come. Being weak will not help me escape. A slave is more likely to die than a warrior. A weak man more likely than a strong man. I can see there is some part of me that thinks that I alone was chosen for death and all the other warriors got to live. But that is not true. Death comes to us all. Death is inevitable. The soul wound and real sorrow in this lifetime and its death was that I was not given a choice. If the priests had told me what was to occur, if they had warned me that I was going to my battle now, not later, and that I would be the one who protected the entire city through my death, I would have proudly said YES! But I was not given that choice. I think that is the real pain. My choices were stolen from me.

I don't have any sense of an Ally or Adversary.

My skills and gifts in this short life were focused on my warrior training and included physical abilities, strength, endurance, and teamwork. Also I was being trained as a sky watcher and taught the movement of the heavens, a skill that gave me great joy in the quiet night watching the sky in its dance.

In my next life, I want to be the one deciding what happens to me. I want to be less focused on the needs of the community and more aware of my own personal needs and desires. I don't want to be so naïve that I fail to see betrayal, and even worse, betrayal by those I trust.

In my present life I express the skills as a sky watcher in my current work as an astrologer. I love the changing patterns of Sun, Moon, and planets. I feel very happy watching the world turn and the heavens change. Also in my current life, lack of trust has been a theme. I hold myself back, watch carefully, wait years, and then I trust. But even then, my trust is overlaid with caution.

I can feel a heaviness in me with the Mayan death that I don't feel with the other lives, indicating that there is still work to be done in releasing the karma carried over from that lifetime. This could be in part because I processed my Atlantis life in some depth during past life therapy sessions. I really did a lot of clearing in those sessions. I haven't done any clearing for this Mayan warrior life. My Soul did not look at my lifeless body and thank it for the wonderful job it did. Soul did not integrate the lessons and then leave that life behind in gratitude. Soul did not move on. Instead Soul stayed with the Body even after its death. As Body and Soul, we both went into the dark, we both soaked in despair. After the Body decayed, Soul finally rose and left the earth to incarnate again. But that time in the Body spent in despair over the betrayal created a soul wound that had consequences on Soul, which is seen in the next lifetime. In some shamanic traditions this is called Soul Loss, and a ceremony can be done to call back the lost fragments.

I now know that I can envision going back to that young warrior and reimagine the death so that Soul does not steep in despair and a healing can begin. Soul speaks to the young warrior: "Thank you, strong young man. You have been a wonderful Body. I loved the feeling of your strength, your pride, your power. You are like a great mountain that radiates protection. I have so enjoyed being in the life with you. I would like to ask you not to despair. It was wrong of them not to let you choose your end, a brave end for the good of your people. I will ignite you and clean out your pain. I will heal your heart so that the failings of other people do not change the way you feel about yourself. I will take your bones and crush them and make them into stars! I will place your star bones in the sky and make you a tall and proud warrior for all to see. Stand proud. Your legs are strong, your arms held high with your bow and arrow. Your belt is made of silver stars and your sword hangs down. You will continue as a warrior and protector for all time. I will place you in the heavens and call you Orion!"

The destruction of my heart was the cause of my Mayan death, just as it was in Atlantis and Egypt. In my current life it is fortunate that I have done work to heal that damage. Many years ago, in one of my shamanic journeys, I was with my Wisdom Council who exist on the inner planes. They drummed and chanted as they performed a ritual to my heart. It was night and they sat in a circle lit by a sparkling fire, with me laying on my back in the center. One elder kneeled next to me and cut out my wounded heart. He replaced it with a beautiful strong crystal heart. I saw the crystal heart blend into my body and shine with radiant light. They healed my heart, and since then I have been more trusting and loving. It was a great gift.

From a universal viewpoint, this Mayan lifetime illustrates how the Body and Soul intersect to share experiences and lessons of an incarnation. When my Body died, my Soul did not just remove it like a coat, an analogy often used to explain how a Soul wears a Body for a single life. My Soul inhabited my Body, like water fills the crevices of a sponge. My Body and Soul were one. As my Body decayed, my Soul was slowly squeezed out. As Soul, I felt unsettled and had no sense of conclusion. I was attached to that Body and did not want to move on.

Ghosts are lost Souls who are so attached to their physical world that they do not want to leave it behind at death. Instead, a Soul Ghost fastens to some reminder of the physical world that was important, like a home, and thus they do not reincarnate to continue their evolution. Instead, they haunt the world. That is a sad thing, really. But now I have some sense of how that can occur.

I feel compassion for a Soul who refuses to move on to the next life because of a deep connection to the current one. I can also see that when the Body is injured, the Soul can be injured as well. The Soul and Body are connected in each lifetime, like a sponge and water, filled with Mind and connected to Spirit. So when the Body is hurt, the Soul is hurt. The Soul has a higher perspective and can heal in a way the Body cannot. But it needs to remember to heal, otherwise the consequences will be seen in the next life.

For you, the reader

Is there anything in this story that resonates with you? Do you give your best to all that you do? Do you feel the inner strength and pride of a warrior? Or do you hide your strength to not bring attention to yourself? Have you ever felt despair or betrayal? Been forced to do something against your will? How did you respond? With rebellion or retreat?

Have you ever felt that you had no place to go, no one to turn to? Do you have control over your life? Your choices? Have you ever had a deep sense of being robbed of fulfilling your individual potential, instead sacrificing (or being sacrificed) for the welfare of family, job, or group? This tension between the needs of the self and the needs of others is widespread.

7
Twisted Heart of a Shaman: Amazon, c. 600 CE

I am a powerful shaman known for my healing abilities. I am a dark-skinned male with long black hair. I am in my prime, lean but powerful, my muscles strong. I think of myself as a panther, tensed and ready to strike. There is an arrogance about me that seems aggressive. But I don't care. I don't care about anything or anyone. I am a shaman, not because I want to heal people. I am a shaman because it gives me power and status. I feel cold inside, heartless.

Chief Banto, the chief of a neighboring tribe, is ill, very ill. No one has been able to heal him and he will most likely die. I receive an urgent message from his family. They are bringing Banto to me. Please, could I heal him?

I stare at the message and gloat. They must be very desperate to send such a plea. I know Chief Banto hates me, and his family wants nothing to do with me. There is a reason for this hatred. Before he was chief of the neighboring tribe he used to be part of my tribe.

We were children together, though our position in village life differed tremendously. Banto's father was chief and he had guided our village well. We were a cohesive and prosperous tribe, at peace with our neighbors and skilled at gaining the necessities of life from the jungle. The huts of the people were placed side by side to form a huge circle that created a barrier to keep out the always encroaching dangers of the jungle. In the center of this circle was the chief's hut, along with the council fire, storage for food, training ground, field for the children to play, and other community necessities. So as the chief's son, Banto grew up in the center of our village, safe and pampered while I lived on the edge, holding back the jungle that seemed like it was trying to devour us, while the screams of panthers echoed in the night. I always felt this pressure as a weight on my back and I resented the safety of Banto.

As we grew into manhood, we became rivals. We competed for everything. I was determined to be the best, and I didn't care how I succeeded in that endeavor. I cheated if it suited me, though I rarely had to. Besides, I didn't really consider it cheating; I thought of it as strategy. When you go to defeat an enemy, nothing matters but the result. Whether you win by killing in battle with a knife, or you defeat an enemy by killing his body in bed with poisons, what difference does it make, as long as he is dead?

Banto was such an enemy. He was the only boy who would stand up to me. All the others were afraid of me. I was cunning and smart and swift. But Banto was not afraid.

As the years passed, it became clear to me that he would likely become chief of our village. My father was a shaman and I knew I would also become a shaman. I was not to be a chief, nor did I want to be. A chief is responsible for the whole tribe and always settling conflicts and making decisions for the good of the whole. No, I did not want to do that. I wanted the power and fear that came from being a shaman, not the responsibility of being the chief.

But I did not want Banto to be chief either. That would give him too much power over me. I needed a chief I could control. And that would not be Banto. It didn't take me long to figure out how to get rid of him. He wanted to marry a girl of our tribe, Whillow. I didn't want that to happen either. She was the most beautiful girl and so I thought she should be mine, since I would need a woman to keep my house clean and provide for my physical needs. But Whillow was also afraid of me and she seemed to favor Banto. When I found out they were meeting in secret, I knew what to do. I would expose them.

In our tribe, the young men and women are not allowed to be together physically until they are joined in a village ceremony. Any physical or sexual contact before such time is forbidden. If it were discovered that they broke this rule, great shame would come on the family of the boy, and especially, the girl.

I watched them many nights until I knew the rhythm of their meetings. I wanted to expose them, but I didn't want the village to know I was the cause of Banto and Whillow's shame. The people of the village already did not like me. If I was found to bring down the hero and future chief of the village, my fate as a hated one would be sealed and I would be shunned, which would not do.

There was a girl, Chano, who wanted to wed Banto and I knew she could be easily manipulated. One day I just casually mentioned to her: "I saw Banto and Whillow last evening by the mossy caves. I have seen them there before and I wonder if they are seeking mushrooms?" Chano looked surprised. "How often have you seen them?" she asked. I shrugged, as if uninterested, "Oh, two or three times. I would like to get some of those mushrooms for my healing remedies. Surely that is the only reason they would be going there at night?"

Chano looked unhappy, which pleased me. It was no surprise the next morning to find that the whole village was talking about Banto and Whillow being found in sexual embrace by Chano down by the mossy caves. Whillow's father was furious and Banto was exposed and humiliated. There would be a decision by the chief as to what to do with them as punishment.

The chief, even though Banto's father, had no choice and banished Banto from the village. Banto would go to live with his uncle in a nearby village. Whillow wanted to go with him. Her father did not want her to go, since he depended on her to clean his house and cook his food. But he also knew that she could not find a good husband now that she had been so exposed. It was decided they would marry and go to the nearby village together.

I had not intended this consequence, and was not pleased. I had planned to take Whillow as my own, since her dishonor would mean that no other man would want her. I had thought this brilliant strategy would both rid me of Banto and gain Whillow as my wife. In that I was wrong.

Banto and Whillow's families were distraught. Their hearts were broken that their children were forced by village law to leave. Word got out that I had told Chano about the meetings at the caves. But I acted innocent, saying I had only wondered about the mushrooms. Banto did not believe me and suspected me of setting them up, but there was no proof strong enough to challenge me.

Although there was no clear evidence I had been the reason of their discovery, there was still rumor of my deception. The exposure of Banto and Whillow caused the village to lose a clear leader, which was a major loss. My reputation grew and now I was not only considered cunning, but cruel. Chano was also blamed and shunned by others in the village. Now an outsider and desperate not to remain an unmarried woman, she agreed to become my wife. But she hates me, for she knows I used her. She denies me her bed, so we have no children. But she cooks and keeps my house orderly, so I am served well enough.

But today, after all these years, Banto is now the chief of that neighboring village and he is ill. Banto's people would only come to me if they had no other choice, which means they have tried every other healer and none succeeded. My reputation as a healer is strong and his village would not let him die without trying every avenue. No one has to like me. And no one does. Normally they would never let Banto near my medicines, for fear I would poison him. But since he is near death anyway, I would have no reason to waste medicines on him. So they come to me now, bringing the limp body of their chief. I wonder if Whillow will be with him.

The sun has already set when they arrive, and my hut is lit with torches and a fire. Four warriors carry Banto to me on a stretcher. Behind them walks Whillow. She keeps her head down as she enters. She still looks lovely and I wonder what will happen to her if Banto dies. She would never marry me, especially if he died under my care. She might not be allowed to come back to the village anyway. If she could... well... Chano is dispensable. It would not take much to rid myself of Chano, and many would not notice her loss.

The warriors carry Banto to the center by the fire. He does not even stir as he is laid on the ground. The warriors cross the room to find a seat on the floor, their bodies casting shadows on the walls, creating the illusion of huge demons shifting and moving across the hut. The fire cracks and red sparks add to the eerie feeling that is beginning to take shape.

Something with Banto is seriously wrong, some evil at play here. I feel a chill run through my body and I pause by the fire opposite where he lays, hesitant to get closer to examine him. I view his body through the flames and I sense there is a curse or evil spirit making him ill. Many would not be willing to approach Banto, but I am not a man easily frightened.

I ask the head warrior, "What do you know about the illness?"

His eyes shift. "It has been two weeks since Banto has been awake. He went into the jungle to hunt but did not return that night. When we went to find him, he was in the state he is now. No one knows what occurred. Perhaps he ate something poisonous. But no one can find the problem and no one can heal him. We ask you to help and to use your great healing powers to save our chief."

I kneel down to examine Banto. I feel for his pulse and am surprised to find his heart still beats in a steady rhythm.

"He is very weak, but he has enough strength yet to live," I say. "He is harboring his life force."

Whillow looks up quickly at me, her eyes wide and imploring. "He might still live?" she gasps. "I was told there is no hope. But I knew you were the greatest healer around, and if anyone could save him, it would be you. I remember your greatness from our youth together."

I feel myself fill with pride and I sit up, looking at her directly. She is still beautiful. "Yes, I might be able to heal him, but it will be very difficult and there is no certainty I can succeed."

She stands up and comes toward me. She moves with the grace of youth, and her hair is lustrous as it falls around her face. She kneels beside me, positioning her body to block sight of the others in the room. Everyone disappears and it is as if we are totally alone. She looks at me, her eyes pleading, and speaks softly, for my ears only. "The others say you will be no more successful than the healers we have seen. But I said you would be. I alone insisted we come to see you. You are more powerful than all the other healers," she says as she puts her hand on my leg. I feel the warmth of her touch go through my body and I am suddenly hot.

I lean into her and say softly, "I could try to heal Banto, but the effort would be much and the cost would be great. I do not know if you would be able to pay me what I require." We stare into each other's eyes and I can see a mixture of fear and desperation move across them, like ripples across a lake.

"I am willing to pay any cost," she says quickly.

My breath quickens. "Any cost?" I say, as my tongue moves slowly across my lips.

"Yes, you save Banto and I will give you whatever you want in return." She does not flinch away from my piercing stare.

I lean back from her and shake my head in order to clear it. I must think. This is the opportunity I have been waiting for. I can show that I am stronger than Banto and he will always be in my debt; I will prove myself as the greatest shaman around, and no one will ever doubt my skills; I will gain prestige and power; and I can have Whillow. She will stay with me and be my wife. If she has children, I can insist on them too. Banto may live, but his life will be ruined. I smile to myself. It is time to see this done.

I return my attention to Banto as Whillow takes a seat on the floor nearby. I lay down next to Banto and move into trance to search his body to find what is draining his life.

I locate the problem quickly. Deep in his stomach there is a very large 'spirit creeper.' I have never encountered one before, but I have heard of them in tales told around the fires at night. A spirit creeper is a demon, an evil energy that takes up residence in a body and lives there, getting larger and larger as it draws energy from its host, until the host body is depleted of all its energy and dies. The stronger the host, the stronger the spirit creeper becomes. Since Banto is a powerful man, the spirit creeper has grown so large it almost fills his belly, where it remains enclosed. But it has tentacles that reach out from Banto's belly to other parts of his body. There is a tentacle that moves toward his lungs, one around his heart, and another moving toward his loins.

It is said that after the host dies, the spirit creeper stays in the decaying body until another live victim comes by. Banto must have unknowingly passed the spirit creeper in the jungle, where it took hold of him.

My body tenses as I diagnose the cause of his illness. I realize this might be beyond my skills, beyond anyone's skills. I come out of trance but still lay quiet as I carefully consider what needs to be done. This is not a physical illness that can be healed with herbs or healing baths. The spirit creeper exists in the realm of spirits and demons. So I will need to work in the same realm and leave the physical body and its corresponding cures behind. I will need to go into trance and in spirit form enter Banto's body, dislodge the spirit creeper and then destroy it before it can reattach to another host. That will be the difficult part.

I could destroy the spirit creeper while it still resides in Banto, of that I have no doubt. My powers are equal to that task, in spite of its formidable size and its expanding tentacles. But if I use the intensity of psychic power needed to kill the spirit creeper while it is still in Banto, Banto will surely be destroyed as well.

Whillow was very clear that she would only give me what I wanted if I saved Banto. If Banto were to die, I would not get any of the things that I desire. I would not get Whillow, nor would I be able to gloat over Banto as I take his wife and children. It would not give me a reputation as a shaman to be respected and feared.

So I will need to dislodge the spirit creeper from Banto's belly while keeping Banto alive, and then kill the spirit creeper before it reattaches itself to another host. I take a deep breath. That will be very hard – like grabbing a snake from its pit and killing it before it has a chance to strike. It would be so much easier to just put a fire to the pit and kill the snake in it. I could tell Whillow and the warriors that Banto cannot be saved. But what is the glory in that? My reputation as a shaman would suffer. No, I must heal him. And I know that if anyone can, it will be me. I am the most powerful shaman in memory. Whillow is right. I am the best.

I sit up and get my medicines to enhance the power of protective spirits. Everything is silent in the fire-lit hut as Banto's people watch me prepare. I throw herbs on the fire and they blaze up with a rich scent. That smoke will diminish the energy in the room so that once I get the spirit creeper out, its energy will be dampened and give me time to destroy it.

I then get my medicine bundle and tie it around my neck. I have spent my life collecting powerful forces to place in my medicine bundle. It will protect me from the spirit creeper, and even if I do fail to save Banto, the creature will not be able to attach to me.

I rub a thick acrid smelling salve on Banto's stomach, again to try and diminish the energy of the spirit creeper so it will be slow and dull when I attack it.

I ask Whillow to sit in the back of the hut, far from Banto. I make an excuse and say that Banto's soul will seek to find hers and the further away she is the more he will need to reach out to find her. But really I want to be sure that if my battle with the spirit creeper fails that Whillow will not be the new host it seeks out. I want her whole so I can have her as my reward for taking on this difficult task.

I lay down again by the fire next to Banto, shoulder to shoulder, and begin to chant, moving myself into a deep trance. As I begin the healing, I call on my ancestors and the powers of my medicine bundle to protect me and give me strength. I move away from the middle world of physical reality. The hut disappears and I am alone with Banto in the spirit world.

The effort and engagement required for a healing is quite different than what I use for diagnosis. To diagnose, I barely connect with the energy of a patient, like skipping stones across a pond. It takes a very light touch for me to find the problem and seek a cure. But to heal a patient means I actually separate my soul from my body, which lays still and unmoving, and then journey with my soul into the body of the one who is sick. Instead of skipping stones across a pond, I am diving deep into the river, holding my breath and swimming against the current.

I enter the life field of Banto and begin to go toward the location of the spirit creeper so I can untangle it from Banto's energy field. But as soon as I enter his life force I am shocked. The tentacles have spread much further than I saw during diagnosis. There are wisps of tentacles throughout his body and I feel them against me, as if the grasses of the river are grabbing at my legs as I swim. I get caught up in them. I can see the glowing energetic body of the spirit creeper ahead of me. I push forward, breaking free from the tentacle wisps and directing my focus to the center of the parasitic form. I blast it with my power and see it begin to dislodge.

My attack causes the spirit creeper to retract its main tentacles that are in Banto's lungs, heart, and groin, and pull them back into its main body. Retracting into itself doubles the size of the spirit creeper and gives it renewed strength.

I am completely taken by surprise. I had not considered that the tentacles could return to the main body of the spirit creeper, nor that it could possibly be as large as it now appears. I blast it again with energy, and I see it begin to dislodge further.

I am starting to think that this is too much. I begin to realize that it might be too big for me to control if it is set free; I need to kill it within Banto's body. But that thought comes too late. As the spirit creeper dislodges, it leaps out of Banto's body and just as quickly enters my own body, which is lying motionless in trance. *No! This cannot be.* My medicine bundle was to protect me. The creeper should have entered another person, not me!

I shift my attention to my own body, now inhabited by a force so large that I am stunned. I attack the spirit creeper inside my body, blasting it with energy in order to destroy it. The battle has now shifted from Banto's body into my own. I can feel my energy weaken, my forceful blasts of power doing little harm to that which now inhabits me. I get weaker and weaker in this battle, until finally there is nothing in me still able to fight.

Silence. Darkness. I realize that my body is near death, victim of the battle with the spirit creeper. I see no light or life force from the spirit creeper's form, and know that the battle destroyed us both.

I have very little life force left as my body fades, but I can still lift my awareness out of my body to rise to the ceiling of the hut and view the scene below. There is no external evidence of the violent battle that just occurred within myself. My body lies there quietly, as if still in trance. Only there is no sign of breath.

Next to me, shoulder to shoulder, lies Banto. But I can see his chest rising and falling with each breath. Whillow leans over him, wiping his head with a cool cloth, talking to him, coaxing him to return to the living. I can see him stir.

I can also see that tied around Banto's neck is my medicine bundle.

Whillow must have realized there was danger involved in the effort to heal Banto when I moved her to the rear of the hut. As soon as I went into trance, she must have come to the fire and untied my protective medicine bundle, then placed it on the neck of Banto instead. She left me unprotected. She took my power and gave it to her husband so that he might live.

I had been made a fool. My anger boils up. I take what little energy I have and send forth a curse to her. I try to curse them all, but what little energy remains is rapidly leaving me. The warriors place Banto on the stretcher and carry him out of my hut and into the moonlight to begin the journey home. Whillow walks next to Banto, touching him and talking to him. I am left alone in my hut, my body lifeless next to the fireplace.

I am full of dismay. I was tricked by Whillow. When my village sees Banto leave with renewed health they will soon come to my hut to be amazed at my skills and ask questions about what riches I gained in payment. I do not want the people to find me helpless like this, dead in my own hut from a cure gone horribly wrong. I do not want to be seen as the victim of my power, my desire, my greed. I want to be remembered as a great shaman, the one to whom great chiefs come to be healed.

My final act, before I leave this life altogether, is to take the last bit of my force and intention and direct it toward the fire. I watch it begin to blaze to life. I breathe energy into the fire, stirring it up, until it roars.

No one will find my body, defenseless, failed. *No*, I think, as the flames jump outside of the pit and begin to feed on the herbs that are drying from the ceiling of my hut. I will go up in a blaze of smoke and no one will know my failure or what happened. They will only know that Banto lives, and that I was the one, the only one, who was able to heal him.

Life Lessons from the Amazon Shaman

This shamanic life came almost immediately after my death as the youthful Mayan warrior. I am even in the same part of the world. When I was sacrificed in the Mayan life, so full of pride and hope, something in me twisted. It was as if the very best in me turned sour, like apple cider into vinegar. All the best qualities I had as the Mayan, all I worked so hard to perfect – for my family, for my tribe, for myself – were turned inside out and curdled.

When I was reborn as the Shaman I believed that being a strong person for the benefit of others was a useless strategy. It just got me killed. I needed to be strong, yes, of that I had no doubt. But I had to be strong for me, and me alone. Other people were to be used, as pawns in my power play. I didn't care what happened to Chano when I manipulated her. I just wanted to destroy Banto as a rival. She was collateral damage, a necessary destruction in my plot to succeed. The fact that I could still use her to cook, clean, and care for me was a side benefit, an unintended consequence. Chano hated me, and I did not care. Everyone hated me, and I did not care. Emotions were unknown to me. I was cold, heartless.

The karmic pattern I brought with me into the Shaman's life was seizing on personal power with no regard for others. This was a reaction to the Mayan life where my dedication had me always putting other people ahead of my own needs. I gave everything for my people only to feel betrayed and sacrificed. It led to the realization as the Shaman that being strong for the community was a waste of time. So this is a rubber band lifetime, springing to the opposite extreme – from over-giving to selfishness.

The soul wound came from the literal destruction of my heart in Atlantis, Egypt, and Maya, which also destroyed my capacity for love and compassion. It made me heartless. It is as if I gave up. Life after life after life left all my best intentions in the dust. The giant hole in my chest was not only the physical emptiness of my real heart, but also the vast wasteland of my symbolic heart. Love became almost unknown to me.

There are no Allies or Adversaries that I am aware of in this life. I saw Banto as an enemy who needed to be destroyed, but I don't have any sense that he had been present in my other lives. Maybe he will show up in a future life of mine, though I doubt it. He played an important part in my lesson of reliance of power for myself alone and the collapse of my pride. In that case he could even have been an Ally who came to help me heal after the intense pain of the Mayan betrayal. I will pay attention if Banto shows up in a future life. Whillow was a trinket that I wanted, a prize that I underestimated. I don't think she is part of any Soul group of mine.

The skill I gained in this life is the directed use of Spirit lifeforce and how that lifeforce can be both depleted and renewed. A trend in entertainment are stories of vampires who live off the lifeforce of other people, represented by the taking of blood. There are also environments that drain us, and foods or drugs that deplete us.

This shamanic life teaches about lifeforce, which comes from Spirit, that mysterious substance that provides the difference between a live physical form and a dead one. Like the Soul essence, Spirit is also a substance that permeates. While Soul is watery like silver mercury, that slips and slides through the crevices of life, Spirit is more like fire, sparkling electricity, and flashes of lightning. The lifeforce given by Spirit is what provides energy and willpower. As a Shaman I had the ability to influence Spirit lifeforce in shape and direction. I could move and direct it not only using the intentions of my Mind but also the force of my will. For example, when I moved into Banto's body to do battle with the spirit creeper, I wasn't just in Banto with the intentions of my Mind. I moved most of my lifeforce from my own physical body, which was in a motionless trance, and directed it into Banto's.

Experiencing something with my Spirit is different than experiencing it with psychic awareness of Soul, or intellectual inquiry of Mind, or with the senses of my body. When I diagnosed Banto, I used psychic awareness to scan, like an X-ray machine that moved over a patient's body and could see the parts that were injured or out of harmony. But an X-ray only photographs the body; it cannot engage or heal the body. When I treated Banto, I went into a deep trance and directed my lifeforce to go into Banto, to do battle with the demon that resided there. I became like a surgeon who consults the image of the X-ray to find the place of illness, and then uses the knife of lifeforce to enter the body to fix it.

When I healed the young princess in Egypt, I used this same technique to pinpoint the location of a physical parasite in her body. Because her disease was physical, I cured her using a knife to cut into her, a reed to enter deeper, and herbs to kill the parasite, and then followed with a salve to heal the cut that I had made. With Banto, I used my psychic awareness and I also found a parasite, but it was not a physical parasite, but rather an energetic one. It was a parasite living on the lifeforce of the body. So I had to remove it using lifeforce means.

This is why it was such a dangerous healing. I calculated that Banto had enough lifeforce left to still maintain his physical body after the spirit creeper was removed. Finding a small bit of Banto's lifeforce that was still his own, and not absorbed by the spirit creeper, was like finding a small spark in a fireplace. That tiny spark, if gently handled, could be made large again until it was a roaring fire. Banto's lifeforce would have to be rejuvenated through food, rest, herbs, exercise, and so on, but it could be done. If his lifeforce was not gently rejuvenated after the healing, he could still die.

For me, I used my own lifeforce to destroy the spirit creeper. By the time it left Banto and entered me, it had been somewhat damaged but not killed. So I had to do to myself what I had planned to do to Banto, which was to kill the spirit creeper while still leaving the host body (me) alive enough to be able to heal. So I directed my lifeforce energy to kill the spirit creeper, but in doing so, I depleted myself and died.

I might have been able to accomplish this task of healing Banto if I had other shamans to help me. If I had worked collaboratively, several of us could have entered Banto and done battle with the spirit creeper while at the same time a few shamans could have used their lifeforce to replenish what we were using. Lifeforce is something like a battery. You can use an appliance or tool on battery life only, but the use of it will drain the battery until the battery is dead and the tool no longer works. The tool will often let you know that you are down to 20 percent of the battery so you can stop before the tool no longer functions. If I had worked with other shamans it would have been like working while the tool is plugged in and the battery getting recharged. There is a lesson in this life about reliance on personal power versus augmenting through collaboration. I can now see how working with others could have benefited both Banto and myself. Greater power comes from alliance with others.

Each physical form – be it human, animal, plant, or mineral – has a certain amount of lifeforce stored within itself. That lifeforce can be seen as a type of personal power. A Soul can bring lifeforce forward into future lives. Like having money in the bank, a Soul either comes into a life in energetic debt, balanced, or with an excess. People with charisma have a larger amount of lifeforce that makes them magnetic. Some people are well aware of their lifeforce and use it, either wisely or not.

In my next life I think that after the wild emotional swing between the Mayan and Shaman lives that I need some balance and centering. A quiet life perhaps. A life of both personal power and collaboration would be a good way to find a balance.

In my present life I am the opposite of the Shaman in many ways. Having personal power and control over others has no appeal to me. Instead of wanting power over others, I value humility, compassion, and empathy, and I have worked my entire life to bring healing energy to the world. But as I write these words, I realize that humility can also be a trap of ego. Instead of being a powerful, engaged, and active force in the world (even if the motives are wrong), humility can make one feel disempowered. I can see how power is not something I have wanted in this current life, and perhaps I use my humility as a way to stay hidden. In this new awareness I see my current life differently. I realize it is important to be directed and powerful as long as the motives have the right spirit and intent. I understand power and action can be a force of good as well as evil.

The universal significance of this life again shows the connection and intersection between the physical Body and the Soul. The Soul doesn't just inhabit a Body like a hotel room, with no commitment. If that were so, there would be no real connection between what happens to the Body and the subsequent effect on the Soul. But there is a connection. The experiences of the physical Body affect the lessons of the Soul. The Soul is "embodied," which means the experiences of life are physical, not just spiritual or intellectual or emotional. It means the Soul fully inhabits the physical form, not contained like water in a vase, but absorbed, like water in a sponge.

For you, the reader

It is important to be aware of your Spirit lifeforce. Notice when you are depleted, and take the time to renew yourself. Admittedly, this is easier to do on a daily basis, when your lifeforce is only a little diminished, than it is when your battery is almost drained before you begin to recharge. An *I Ching* quatrain describes how one lake can dissipate and go dry, but two adjacent lakes feed each other and both remain strong. You build your lifeforce through exchange with other things – people, plants, minerals – and in doing so, gain wisdom or knowledge through that exchange.

You can increase your lifeforce through various means. There must be thousands of ways, and each person will resonate with their favorite methods. Any of the four elements of Fire, Earth, Air, and Water can renew your lifeforce. The Fire element is attained by actual fire, like being beside a fireplace or campfire, and also the fire of the heavens, like Sun and Moon bathing, star gazing, and connecting to the celestial sphere. Meditation and yoga, especially energetic forms like kundalini, can activate and charge your lifeforce.

Earth element is attained by connecting to anything physical, like nature, which is abundant with lifeforce. You can lie down on the earth. If I am feeling depleted I will often lean against a tree or hug a tree. I offer the tree the ability to take my lifeforce too, and in doing this, we are making an exchange. So instead of me just using the lifeforce in the tree, like draining a battery, I am offering my lifeforce back to it. Being around people who have good energy can be renewing as well as engaging in physical activities that enliven you. Good food is another way to build your lifeforce. Stones and herbs also have specific energies that are available when used.

The Air element lifeforce is found in the different types of winds, watching the sky and the movement of clouds, sounds such as bird song and music of all types, as well as intellectual activities of poetry, good conversation, reading, and writing. Deep breaths also bring in lifeforce and build it up in your body.

Water element lifeforce is found in all bodies of water, which may appeal to you in different ways. The oceans can stir and invigorate your lifeforce with their crashing waves, while quiet ponds will bring your lifeforce a gentle lift. A bubbling brook can enliven your heart and bring joy. Drinking good healthy water will replenish you, as well as baths, swimming, and hot springs.

Once you have enough and are aware of your lifeforce, then you can begin to use it. Using lifeforce is done through intention and direction of the Mind, mostly accomplished through the breath, which I discussed as the skill from the Atlantis life.

Each lifetime contains knowledge and abilities that are learned, and by bringing each past lifetime to awareness, the skills become available in this current life. You have lifetimes of knowledge and abilities that you might not remember, and hence are under-used. Connection to your Soul through the memory of your past lives can activate these skills and make them more available.

What skills do you think you have that come from a past life? Do you use them in this life now? For better or for worse? Can you sense skills that are available for you to discover? Is there something that comes so naturally to you, or that you love so much that it feels like you were born with it? What is the state of your lifeforce? How do you deplete it? How do you keep your lifeforce strong?

8
Priest's Lesson in Humility: Germany, c. 1000 CE

Humility. That seems to be what we are taught here in the monastery. It appears to be the only thing that we are taught. I am told quite often that we are nothing before God. I am to keep my head bowed, my eyes cast down, and my shoulders stooped as I walk. I am not to look at a person directly in the eye nor engage anyone in conversation, for it should be clear to me that I have nothing to say.

My main task is to pray. I sit inside the church and pray for hours a day, and I pray in my small room when I wake in the morning and when I go to bed at night. I pray at each meal, and every time I am given a directive from a priest who ranks above me. My response is always, "Glory to God the Almighty, and to his son, Jesus Christ, who died on the cross for our sins."

I spend so much time praying and doing my duties, which include such things as cleaning, gardening, or tending to the sick, that I find I have little time for anything else. Not that there is much else to do.

I am dressed in a rough brown robe with a hood and a braided grass belt. I wear simple sandals on my feet. The arms of the robe are very long, which serves several purposes. They cover my hands, which are folded together in front of me in a sign of submission to God, and they are like giant pockets that can hide anything I don't want the senior Fathers finding out that I have.

Our monastery is utilitarian and harsh and there are not many items beyond those necessary to daily life, and certainly nothing of beauty. But I discover little treasures that strike my fancy, and although it is quite forbidden to have anything personal or special, I find it is a small pleasure to gather objects that I consider mine.

It began when I found a button – a beautiful delicate thing made from the tusk of an elephant. I found it on the ground while I was walking in prayer, with my head down. I quickly glanced around and saw no one near to me, so I bent down and picked it up. I held it in my hands, which were hidden under the long sleeves of my robe, and continued on my way. I could feel its smoothness and intricacy. When I had a chance in my room to study it closer, I felt like I had a king's treasure in front of me, something that was mine alone. I felt elated. This was the first object I found, but it started my small collection of treasures, for my eyes and touch alone. A butterfly wing, a stone shaped like the sun, a bright blue bird feather, a coin (which I should have given to the church, but kept for myself instead), and an old key. Having these treasures seems like a small thing, but they give me an identity beyond the monastery and a life outside of being a monk.

I wasn't always a monk. I came to the monastery when I was 16 years old, a young man in my prime. I was my father's third son and as a nobleman he really didn't need more than two sons. I was the extra. He kept me around until it was clear my two older brothers would survive. My eldest brother would inherit the estate. He would get all the land, home, and money. My second brother was a spare, to keep in case my eldest brother would die before having an heir. This brother was made the estate manager and given a fine home of his own, with enough money to marry well and have children. I was the third son. Since my father had no need of me, I was sent to join the church.

Perhaps I would make my way up to Bishop, or Cardinal, and bring power and respect to my family. There was no expectation that I actually believe in Christ or God or salvation. I hadn't much time to consider my thoughts on these things since I was so busy learning to fight and hunt and ride. I was full of myself, a strong young man without thought for tomorrow. I just assumed I'd marry one day since I was very fond of women.

One evening when I was 16 years old, I was called to my father's rooms, and with little time or concern, I was told that I was leaving in the morning for the monastery where I would begin my time with the church. My father made a donation to the church, enough for my room and board for a few years. I complained of this future of mine, threatened to run away, and threw words of hatred and venom to the whole family. But it made no difference. I had no money of my own, and I didn't know what I would do if I should run away. Where would I go? Little was said to me that night. I was to pack nothing. I was to take only the clothes on my back. I was brought to the monastery in a carriage by a servant, which was a three-day drive, and left at the door. Yes, I was humbled. I realized I really was nothing. My name was changed to Brother John and my past was entirely unknown and unimportant, at least to everyone else but me.

So even though my treasures were few, at least they were mine.

Ten years have now passed since I first arrived and no one from my family has ever come by or inquired about me. It is as if I were dead. My only hope is to move up in the church, becoming a Bishop at least. Then

I could contact my family and have something to offer them, something to make them pay attention again.

I miss my life as a free man. I miss hunting and horses and women. But I have done all I could to become the monk that was expected of me. I ignored my wet dreams and kept my fantasies at a distance. I directed my physical vitality to outdoor pursuits, mostly gardening and caring for the extensive grounds of the monastery. I apprenticed under the master herbalist and learned all about the healing and culinary qualities of herbs. When he died, I became the master herbalist in charge of keeping the herbs plentiful so the healers have all they need. I don't do any healing myself, but I know how to prepare the medicines and provide many of the cures the healers use.

I was content enough. But when an elderly priest of a nearby village church passed on, I was pleased to be chosen to take his place. I would now have my own church, my own flock to care for. I am 26 years of age and gratified with this new change. It was made clear to me that although I would be in charge of the church and the parishioners, I am still under the direct supervision of the Fathers at the monastery. I understand I will need to report to them on a regular basis and that they will choose the deacons and novices who help me in my duties. But I will no longer be at the monastery or have the elder Fathers watching my every move. As I look around my small monastery cell and gather my few belongings, I feel like a bird set free from its cage.

I become pastor of a lovely village church which is surrounded by a stone wall that holds fruit trees, a wonderful herb garden, and the cemetery for the village dead. This church is the very heart of the village and all the important rituals of life – birth, baptism, marriage, and death – are held within its walls. The villagers come together each Sunday, and in the crowded church I share the word of God and give the holy sacraments to the parishioners. At Christmas we celebrate Christ's birth and at Easter his resurrection with colorful festivities and song.

A year goes by and I am happy with the seasons of my life. Within these stone walls I relax and feel like maybe this small church could become my home, and that one day I too will be buried within these stone walls. I feel whole again for the first time since I was sent from my home. With no more need for a secret inner life, I take my small box of treasures and bury it in the cemetery with the village dead.

When I am not ministering to my flock I am in the walled garden tending to my herbs. Soon it becomes clear to the townspeople that I have a gift with my knowledge of herbs. I allow the women to come and harvest the healing herbs whenever they need. Many people grow a few of the most common at their homes, like comfrey or mint. But I grow all those plus exotic herbs like nightshade and healewell. I fall into an easy rhythm and am at peace.

Then one day it all changes. I am tending my herbs and I look up to see the silhouette of a woman walking toward me. The setting sun is behind her so I cannot see her face, but I can tell from how she walks that she is a woman of some beauty and substance. A chill runs over me, as if a cold wind blew into my heart. At the same time my hands feel hot, as if they want nothing more than to touch her soft skin. As she comes closer I realize she is the most beautiful woman I have ever seen, so soft, dressed in silks, wearing an emerald necklace and smelling like a lavender field.

"My name is Sybil and I have come to see your herb garden," she purrs softly, "for it is quite famous and I have been told that it is a great pleasure to admire."

For some reason it goes through my mind that instead of the garden, she is referring to me, as if I were quite famous and she wanted to see for herself if I was as admirable as she had been told. I had never considered that I might be a subject of talk among the village women but the way Sybil looks at me, as if it were my delicacies she wanted to pluck, I suddenly remember I am a 26-year-old man, strong, handsome, and now apparently quite in demand.

My face flushes. I put my hands inside my robe, so that she does not see them clench and tremble. I stand up. "Do you enjoy working with herbs?" I ask, quite innocently.

Sybil smiles. "I have never been familiar with such an herb garden as this, for it is a rarity in these parts. But I would like to know everything that it has to offer."

"This garden is available for all who live in the village. I have never seen you here before. Are you new to the area?"

She looks me fully in the face and holds my eyes as she speaks. "I recently moved here with my husband, who owns a large estate outside of town. He is older than I am and doesn't enjoy my same pursuits. I thought I could find some diversion here."

I am taken aback at how brash she is. I have never met a lady such as this; only a bar maid from my youth would have spoken such thoughts.

She looks at me from head to feet, slowly, as if examining me for flaws. "You seem quite young to be a village priest. You are not feeble like most priests. Your hands are strong, your body powerful."

I lean over to gather my gardening tools and begin to leave. "I assure you that I am quite capable of the position for which I am entrusted. If you want to gather herbs from the garden, you can return on Sunday after church, when most of the women come to cut their herbs." I turn my back to her and begin to walk away. I can feel her watching my every move. I feet hot, and my body starts to harden and raise in a way it has not in many years.

That night I have a wet dream, and when I awake I pleasure myself further, thinking of Sybil and her bold ways. I know such pleasure is a sin, so I deny myself breakfast and confess and give myself penance in my morning prayers. I stay away from my garden that day and keep myself busy visiting the sick.

The next few days it rains, and thoughts of Sybil begin to lessen. When the rain stops and the sun returns, I eagerly go to the garden, ready to weed out what is unnecessary, something so easy when the soil is damp. I am lost in the feel of the earth and the smell of the herbs when I see her approach again.

She is less formally garbed than before, in a soft cotton dress like the villagers wear. She looks younger and more innocent. But as soon as she speaks, her voice sultry and thick like honey, I know that her innocent appearance is deceiving. "I decided I should learn from you how to tell one herb from the next. I have very little to do all day and am quite bored. I thought that giving my time to the church would find favor with God and satisfy my husband's questions as to where I go every day." She leans down and touches an herb still wet with the rain, rubbing her fingers along its ridges. "He is pleased that I am giving my time to the church, for what trouble could I find in the house of God?"

There is little I can do, as she shows up daily to work next to me in the garden. She says little, but manages to move up against me whenever she can. It becomes clear that she is teasing me, flirting with me. She only does it when we are alone. If others are around, she works in a different part of the garden.

One evening after a long day in the garden, I take the short walk to the small wooden barn that sits right outside the stone walls. It is a simple rustic structure where I keep all my supplies, a quiet place with a dirt floor covered with straw and a soft light that filters in from the open beams. I love the earthy smell, and aside from the occasional horse kept here when a traveling priest visits, I consider this small space as my own refuge. Right outside this barn is a water pump which supplies water to the herbs when needed and where I clean up before returning to the tidiness of my small quarters, which I share with a few novices who help in the kitchen and with the services.

I am washing my hands underneath the streaming water of the pump and watching the sun go down below the horizon when Sybil comes up silently next to me. She crushes the soap herb between her wet hands and then takes my hands in hers. She begins to wash my hands, slowly moving the soap between my fingers to my palms, then placing her hands in mine, encouraging me to do the same. Our hands are locked together, moving around each other's, touching intimately in a way I have not touched a woman, or any person, in many years. My desire for her increases with each touch and I feel myself grow hard. I want her to touch me everywhere. I can imagine her wet soapy hands going over my body, touching me, me touching her. I lose myself to the thought. It is as if I am in a trance, and I feel her wet hands on my face, her lips on my mouth. I forget where I am. I am not a priest, not a monk. I am a young powerful male, my manhood calling for my attention.

I pull her to me and return her kiss, my hands feeling for her breasts, bringing her to me. I am not sure what happens next. I lose myself to passion and I don't remember where I end and she begins. Night falls and I am pushing her against the barn, her legs wrapped around my rough brown cloak as she moans in pleasure.

The barn becomes our refuge. We devour each other, night after night. All I think about is when I will see her. We work together in the day, touching when we can. We sometimes sneak off to the barn in the middle of the day, our passion is so great. But mostly we wait until dusk falls and the village is quiet, when families join to eat their evening meal. Our lovemaking is wild, full of abandon. I cannot be contained, and she urges me on. I am a stallion and she is riding me until I am lathered and worn out. Our gasping is all that is heard.

We become less careful and it should have been obvious to me that we would be found out eventually. We are in full embrace, lying on the straw floor. She is on top of me, riding me like a wild demon of the night. I urge her to go faster and ride me even harder. I am lost in my passion when the door opens and a novice priest comes in. He looks at us in shock, closes the door, and hurries away.

I leap up and rush after him. I catch up to him just as he is entering the church. I am panting and my heart is racing as I grab his arm and pull him away before he can go in. Anger flows through me and I slam him repeatedly against the stone walls of the church. I feel him struggle, but I push harder. I am punishing him... punishing him for finding me and Sybil, for ending our secrecy, for bringing my treasure into the light. In anger I begin to pummel him, hating him for ruining me.

His body finally goes limp. I know he is dead. I pick him up and carry him back to the barn. Sybil is gone. I feel like an animal, unleashed, wild, cruel. I roar in rage.

I want to go after Sybil, to punish her for ruining me. But in the dark night in the quiet of the barn I begin to calm down, and I realize that I have ruined myself. My own nature brought me low. I have to get away from here, for now everyone will know. I know with near certainty that the novice had been told to come to the barn with the expectation that he would discover me, for why else would he have come?

I have gotten too lax. I need to leave, but I have nothing, and I have no place to go. I look round me in the dim light and see that Sybil has left me a gift. There in the straw is her emerald necklace. It will bring me much money, enough to leave this town, this country, and start again.

My own nature cannot be denied. I am a man, with a man's needs. I cannot be contained in a monastery, as a gardener and a priest. Sybil set free what was held captive inside of me. Surely God would forgive me for my lust. But he would not be likely to forgive me for murder.

I do not go back to my room since there is nothing for me there. Dressed in my brown robe, I leave quietly in the night. I take the body of the novice and throw him in the river on my way out of town. I walk for miles until I find an empty house where I sleep. When I leave the next morning, I am wearing someone else's pants, shirt, and shoes, with Sybil's emerald necklace in my pocket. I do not know where I am going, only that I am leaving. I do not think too much about what I have done, for there is no way to bring my many feelings into harmony.

I will miss the quiet of the monastery, the comfort of the garden, the care of my parish, my acceptance of a life of God. But I know that I cannot go back to that life; my fierce power has been reawakened and I cannot live as a eunuch, denying the animal within me. These two sides of myself – the spirit and the body – hold each other at bay, neither giving in nor allowing regret.

I walk for many months, doing odd jobs just to get by and to have a roof over my head while I sleep. I am not willing to take a chance selling the emerald necklace to just anyone, for I realize it could bring attention to me if Sybil has listed it as stolen. It could also bring attention to me as a man with money, and therefore a man worthy of robbing. I like my anonymous existence. I keep the necklace well-hidden and do not bring attention to myself.

I find myself in a fairly large town during a festival. Many outsiders have come to the festival and there is a huge market where everything under the sun is bought and sold. I think this will be a good time to sell the necklace without bringing undue attention to myself. I make inquiries to sellers at many booths. After a morning's research, I have a sense of the necklace's worth and the man I will sell it to. I then sit near his shop and watch the comings and goings. I want to see who frequents his shop and who else is watching the purchases that occur there. By evening I am convinced he sells mostly to wealthy nobility, and since guards accompany most of them, there is less riff-raff waiting to try to steal either merchandise or money.

The next day I approach this booth at mid-morning while there is a lull in activity. I tell the man that the necklace is the only piece of value of a beloved, but newly deceased mother. I am looking to sell it to make my way. Because I have been raised as a nobleman's son, I was able to put on the airs of a destitute, but otherwise well-bred man, which in fact is the truth. He pays me a fair price. As best as I can tell, our exchange is not seen. I wander a bit more through the market, watching to see if I am being followed. Convinced I am not, I leave the town and continue on my way, moving quickly to put as many miles as I can between me and the festival.

I have a huge sense of relief that the necklace has been sold, since now I have money to begin an occupation and start a new life. Within the next Moon I find a town that suits me quite well for my new home. It is a prosperous town, has a fair climate, and a good growing season. Plus there are many healers but no apothecary, no place to buy herbal remedies, tinctures, or salves.

With my skill as a maker of herbal mixtures, the best line of work for me is to open a pharmacy. I find a small shop at the edge of town with some acres of good land where I can plant my herb garden. I buy it outright for a fair price. For now I will live in the shop, but as I make more money I will build a house in the back.

I left the monastery with nothing. But during my travels I collected seeds and herbs. Anytime I met someone with knowledge about medicinal plants I asked questions. In this way, by the time I bought my shop, I had seeds to plant and new healing potions that were popular, as well as some that were not used often but could bring a large price. I had even learned of poisons to dull or kill, and potions to end a pregnancy or to start one. Those would all bring a good price if sold to the right person.

I settle in, plant my garden, and within one year I have a successful pharmacy. I marry a young widow who has some money, which enables us to build a lovely house. We have four children and are very happy.

With my knowledge and skill, I could have made a great reputation for myself. At least that is what my clients and my wife often say. But I do not want a great reputation. I do not want to bring attention to myself. I have a dark past and I do not want it coming back to haunt me. I have a feeling that if I brag of my skills and make a fancy shop known throughout the region that someone will show up one day who will recognize me. I know I need to lie low, do my work, and be satisfied with a peaceful and productive life.

And so I do for many years. I die an old man in my bed, surrounded by children and grandchildren. I have trained my children well in the skills of pharmacy arts. Once I am buried in the cemetery within the walls of the local village church, they expand the store and thus become rich and well known. I am glad I could leave them this. It is more than my father left for me. I rarely thought of my old life as a noble or wondered about the church. My work in the gardens and my love of my family brought me all the contentment I needed. That was the path to my peace and I have no regrets when I die.

Life Lessons from the Priest

This life as a Priest was the first past life I recalled. It came to me spontaneously in the early morning after a night's sleep when I was 25 years old, rather than through a Past Life Therapy session. It felt so real. I was a young Priest, seduced by a married parishioner, an event that caused me to destroy my livelihood, fail in my vows, and commit murder. I sensed at the time that the themes of the Priest's life must be important for me to consider in my current life.

The main theme of the Priest's life is tension between the physical world and the spiritual world. Living a robust physical life with a home and family was incompatible with living an interior isolated life of a spiritual man of God. It is a clash between two entirely different systems of socialization, that process where you learn who and what you are through the context of your surroundings.

Growing up as a rich nobleman's son, I had been socialized to be a free-willed knight, a sexual married man, a responsible father. The monastic life of prayer, poverty, isolation, and humility was opposite my earlier upbringing in almost every way. To live the monastic life I had to deny all my sexual feelings and instincts for freedom and power that had been part of my upbringing. Through hard work and commitment I managed to keep separate the lives of nobleman and Priest, but once the desires and lusts were reawakened by the seductions of Sybil, I could no longer keep them apart. I could no longer live as a celibate Priest cut off from the physical world of desire.

My life as a Priest is a clear demonstration of what happens when a person denies an essential part of who they are. In that life I was a strong, robust young man, primed for battle, leadership, and love. When I joined the monastery, all those qualities were suppressed and I took on a life of solitude, celibacy, and prayer. There was some type of assumption that I could just turn off the young male essence of who I was and turn on the priest. But that was clearly not the case. Instead, I repressed those male needs, those physical needs, and pushed them deep inside of me. As long as nothing reminded me of them, I was safe to pursue the life of a Priest. As long as I was separate from society and spent most of my time in prayer or work, there was little chance that the repressed part would call for my attention.

But once Sybil entered my life, all it took was her touch. Her hand on mine set me afire. That shows how large and unwieldy the repressed part of myself was. It was like a demon inside of me just waiting for a chance to escape. Once I unleashed my physical needs they consumed me. I did not have control over them. I was not able to balance them or rationalize whether what I did was right or wrong, good or bad.

The problem was that the power of my repressed sexuality grew outside of my sight, in the depths of the unconscious. My physical needs never went away; they were hidden, left alone to fester, like a fungus in the dark. When the sunlight was let in, even just a sliver, they began to bloom uncontrollably. The dark shadow was unleashed. A clear indication that my sexual and physical needs were out of control was my response to the novice. My sexual desire with Sybil turned into anger and violence with him. If sexual and physical desires are kept repressed, they can become out of control. These are probably some of the issues with the sexual abuse of young children by church leaders.

And it wasn't just sexual repression. This life also shows how much I was longing for a simple touch. My secret treasures were important because they were my only private existence. But they also provided me with a tactile life; I loved not just looking at my treasures but also touching them. It is as if I buried my desire for touch in the earth and directed it toward gardening. But when Sybil took my hands to wash them, I was completely undone. If physical touch had been part of my life – if getting a hug, or having someone touch my arm when they talked to me, or if I had curled up around someone in bed – I doubt if just the feel of Sybil's hands on mine would have been such an unlocking of my buried needs.

I am grateful for this life as a Priest because a continuation of the selfish arrogance and hatred of the Shaman is not a path I would want to go down any further. The humility of the Priest feels like a life of redemption for the hateful Shaman. Confidence and belief in self is an important feature, but when taken too far it becomes arrogance, as seen in the Shaman. The Priest is also a lifetime of finding a way to have both a spiritual life of service and a vigorous physical life. Once I left the church and became an herbalist, I found a way to be of service to the community while still living a fully physical existence with a home, wife, and children.

There is a karmic pattern of betrayal by my father when he cast me off to the church as I was entering the prime of manhood, similar to the betrayal of the Mayan warrior who was forced to a sacrifice that I did not choose. As the Mayan warrior I thought of running, but felt trapped by duty and circumstance. I changed that pattern as the Priest in that I did make the choice to run and begin a life on my own away from birth family and church obligations.

This Priest life continued a pattern repeated over many lifetimes that being noticed could only be a bad thing for me. Either someone wanted to steal my gift (Atlantis), or got jealous of my gift (Egypt), or wanted to sacrifice my gift (Mayan), or used my gift against me (Shaman). Even after I left the monastery and started my pharmacy, I kept a low profile. I quickly hired someone to work the store so that I would not have to talk to customers. I spent most of my time growing herbs and making medicines. I was rarely seen. This pattern of keeping a low profile is one that I still continue in my current life.

The karmic pattern played out through the young novice who was sent to the barn to discover that I was involved in illicit sex, a discovery that ruined me in the priesthood and led me to leave the church. This is similar to my actions as the Shaman, when I set up the discovery of my rival Banto having illicit sex, which ruined his leadership role and got him banished from our village.

The soul wound was the split in myself between what I felt was duty to family and church and my own inner needs and desires. I would never have left the church on my own, though now that I look back, I could have left at any time. But it never occurred to me since I had my family honor to uphold and the vows I took to God and the Church. Yet my family had betrayed me and tossed me out, so I had no duty to them. And God and the Church? Well, would God want to accept the pledge of a person who did not know what he was pledging? I did what I was supposed to do, and though I didn't like it, I still did the best I could. Does one have to accept one's position in life? Do we have to accept our fate, especially if another person chooses that fate for us? Would God want me to take vows that deny an essential part of who I am?

I suspect Sybil was an Adversary following me through lifetimes and trying to take me down. When I first laid eyes on her I felt a chill in my heart. That is the same feeling I had around Dem Majer in Atlantis and Ben Mal in Egypt. Sybil used me for her own needs with no consideration of the effect on my life. This shows how Adversaries can take many forms and sexes, but their intention remains.

The skills I gained in this life are a continuation of the herbal skills I had in Egypt. But instead of being the actual healer, I became a behind the scenes person who grew and developed herbal medicines. I have had a lifelong interest in herbal medicines in this current life.

In my next life I want more balance. I want to have more autonomy and more ability to make my own decisions. I don't want to be a sacrifice, especially an unwilling sacrifice. And I don't want to repress physical needs. I want to have both a spiritual life and a life of the natural world, to be physically sexual and spiritually sacred.

In my present life, I think the reason the Priest was the first life I remembered is because it clearly illustrated the themes I was working with at the time. As a woman in my 20s on a spiritual journey, I strongly believed that I had to choose between a life of spirit and a life of matter. There was a core sense that if I lived the life of a spiritual seeker then I couldn't have the trappings of an everyday life. I was on a spiritual journey and that meant that I was alone. One of my sayings was "You come in alone, you go out alone." I never thought that I could have a home, a family, children, or money. I was on a spiritual search, alone. God would take care of my basic needs, so I knew I would never starve. But I did not think I could be on a spiritual path as a mother, or wife, or business owner. Those things would only distract me from my goal of a spiritual awakening and to be of greater service.

I think this belief, that was both conscious and unconscious, is the reason that I lived largely alone, never settling down in one place but moving to new towns as I followed my own path. Now that I am older and more illuminated, I realize that an everyday life can provide the foundation for a spiritual approach to the world; if I have my basic needs met, like food, physical contact, companionship, housing, and safety, then I can better serve the world as a spiritual teacher.

As I have grown in my own path, the reconnection and balance of this split between spirit and matter, between heaven and earth, has been a central part of my spiritual work. During the times in my current life when I was very tuned into Soul and Spirit, I had little knowledge of what it took to flourish financially or the pragmatic benefits of a solid foundation. Then other times, when I was at university earning my doctorate, my Mind and intellect became strong and dominant while my Spiritual connection lessened. I now work to have an integrated balance between Mind, Spirit, Body, and Soul on a daily basis. An awareness of my past lives and reincarnation has helped me to bring Spirit into my Physical life, to have control over Mind and listen to the prompting of my Soul.

There is a universal aspect to this life, since the split between a physical and spiritual life is a recognizable theme in many religions, where the separation between spirit and flesh permeates much of religious literature and teachings. In the Catholic Church one must be unmarried and celibate to be a monk, nun, or priest. The Bible tells that the apostles had to leave their families behind in order to follow Christ. In Buddhism, monks and nuns do not marry. In Hindu India, there is more integration between the two, but instead of creating a world where you must choose one or the other, the experiences of life are divided to accommodate this reality. So, in the first part of life you are a householder, where the job of being a parent, provider, and responsible community member are highly regarded and expected occupations. Once those duties are met, at around age 40, you can move on to another stage of life where the main focus is a spiritual existence. Some people will leave their households for good, even changing their name. Others will move into seclusion, or become the wise elder.

Also in many contexts spiritual pursuits are seen as incompatible with financial profits. Most churches, meditation centers, healing, and missionary work are non-profit. In some Native American traditions a shaman or healer does not accept money for their work. If someone wants to leave money instead of giving it directly to the healer, they place it on the ground as a symbolic gesture that says that Mother Earth is the one providing the sustenance. Why is the split between spirit and matter, between heaven and earth, emphasized in many religions? Is it because the demands of the flesh distract from the spiritual work? Is it based on some idea that this physical world is somehow less important than the spiritual world?

For you, the reader

Ponder if anything in the Priest's life resonates with you. Have you been separated from your family of birth? Have you repressed any desire because you thought it would not be accepted by others? Have you kept a secret that was important to you, like the Priest had with his treasures? Have you had to find your own way in troubling times? Have you felt the tension between a life of spirit and a life of matter? Are you called to live a spiritually-oriented life?

Think also about actions you may have done in this lifetime for which you feel guilt or regret. These are common emotions in the Soul's evolution, as we figure out how to be human and navigate the physical world.

You will have both successes and failures in any life. And you may be punished for misdeeds. But in the larger sense, in the context of the Soul, such misdeeds are part of learning and you need to bring compassion and forgiveness to your imperfections.

9
Cather Trapped in a Vice Grip: Montsegur, France, 1240 CE

It seems like forever since I left the Mont, but I can remember it as if it were yesterday. My mind wanders back and I can see it all as it was happening in those last days of 1244, the last days of my people.

"Come!" calls my uncle, breaking my inner musings. "You cannot spend all day in a dream! There is work to do."

Ah, but I am so tired of work, and who wants to work after the pleasure of one's first kiss? I can still feel Justine's softness on my lips. Surely this is more important than lifting and hauling bales of food and water up and down the steep slopes of the Mont. That task happens every day. Today I want to be left alone to bask in the memory of Justine.

"But I do not feel so well today," I reply, trying to get out of work. Maybe I can meet up with Justine later and we can kiss again, and longer this time, not a quick touch like last night. "I think I should head home."

"Head home!" replies Uncle, his brows furrowed. "This is home, and we are defending it right now. If you do not put these bales on your back and start your descent down the Mont, there might soon be nothing left to defend. One hundred days we have been cut off from the world. One hundred days we are trapped here like mice by a very large cat. One hundred days and no relief in sight. And you want to go home and nap!"

The anger in his voice wakes me from my dream of Justine and I slowly stretch out my legs which are folded under me as I sit on the stone walls at the top of the Mont. I look over the vast green countryside as it expands out to the base of the forbidding mountains in the distance. I am quite tall and lanky, but there is a gift in this. I am nimble, like a spider. In fact, they call me Spider, since for as long as I have been able to walk, I have been climbing and scurrying the walls of the Mont.

The Mont is our castle, home, and refuge located at the top of a very tall and rocky mountain called Montsegur near the Pyrenees Mountains. The sides of Montsegur are nearly vertical walls of rock. There is only one side that can be approached directly and even that is by a steep, narrow, and winding horse path that leads to the large gates of our castle. The Mont is made of huge blocks of stone and is so much a part of Montsegur that it looks as if it erupted right out of the peak of the mountain, instead of having been built carefully by hard labor many years ago. The Mont and the mountain of Montsegur are so connected that we think of them as one. I was born here and my ancestors were some of the first to seek protection in these walls of stone. My family, including my two brothers and my uncle, all live within the castle. My father is the Leader for all who live in the Mont as well as for the villagers who surround our base.

The height and inaccessibility of Montsegur gives us great protection. Our view from such a height allows us to see all that happens for miles around us. Even a single traveler catches our attention, and unless we open the gates, that traveler will have to move on. We control who comes and who goes.

But from such a vaulted refuge we have no water source or farmland. We have to count on the valleys below for our food and water. The villagers in the valley gladly sell their crops to us and in turn we nourish them with money, tales of the truth, stories of the past, healing balms, and the school where villagers send their children if they can afford to have them absent from the fields. For me, since I live at the Mont I have to go to school. I have no such luxury as spending my days in a village.

Justine is from the closest small village, only an hour ride down the valley. She comes up to the Mont once a week for school and I have been pining over her for years. Her hair is red and curly and falls in waves like the ocean down her back and around her face. Luck came my way one hundred days ago when she and her family moved from their home in the valley into a tiny group of houses that perch on the slopes of Montsegur. The houses are small and scattered about like rocks tossed on a shore. We call it the Pog. A sturdy wall surrounds it and narrow paths weave together the homes there. When the Catholic army began their march toward us, many of the families in the nearby valley moved to the Pog for protection. So now I get to see Justine every day.

My family is part of a religious group known as Cathars. We are Christians who live according to the life of Christ. But we do not believe in the Catholic Church or its Pope, as we consider it too worldly, attached to material wealth and putting great emphasis on the physical world. The Catholics even think that God came to earth in the form of a man called Jesus, and that the death of Jesus's body by torture was the salvation of mankind! None of these Catholic beliefs make sense to us. So we live our own way as Pure Ones, emulating the life and teachings of the spiritual being we know as Christ, while living in peace with our neighbors.

But the Catholic Church will not leave us in peace. They have tried for many years to get us to set aside our beliefs and accept their teachings. Many times they have sent their fancy priests to debate with our humble teachers, the Good Men and Good Women, to try to reason their faith into us. When that failed they took to force and set a Crusade upon us. They have vowed to bring us into their way of thinking or destroy us all.

We knew the Catholic troops would come to the Mont. They had conquered every other nearby Cathar town and village. We knew they would come sooner or later so we have been preparing. We worked for nearly a year, making our Mont as strong as possible and setting up supplies that would last. And now the Catholic troops are camped at the base of Montsegur, tossing up threats and stones every now and then to remind us they are there. I am quite bored with all the Councils and speeches and prayers and admonitions. I spend my nights looking forward to school so I can see Justine. Afternoons I haul bales of food and water up the mountain, and my evenings after prayers are spent wondering how I can find time alone. It feels like an old man's war, an old man's task, an old man's battle.

"Another day, another siege," I murmur to myself as I stand up from the wall.

"What!" cries Uncle, for apparently I had spoken my complaint out loud. "Another day, another siege! As if this is a game! Do you not understand what is at stake? Your entire family could be killed. Your entire people slaughtered. We could be driven to the ground!"

"I am sorry, Uncle, that I spoke thus," I say, though I am only sorry I had spoken out loud. "But the Mont has never been taken before. The troops cannot come up even to the gate without us stopping them. How can they take the Mont? It is impossible. They will tire of this game, as they have in the past, and leave us in peace."

"No, you are wrong. They will not give up this time. They are intent on destroying us all. Look at the burnings of Cathars in Besiers, Carcassonne, and Foix. Thousands... no, tens of thousands of Cathars are dead. Those who survived have come here. The Mont is filled to the brim with all the people who were able to escape those massacres. We are now the eye of the Crusader storm as well as the pot of gold that Pope Innocent wants to claim in order to prove that the Catholic teachings are the only truth of Christ. We Pure Ones are a threat to his power."

"How can we be a threat? We have nothing. We are nothing. We hold no lands, nor seek power or prestige."

Uncle shakes his head and sighs deeply. "Although you are 18 you speak like a child. Have you not been paying attention in school? To the stories of the Good Men and Good Women who are our teachers? For hundreds of years we Cathars have lived in peace with the Catholics around us. Our way of Christ was accepted by many as the real path, the pure way to salvation, or at least we were respected as lovers of Christ and those who emulate his life. The Catholic priests and their fancy rich ways had little effect on us in the villages.

"But once the Dominican priests began their preaching, everything changed. They look and act like simple men, like Pure men; they act like us. So people listen to them and think they tell the truth when they spread the stories that we are heretics and of the devil. They have seeded suspicion and persecution. The Dominicans look like Pure Ones, but they are wolves in sheep's clothing. They only act like Good Men so that they can make their way into our flock. Pretending trust and friendship, they gather the names of the followers of our faith and then have them arrested one by one. Tortured, some fall from the path and claim to be of Catholic faith. To save their body, or their family, they tell where others of us live, and name the Good Men and Good Women who lead us through their inspiration and guidance. We are being destroyed on the inside by betrayal caused by Dominican lies and from the outside by Catholic troops. This Mont is pushed from both sides, like a vice grip; we are being pressured until I can feel the crumbling of the very foundation on which we live. This is not just another siege. God only knows that I wish that were true."

After so many words, Uncle sits down heavily, as if exhausted. His head falls into his hands and I can see him taken over by the weight of it all.

"If it is as bad as you say, then why are we still here? Why don't we leave? You know there is a secret way from the Mont. Why don't we all escape?"

Uncle raises his head and looks around quickly to be sure we are alone. "You know of the secret way since you were raised here and know every stone of this mountain. But others do not know it, nor should they. Not everyone could make the rough trip through the mountain that way, as you well know. Only those nimble and strong, like you, could make it."

"Then why not send out those who are able to leave? The fact that we stay here and do nothing only gives the sense that we are not in peril. If it is as bad as you say, wouldn't it be best for at least some to flee?"

"And who would you have leave?" questions Uncle, looking up at me, his face in shadow as I stand over him. "Would you leave? Leave your family to face the threat alone?"

I ponder the idea, looking at his dark eyes and realizing that if those young and strong enough to escape by the secret way did leave, then the Mont would lose anyone capable of bringing up food and water, or to work for our defense. It became clear that all my questions had been asked, debated, and answered in Councils that were not attended by the likes of me.

I take a deep breath and regret that I have not been paying more attention to the events. Standing tall, I hold out my arms and say, "Then Uncle, it is best for you to put the bales on my back and let me begin my work. For clearly there is much to be done."

This brings Uncle out of his despair. He grabs the empty food bale and the two empty leather casts for water. Each holds only five gallons, but if I make the trip three times daily it will be 30 gallons of water for the Mont. If my brothers also work with me, it could be 100 gallons a day, which keeps the stores refreshed. Independence is important to us. We will do our part. I know that from my very heart.

I wonder why Uncle feels we are in such danger. Montsegur means "secure mountain." It has never been taken, not in its entire history. There is only one path up the mountain to the gates of the Mont and it is narrow and steep. An enemy could only advance very slowly, no wider than a few men across, making their position extremely weak. In the past, enemy troops were easily shot with arrows or crushed by stones if they got too close. But Cathars are not a fighting people; we are a religious group committed to non-violence and hence we do not try to kill the enemy that stalks us from below. The Mont is a defensive fortress only and we do not fight. Our strategy has always been to wait out a siege. Eventually the enemy troops run out of food and tire of the endless waiting. We have learned patience and strategic organization through this game, a contest we have always won.

The only way we can be defeated is if troops outlast our food and water supply. This is why it is so important to keep our people healthy, since disease can spread quickly and do more destruction than any enemy troop. So we have created a way to go down the Mont on the fourth side, a sheer drop-off to the rocks below, where no enemy could begin an attack nor camp beneath it. Few know that it can be scaled, but over centuries a climbing wall has been dug into the rock face. No enemy can see the cliff from this position, which allows us to get news from outside, send messages, and bring up supplies to replenish our storage.

But a frustrated enemy will tire of waiting, then troops circle Montsegur like vultures, seeking some hidden entrance. From our superior position, we see their movements and if they get close to the fourth side I do not climb. If our fourth side were discovered by crusading troops, it would be worse than the loss of the Mont itself. We would be truly stuck.

I look out over the expanse of land beneath me. The white clouds dancing over blue skies remind me that rain is on its way. Swallows call out their cheer as they fly in loops and daring acts of aerial courage above my head. I love the swallows. They look so free to me. Free to fly, to soar, to dance, to spin. Unlike other birds, they do not seem to have a single intent or destination, nor do they pump their wings in quiet desperation. Swallows play with each other, flying in pairs, like they belong to each other, as well as to their flock.

My mind drifts again to Justine. I wonder what it would be like to just fly away with her, to leave the Mont and start a new life in the valley below. We could leave by the secret passage. I know the way and she is strong enough to follow. Images of us living in a small home surrounded by trees and flowers drift through my head. We would laugh and be free like the swallows.

My thoughts are interrupted by the weight of the bales and leather casts as Uncle lifts them over my shoulders and straps them around my body. I situate them so they are stable and secure. I can't have the weight shift as I climb down the mountain. There is no way to survive a fall down such a steep slope. I shift from daydreams into the reality of work. With empty packs it takes half an hour to scamper down the Mont. But climbing back up with the full weight of food and water can take two hours.

I love scaling the sides of the Mont like a spider. And I love the freedom of being alone, with just the sky and the valley stretching out in front of me. I'm not always alone.

I look into my uncle's worried face and give him a smile. He is always worried when I climb. Not so much that I will have a misstep, but that I might be seen and captured. Worse than the possibility of my death is that the troops would discover how we get our food and water when under siege. The villagers who supply us would then also be in danger. I know all this and put my focus on making as little noise as possible. I cannot sing like the swallows when they fly. I must remain silent.

That evening, I stand outside my father's study not long after our evening meal. I have been pondering my conversation with Uncle all day and I feel a great unease.

He looks up from his large wooden desk that is covered in books and writing implements. We are not wealthy people. Money means nothing to us. But we do value knowledge and books and learning. We have acquired many of the comforts that come from a life of settled study. I am sure to the villagers in the Pog we must seem rich.

Today as I thought of Justine and the possibility of having a home with her, I realized that I have no way to make a living. No one pays me to haul goods up and down the Mont, or to explore the secrets of the castle. How could I provide a home for Justine? I cannot ask her to be my wife if I have nothing to give her.

"Are we really in danger from the Catholic troops below us? I met Johan at the base of the mountain where he gave me the food and water from the village. He told me that the troops have quit raiding the villages for food and are instead bringing their own supplies with them. He said they have become settled in tents and that more come every day. Some even come with women, though he does not think they are wives, but rather women to entertain the troops."

My father's eyes briefly smile as he considers that his elder son is gossiping about village whores. Then he looks at me up and down, as if seeing me for the first time. "You have grown to be a strong and handsome man and you now are having interest in young ladies." I am always surprised how he knows what is on my mind. I feel suddenly shy. "What is it you wish to discuss?" he says.

"I want to know the state of Montsegur. Uncle says we are in grave danger. What decisions have been made about our defense and the care of our people?"

Father continues to eye me carefully, as if coming to a decision. "We have received terrible news this evening," he says, pointing to a letter before him. "Catholic troops saw Johan leaving the rocky place after he gave you the food and water. He had an empty cart and the troops took him. He was tortured. They threatened to kill his mother and father if he did not tell them where the meeting place was, and so he took them there. He was badly beaten and the enemy would have killed him except they think he may have more secrets still. They took his sister into captivity as well. The family is in shock and despair. They have risked and lost much."

I stand, speechless. Just a few hours ago Johan was laughing with me as he described the women who were encamped with the troops. Now it has all changed.

"Fortunately," continues my father, "he did not show them the path up the Mont, because he did not know it. Otherwise they might scale our heights right now. But they will be on alert to any villager who may try to help us."

My mind goes to Johan's sister who is young and beautiful. I do not need to wonder what the troops would do to her. I feel deep despair, and also great relief that Justine is safe in the Pog. I want to run to find her, to be sure she has not gone down into the village for the day.

"How did you find this out?" I ask, getting weak as the implications grow in my mind.

"Allies in the village shot a message arrow, so we sent down one of the hawks to fly back with their letter. I have just called a Council meeting to consider what this means and how we should respond. It is likely that our source of food and water has been cut off."

He said those words simply, but I knew what they meant. How could we wait out the Catholic troops if we cannot replenish our supplies? How can the villagers help us when they are being watched and tortured? I realize that my uncle's words were correct and I am awash in shame that I did not take this siege seriously.

"You are now 18," says Father. "You can come to the Council if you wish, and speak if you are moved."

I want to run to the top of the Mont and fly free like the swallows. But that route has been cut off from me. To think that I tried to get out of work today, but if I had, would Johan have been found? Yes, he would have, only worse, he would have been found with a full cart because I would not have been there to take the goods. I want to run, but there is no place to run in our perch at the top of the world. I feel trapped, and remember my uncle's words that we are caught in a vice grip.

I feel my father's hand on my shoulder. The warmth of his touch comforts me and brings me back to the room. "I am sorry for you, as I know Johan is a friend and close to your heart." I am afraid I will begin to weep if I don't leave this room. I find it hard to breathe.

My father again knows what is inside of me. and he pulls me down to my knees and begins to pray. I don't know what he says, but the sound of his voice comforts me, and now that I am on the cool stone floor I do not feel like I will faint. It is as if the armor of my childhood is cracking around me and falling off in chunks. I feel exposed. I am not a child anymore, but I am not yet ready to be a man. I want to chase my brothers around the house and play hide and seek, or curl up in bed and have Mother sing to me. But all these options are gone, stripped away. In front of my eyes now are only blood and tears.

The Council is made of twelve men and women, usually elders, business owners, or those with more experience. Their meetings are held in the largest hall of the Mont, which is made entirely of stone. Seating is designed like an old Roman theater, with the Council seated around a table at the front, and stone benches for spectators rising up around them.

Nothing is decided quickly among my people and there are many Council meetings in the month since Johan's capture. While the Good Men and Good Women lead us in spiritual matters, the Council makes all other decisions. With this crisis, the Council hall is overflowing.

Crusading troops have not yet found our climbing wall, but dozens of them search daily and my trips have become impossible.

The endless Council meetings focus on how long the Mont and the Pog can last without replenishment of provisions. The answer is not good, with only a 90-day supply of water left. Everyone is put on rationing. Even baths are forbidden.

I wonder what that means. Would we surrender in 90 days? Would we pray for rain? The Council, and especially the Good Men and Women who attend, spend much time talking about how, if captured, the Catholic Pope would end our Teachings forever, making it as if we had never lived. That is of greater concern than how long our water can last.

I am the youngest in attendance. I sit in the back, listening, but never speaking. I do not want to be seen a fool, as my uncle saw me that last day when I scaled the wall.

I learn that there are 450 Cathars at Montsegur, the Mont and Pog. Over half are elderly or hurt, the remains of our people who escaped other towns that were besieged.

One particularly old man seated near the front stands to speak. "I came from the small town of Beziers, where we Cathars and our Catholic friends lived together in peace and brotherhood. As families and friends we were entwined as one, impossible to tell by sight which was which. When the crusaders came, they demanded that our Catholic neighbors identify their Cathar brethren, since the troops could not distinguish between us. The Catholic townspeople refused. They thought surely their refusal would stop the bloodshed and save the community they had come to love."

The old man became tearful and agitated. "Alas, they were wrong. When the troops could not distinguish who they should kill and who they should spare, the Bishop said, 'Kill them all. God will know his own.' The crusaders rampaged and the whole town was destroyed – all 5000, Cathar and Catholic alike."

Tears pour down his face. "I was in the fields and heard the screams of the dying and cries of children. By the time I got to the village the killing was done and the troops were gone. I will never forget the dead, piled upon one another. Friends and kin, young and old. Not one Cathar had been given the Consolamentum, the rite that promises eternity with Christ after death. It is for that loss I weep the most, for as we know, the body is only the container for Spirit and has no value on its own." He hangs his head in sorrow and slowly sits back down. Silence surrounds the Council and I hear soft weeping and whispered prayers.

Under normal conditions, two or three Good Men and Good Women are present in Montsegur. They live a life in emulation of Christ, a perfection that is not expected of us lay believers. They travel the countryside and teach the ways of Christ, and hence do not settle anywhere for long. With the Crusade it is now dangerous for them to leave. Fifty Good Men and Women in one place is very unusual. Montsegur is the remaining Cathar stronghold and the final place that offers protection for our people.

Today in the Council, some suggest the Good Men and Women should leave the Mont to continue teaching for as long as they are able, to carry our faith forward. Others think they should stay at the Mont to provide spiritual and moral support to the Believers, since we are trapped by this siege. Since the climbing wall has been compromised, there is a broad consensus that the Good Men and Women are needed at the Mont to provide the rite of Consolamentum.

The Consolamentum is our only ceremony, the laying of hands and the Gospels on the head of a Believer, a blessing that instills the Holy Spirit and ensures salvation and an eternity with Christ. To know that we will be with Christ when we die strengthens our faith. This belief in everlasting life makes it easier to die if the Catholic troops overtake the Mont. Our deaths will come, most likely by flame and fire, if the massacres in the other Cathar towns are any indication.

No one suggests renouncing our Cathar faith and converting to Catholicism, even though it is known that such a move will save us.

A few are hopeful that the crusaders will leave and everything will return to normal. I recall my own voice as I suggested the same words to Uncle. That seems like a lifetime ago, and I realize how simplistic and naive such ideas are. The troops will not leave us this time. Winter is nearing and it is clear that they are planning to stay. More and more come weekly and none leave.

When not at the Council meetings I spend my days walking the walls of the keep, looking out over the land and sky. I think I will lose my mind.

One day Uncle meets me at the walls and gives me a task. He looks around to be sure no one is near. "We need you to go to the secret passage in the heart of the Mont. Clear it of any stones and dirt and make the path as clear as possible. Report back to me with any ideas of how to improve the passage. Do not, under any circumstances, go outside. And do not tell anyone of this task. Do you understand?"

The secret passage? I am given permission to walk the secret passage? I have done it many times in my life, but never with permission. And I am to see what needs to be done to improve it? I have many thoughts on that, including where to put torches to give more light. There are many questions I want to ask, but I can see in my uncle's face that I should not. I straighten up and look him clearly in the eyes. "Yes, I understand. I am to work on the passage to make it easier to traverse. I am not to go outside. I am to keep quiet, and I am to report back to you with ideas for improvement."

Uncle gives me a small grin and a grunt and walks away, but I notice his step is lighter.

I take the first deep breath that I have allowed into my lungs in over a month. I look up into the sky and see the swallows dancing and playing and hear the sound of their song. I decide to go down to the Pog to see Justine, the first time I have sought her out since I heard of Johan's capture and the ending of our supplies. It will be the first time I have seen her since our sweet kiss.

My heart beats wildly and the strength of purpose grows inside of me again. I feel a bit of joy growing in my heart and I run from the castle to the streets below, hoping I can find her at her home, where we can have some time alone. I wonder how much I can tell her.

My day does not go well. When I find Justine, she will not speak to me. I had kissed her a month ago and then did not return. She was embarrassed and ashamed. I had to spend the entire day following her around to prove my good intentions and apologize for my long absence. Any thought of a repeat kiss is gone the moment I see her eyes, hooded and cloaked. I leave her in the early evening to go to prayers, but since I don't feel I can share what I know, my silence still creates a distance between us. I need to find out what I can say, get a sense of what I can do. I need to speak to Father again to find out what the people know about our fate.

"Father," I begin. My insides are churning and I want to hop from foot to foot in sheer nervousness, but I stand perfectly still.

He looks up from his desk and puts down the letter he is reading. The boy he saw in front of him only months ago is gone. In his place is a man, young and worn out. I have lost weight due to food rationing, and lost strength from the absence of my daily trips up and down the mountain. My eyes hold little joy or curiosity. I feel like an old man.

"What is it?" Father asks quietly.

"You know of my new task to improve the secret passageway?" Father affirms with a nod. "Why am I to do this task? I have been to every Council meeting since Johan's arrest and the end of our supply climbs and no one has mentioned the secret passage. No one has mentioned escaping the Mont."

"Is it not enough for you to have the task?" Father asks.

I pause as I consider the question. At one time it might have been enough, but now there is Justine. I know I want her to be my wife. Will I be alive to ask her? Will she be alive to answer? I am surprised to see that Father no longer intimidates me. I look him in the eyes.

"From what I have gathered in the Council meetings," I say, "we have about 30 days left before our water ends. No one has mentioned an escape. Why prepare the secret passageway if no one is to escape? Are the Good Men and Good Women planning to leave to continue to share our teachings?"

Again he looks at me. I get the sense he wishes I would go away. But I do not move. "These are not questions to which you need to know the answer," he finally says.

"But I do need to know. We all need to know. Is the fate of all 450 of us to be decided by the Council of 12? Do we not have the right to know and decide for ourselves? What good is a sacrifice if it is not freely given?" I have heard enough in the Council to know that being burnt at the stake is the most likely end we will face.

I look at Father and realize I am not the only one who has aged. He looks old, tired, weak. I want to feel badly for him, but I do not. "What is my fate? I have a right to know."

"Why do you care?" Father asks me calmly. "Are you afraid to die? Are you not ready to let go of your body and enter Christ?"

"I do not want to die; I want to live. I want to marry Justine and have a family with her and live in the valley and be free from war. I want to live the life that has been mine since my beginning. I am not ready to go to the fires. I am ready to fight if need be, fight for my life, for my family, for Justine."

"You know we do not fight, that we are peaceful people." Father looks at me askance.

"I do not mean to fight with weapons, but to fight with actions and words. Fight for our way of life by taking actions that will sustain our lives. I am not ready to surrender. I will not kill another, yet I do not want to be killed. I can fight with my choices, by refusing to surrender and by leaving this Mont to live a life of peace. The Catholic crusaders do not control my life or my choices."

All of these words come as a surprise to me. I had not intended to say such things. But as they fall from my lips I know they are true. There are ways to fight that do not include weapons, war, and killing. I can stand up for my life, my family, my faith. That will be fight enough.

I can see surprise cross Father's face. He looks into my eyes as if deciding what to do. Finally, he says, "We have had terrible news tonight. The Catholic troops have gone into the Pyrenees Mountains and found men from the Basque country who will show them the way of the mountains. The route up the Mont walls will be clear to those men who climb every day of their lives. It is only a matter of time before the Mont will be scaled. The period of talking is over; we must meet in Council tomorrow and decide our fate."

"Why would the Pyrenees Basque help the Catholics? They are not friends of that faith." I am surprised at such a turn of events. I thought that the way up the Mont would never be discovered.

"They are being offered much money. Helping the Catholics conquer us proves their fidelity to the Church and relieves them from the same fate as ours."

I cannot believe that the Basques, a solitary and independent race, would turn on us in such a way. We have traded with them for years, and though not friends, we have certainly been respectful of each other's ways. "I cannot believe it," I murmur, looking down.

"Believe it," replies Father. "There will be a Council meeting tomorrow to address this new threat. Do not come to complain or bemoan our fate. Come with a plan of action to be voted up or down. You are young, but the Council also knows you are wise and serious and know more than most. They will listen to you. Be bold if you have any desire to leave the Mont. This will be your last time to convince anyone of such a plan, for we must make final decisions tomorrow between all the ideas we have been discussing this past month."

With a short nod of his head I know I am dismissed. I have all night to consider what I want to do. I bow slightly and turn to leave. I head straight to the walls at the top of the Mont, where I walk round and round all through the night, looking out to the valleys below, to the Pog where Justine is settling into her bed, to the fires of thousands of crusading troops that are camped below. I spend the whole night walking the walls, talking out loud to the stars and the Moon, trying to figure out a plan.

It strikes me as odd that only the previous day I was told to keep the passage in the heart of the mountain a secret, and now today, I am going to announce it to the entire Council and all the Believers who are present. I do not know how such a declaration will be received. But Father said this meeting would be my only chance to present a plan.

I love my faith and am true to God, and if necessary, I would die before I would deny it. But that does not mean I am ready to die, and I do not want my family and faith to die. To surrender quietly to the Catholic crusaders does not appeal to me. I want to try to escape, to leave the Mont and continue my beliefs. Surely others will want that as well.

As I enter the Council meeting, I breathe deeply and center myself. I feel small in the cavernous room and feel a chill in the walls and in my bones. I take a seat midway back with a clear view. I look down and see both Uncle and Father in deep conversation with several other elders.

I decide to listen to all the ideas of the Council and other brethren before I share my plan. I also want to get a sense of what the Good Men and Women propose to do. From Father's tone the previous night, I sense that the plight of the lay Believer has not been considered an important factor; it has been assumed we are ready to die for our faith. The Council's only real concern has been for the continuation of our Teaching, especially as it relates to the Good Men and Women who can share the faith if they leave the Mont, or who can give the Consolamentum if they stay. To be successful in my plan I need to acknowledge these central concerns. The personal desires of a young man would mean nothing to the Council; any plan that would matter needs to fit these larger aims. My time attending meetings has been time well spent.

The passage in the heart of the Mont is known by very few. I discovered it as a small child in my endless searching for new places to climb. When I told my family about it, I was forbidden to return. Naturally that did not stop me. But it did make me more circumspect, so I did not share the knowledge with my brothers or friends. I explored it on my own, year after year. I crawled through the open crevices and dark hallways, finding every turn and twist.

I loved going to the secret passage. It was my place to be free. If I could not fly away like the swallows, then I could scamper away like the spiders. Every once in a while someone would enter the secret passage, but I knew how to hide. In spite of my secrecy, it became known that I spent time down in the hidden paths. Once Uncle caught me down there, but instead of forbidding me to return he told me to be silent. I alone was allowed.

The passage led to an exit that was a far distance from the Mont. It opened up amid fallen rocks onto a valley with a flowing river and green trees. Sometimes I would spend the day in the river and fall asleep in the soft green grass. It was a magical world that was mine alone. I had never heard the passage mentioned again until the previous day when I was asked to make it more passable. Uncle, at least, must know where it leads. It is rough passage with climbing on rocks and crawling on knees, so not everyone would be able to use it as an escape route. But plenty would be able to traverse its tumbled paths, and this is what I will say in Council.

Hours pass in the meeting and I hear many of the same plans that had been previously presented, though with more intensity now. With the capture of Johan our supplies have been cut off. Everyone agrees that with the Basque help it is only a matter of time before our fourth wall is found. Guards are posted overlooking the rocky cliff to keep track of the Basque progress and to alert Council if discovery seems imminent. The general consensus is that we have only days left.

It will be impossible for the crusaders to mount an effective assault up the rock wall, since only one person can climb at a time. Troops would be single file, strung out like ants, thus exposed and easy to kill. The rock climb would only be useful if the Basques make it to the top, enter the castle, and open the main gate to allow the crusading troops to enter the Mont.

Dozens of fighting knights from other besieged Cathar towns make the request that they be allowed to kill the Basques as they climb to the top. But we are non-violent and killing the Basques, or Catholic crusaders for that matter, is against our beliefs.

"Better a willing death now than a weak death later!" cries out one of the Good Men. "I do not need to remind you that our body is flesh of the dark world and that it is our spirit alone that holds the light. We know that the Catholic fantasy that Christ took a physical body is not true and therefore Christ's death on the cross has no reality, glory, or saving grace for humankind. The only saving grace we Cathars can hope for is to leave our physical body behind in this dark world at death and join Christ in the light of spirit. We need not be afraid of our fate."

Another Good Man stands to speak. "If we accept this fate that lies before us then our death is anticipated and becomes a willing sacrifice for God. More importantly, all our brethren would have time to receive the final rite of Consolamentum. Under normal circumstances the Consolamentum is given to the sick near the time of death to open the gates of heaven so that the dying can walk through to be with Christ. If we decided now to face the fires," the Good Man continued, "there will be time for the Good Men and Women here at Montsegur to give the Consolamentum to all the lay Believers in the castle and in the Pog. We would all go to the fires in peace, knowing that Christ awaits us. If we wait to see what the crusading troops will do, then we might lose the opportunity for the Consolamentum, and the final rite might not be given. Without the rite, then the reunion with Christ in Heaven is not guaranteed." He sat down heavily, as if the weight of this dark world was becoming too much for him to bear.

Though it is true that we are not attached to the physical world, I cannot see the honor in dying sooner rather than later. Either way, the Catholics who hate us will hunt us down like animals for the slaughter. Thoughts of the Dominicans who made us their sworn enemies – and the mercenary troops who kill us for money – make my heart beat fast and I feel my face become hot. Such anger and fear are not useful to me. They would be seen by the Council as a sign of weakness. I need to be cool, detached, and logical. My people love logic and we are taught the reasoned arguments of Aristotle from an early age. I keep my silence.

After all is said and done, the main option appears to be surrender. The only question that remains is whether we do it sooner rather than later.

I wait until I hear the words: "Does anyone else want to speak before we make a decision?"

People begin to murmur among themselves. I stand up tall and let my voice ring through the hall. "Let us use the secret passage in the heart of the Mont to leave Montsegur so that we can worship elsewhere according to our faith. In this way our Teachings can continue."

All voices stop and there is total silence. I pause to let my words take hold before I continue. This will also give Father the time to cut me off if he feels this disclosure should not be voiced. I do not think he will stop me, since he encouraged me to come to Council and speak. But I will abide by his wisdom. I look at him for a brief moment and see the slightest nod of his head. I take another deep breath and continue.

"The Catholics should not be allowed to determine our fate. Guided by the light of Christ, we should decide for ourselves. The Catholics have hunted us down until all that are left are here in Montsegur. This Council speaks as if our death and the end of our religion is inevitable. How would that benefit our religion if we allow the Catholics to kill us now? What will become of our Teachings? Are not our Teachings true? And it is not just our bodies they will burn. They will burn all our books, all our knowledge. What of those who will come later? Do they not deserve to know the Pure Way? Will the teachings of the Catholics be all that is known and taught of Christ?"

I pause and again take a deep breath. I want to say that I love Justine and I want to marry her and raise our children as Cathars and share our lifestyle of peace and nonviolence with my grandchildren. But I know that would sound as if I were only concerned about myself. I would be dismissed as one who speaks only out of selfishness and ignorance.

"There is a secret passage in the heart of the Mont that leads to a valley well past where the Catholic troops are camped. It is a difficult journey and only the young and strong will be able to succeed. But it does provide a choice for us; some could leave Montsegur with our books, Teachings, and Good Men and Women to guide us in the creation of a new community where we can continue to teach the true way of Christ. Those who cannot or choose not to take the difficult road can stay here in the Mont and prepare to make the sacrifice by flame, supported by their faithful brothers and sisters and the final rite of Consolamentum." Again, I pause, for I know these are new ideas that have not been stated before.

I continue, gaining strength in my voice. "The 12 men and women in this Council are wise and have guided us well. But there are over 400 more men, women, and children who do not know about these decisions that are being made for them. I ask the Council to call a meeting with all the people at the Castle and in the Pog and let each person make the choice to either stay here and die freely as a sacrifice for our faith and for Christ, or to leave the Mont with our Teachings in order to share our faith in another land and another future."

I wait another moment to let the words sink in before I sit down. There is total silence.

A Good Woman, an elder with long gray-streaked hair, stands up. Looking at me but also at the members of the Council, she asks, "Is it true that there is a way out of Montsegur, even with the troops below and the rock wall no longer available?"

Uncle, who is in charge of the Mont, stands. "It is true. The way is rarely used and is in rough shape. But it is passable for those of enough strength and perseverance. Remy," he nods in my direction, "found it when he was a child and has traversed it many times through the years. We were just beginning to make it more passable after the wall climb was cut off in case we could use it to bring in supplies."

The Good Woman continues. "I did not know that we had a way out. The Catholics will tear this castle to the ground and destroy all the houses in the Pog. They will find any writings or books and burn them too. They have done this in every other town they have taken. This is the last stand for our people. All the books and treasured items from the other destroyed towns have been brought here. We were hoping these items would be safe on the secure mountain, but alas they are not. I willingly give my body as a sacrifice to Christ, but I would like to be able to save our knowledge, our Teachings, and our books." With these words, she sits.

It is as if a fire has been lit and the meeting explodes with everyone talking at once. Many do not think we should be divided. Who would stay and who would go? Others say that if some did leave it would allow more rations of food and water to those who remain, and the Mont could hold out longer. This would allow the people who choose to leave the opportunity to get far away and settled before the troops disperse.

People want to see the secret heart of the Mont and decide for themselves if such a plan is foolhardy. Others start talking about how we could get the books and Teachings out, while burdened with provisions for the trip. And where would we go? Would we be openly Cathars to be hunted down at a later date? Or would we practice our faith in secret? And if we did so, would that mean we were denying who we were, pretending to be Catholics? Some suggest we go to the Pyrenees Mountains where we could live in isolation, never to be found. Others wonder if the Basques would report our presence now that they are working for the crusaders at our doorstep.

The questions and ideas continue as light fades into evening. Finally, a Council Elder stands up. "It is late and we have discussed much. It is time for a vote. We have before us two options. One: Surrender to the Catholic crusaders to face death by fire. Each Cathar will have the rite of Consolamentum and the support and faith of their brothers and sisters in Christ to uphold them. Two: Bring together all people in the Castle and the Pog and give them the choice of staying with the Mont and dying for their faith, or leaving by the secret passage to take the Teachings to a new land and continue to live according to our faith. Which way do you vote?"

I am not a voting member so I close my eyes and begin to silently pray. I cannot bear to know how my father and uncle vote.

I hear the Council Elder's voice again: "The second option has passed – to bring together the people of the Mont and the Pog to make the choice to stay or to go. The Council will meet tomorrow to figure out the details of implementing this decision."

My heart leaps and my eyes open wide. I jump from my seat and run from the hall and out to the Pog to my Justine. She must know how I feel and that I want to marry her right away. Tomorrow will not be too soon. I want us to have a family and a farm where we grow our own food and draw water from our own well. I must convince her to make the journey from the top of the Mont through its heart and that we must be part of those who choose to leave to carry our Teaching forth. I run down the lane to her house and I fling my arms wide. I feel like I am flying, free like the swallows, and I open my mouth and begin to sing.

The next morning I sit silently as Council members take their seats around a large table. Since I know more about the passage than anyone else, all my years of breaking the rules turn out to be of value. I am not accustomed to being treated like an adult. I squirm in my seat and am uncomfortable in this new role.

There are 50 Good Men and Good Women among the 450 Believers currently living in the Mont and Pog. The Good Men and Women are meeting separately to decide which Teachings must leave the Mont and which can be left behind. There are a thousand books, from ancient Greek philosophy to the writings of Jesus, to instructions for our faith. We also need to carry food and water, blankets and cooking implements, in addition to the tools of our crafts. Priorities have to be made. After all, the main reason the Council has decided on this course of action is so that we can save our Teachings.

Before alerting the Lay people, the Ruling Council wants to be certain that the passage at the heart of the Mont can be traversed, and if so, what degree of physical strength and dexterity will be needed. That is my job. I want to go alone to assess the passage as I have not seen it since the siege began, but the Ruling Council thinks that others should go with me, both to see the path and also to judge its difficulty.

I am certain the path can be improved but there will not be much time. Lighting with torches seems the quickest and most reasonable approach, though I am also hopeful for hand ropes and additional toe holds. The smithy, a strong man able to work with fire and iron, volunteers to accompany me. His assistant, a younger man about my age who is both strong and bright, will also come to write down the changes that are needed. A fourth man, a hunter, will complete our party. He is very good at tracking and remembering trails. He will mark the route as we go, and then create a rough map to show the Ruling Council and to better judge its distance and the time it will take.

As these companions are being chosen, I look at Uncle. I hope he will volunteer to come with us, since I know he has been on the passage before. Uncle is strong enough, but I can see he has aged. His short and stocky frame does not favor agility. He does not raise his eyes to look at mine, so I say nothing.

It had taken two years of my youthful explorations until I found the exit into the valley below. On my 13th birthday, I thought that was a lucky gift to me from the Mont. The day I walked out into the green valley I gasped with surprise and delight. There was a lovely river rushing by and I took off all my clothes and jumped in, swimming like a fish. I spent many hours along that river in the valley and never saw another person. Only the swallows seemed to know of its existence.

Now, five years later I am to lead my elders along this path and help my people find a way to escape the Mont.

The torches I had left behind are still there, and we have brought extra oil. The four of us traverse much slower than on any of my other trips. I quickly realize that taking a hundred people, if that many want to come, will be difficult. We would probably need to go in groups of ten at the most, and all must be physically capable, for one person unable to complete the passage would put the rest in peril.

I decide to construct a test course with similar obstacles – crawling under small outcroppings, climbing down rock faces, and walking along narrow courses. The smith suggests we just take everyone down the crevice and into the passage and see how they fare. But remembering Johan, I sense we do not want others to know of the secret passage. It would not do for the Catholics to come and torture people who could share the direction of our route.

The next day at the Ruling Council meeting, I suggest such a test course, and am supported by the other companions who state that the passage is difficult and not all who want to leave the Mont will be able to succeed.

It had taken nearly two hours for the four of us to go the entire passage out into the valley. If we did it in groups of ten, it could take a full day to move 100 people. But I underestimated those who would want to leave. Nearly half the townspeople preferred to start anew, which would require two full days. Those who wanted to stay were the leaders of Montsegur, the old and feeble, and those who had already left other cities under siege. Some parents preferred to stay at the Mont, but didn't want to make such a decision for their children. Since our faith sees the physical world as a place of turmoil and does not encourage bringing other souls into it, there are thankfully not many children. The Ruling Council decide that children 14 and older can make their own decision, though the unexpected problem – even in my own family – is that the children feel they should not leave their parents behind.

I beg my siblings to come with me. Finally they decide to draw lots to see which one will stay and care for our parents. My heart breaks as my youngest brother draws the shorter straw and insists that he will stay, in spite of my parents asking him to go.

Emotions run high as family decisions are made, and it is in the middle of all of this that we receive word that the Basques have discovered the climbing wall. We expect they will begin their ascent the next morning with plans to enter the Mont.

At dawn we wait high on the walls that have been both my playground and refuge. We see the Basques and over 100 Catholic troops coming to the base of our climbing wall. Council decided to allow the Basques to climb to the top, but not to allow any Catholics to enter the Mont. When it becomes clear that Catholic troops are going to climb, we send out an emissary to negotiate surrender.

The Catholic troops know we have enough fighting Knights who would relish the opportunity to kill those who scale the walls. For this reason they are willing to discuss a plan for surrender. We ask for 30 days to prepare ourselves in prayer, after which time we will surrender to the crusading troops below. Each Believer will have an opportunity to either confess their loyalty to the Pope and join the Catholic faith, or declare themselves a Cathar and go to death in the fire as a heretic.

We are a bit surprised when the Catholics accept our terms, for if they had known us better they would realize we would never kill anyone who scaled the walls. But the 30 days give us time to prepare, and we hope it will allow those who escape to get as far from the Mont as possible before the end comes and the troops disperse. We do not want to be anywhere near the Mont when the crusaders dismantle their camp and begin their journey home. The blood lust of a victory would make them a continued danger.

In the middle of all of this I marry Justine. She looks beautiful in a pale lace dress with flowers in her hair. We spend our first night under the stars on a soft bed of blankets. Since we know the Mont will not be our home, we ask the Moon, the stars, and God to care for us as we prepare to leave and start a new life together.

The details of my last days at the Mont rush through my head so fast I cannot grasp them. But in the night when I am alone with Justine, in our soft and starry bed, I forget about my exhaustion and remember all the reasons why I am working so hard for this escape to occur.

The Good Men and Good Women are concerned about the continuation of our Teachings, while I am concerned about my continuation with Justine. She is sad to leave her parents, but has willingly decided to follow me out of the Mont. Each night I fall to sleep with images of a life with her that is free from war and strife. I see just the two of us in a small cottage on a fertile field near a stream, growing our own food and having a well that has plentiful water. All my life I have lived on the top of the Mont and I have had to depend on others for food and water. The fact that soon I will have my own source of water puts a smile on my face as I drift off to sleep.

"Son," Father begins as I stand silently before his desk. This time he has asked me to come, so I wait to see what he will say. "These are difficult times and you have done well. I am proud of you. Your knowledge of the passage at the heart of the Mont has given our people hope for the future of our religion and a choice in their own destiny. Even those who have chosen to stay behind rejoice that our children and friends will live and continue the Teachings."

I am so tired and I would like to sit down, but I dare not suggest such a move. This might be the last time I see Father and I want to give him full respect.

He says, "Your test course was a good idea. Half of those who wanted to leave the Mont did not have the stamina or strength to make the passage. The final count for those who will leave is 115, including 25 Good Men and Women who will accompany you. The other 25 will stay behind to give the rest of us the rite of Consolamentum and guide us so that we will be ready to meet Christ."

"And what of my brother?" I ask. "Has he changed his mind? Will he come with us?"

"No, he has decided to stay here. We must honor his choice." There is defeat in Father's voice.

My heart sinks. The actuality of leaving is so much harder than the planning of it. But there is no other option before me. To stay is to die.

My mind drifts and I imagine Justine having a similar conversation with her parents. Her 14-year-old sister will accompany us, even as her older brother stays behind with her parents. I imagine many such conversations taking place all over the Mont and in the Pog tonight. So many goodbyes being said, for tomorrow we leave. With sadness, we are ripped apart. I find myself thinking of the Catholics and Dominicans and rage begins to grow in my heart. I calm my breathing. Hate will not be helpful now.

Father continues, "The task at hand is to assure your safe passage. At first light, all who are staying will go about their daily tasks. The exit must remain a secret to those who stay behind. Even for me."

After a pause he adds, "Your uncle, who has been on the passage, has volunteered to help in the organization of those who are leaving. He will be at the crevice and divide the people into groups of 10 and time their exit so that each group is 30 minutes apart. As you have trained 12 leaders who now know the passage well, one leader will be assigned to each group. Uncle will follow the last group into the crevice and onto the passage. Then he will destroy the passage behind you. You will never be able to turn back. But the crusaders will never be able to follow."

I vaguely wonder how Uncle will destroy the passage. He must do it from inside, for if he tore up the crevice rock in the courtyard it would surely bring attention. I know Uncle will be thorough and a thought flickers through my mind that he will likely die in the task. But better to die taking action to defeat the Crusaders than to jump willingly into the fire.

As despair seeps through me, Father's next words bring me back to the room.

"The 25 Good Men and Good Women who accompany you will carry the Teachings, and all the laypeople will be responsible for keeping them alive and healthy. These Good Men and Women will not carry food or water or shelter with them. These things must be shared with them."

I already know this and wonder why he is telling me again.

"You will be responsible for sharing food and resources. You will be the one responsible for the continuation and prosperity of the group. You will be their leader."

I gasp. A voice in my head says that I am only a child. I don't want to be a leader. I just want to be left alone and live my life in peace.

"Me? Leader? Surely not. There are older and more experienced people than me on the passage. And any of the Good Men and Women would be capable leaders. Not me."

I feel panicked. My insides are in knots and I want to flee. I have grown up too fast. I do not want this task.

Father looks at me closely and I think I see sadness in his eyes. "You have done a great job this last month. The Ruling Council has decided. You know more than anyone else about the passage and the land beyond. You have attended many Council meetings and have shown yourself to be wise and calm, and you have a steady heart and make good decisions. You are strong and brave. You have been a leader this past month. It is time you accept this fact and do your duty for your people."

But I feel smothered by duty, exhausted by obligation, beaten down with responsibility. I just want to be free. I have been thinking that Justine and I could split off from the group as soon as we found a path or valley that invited us to make our new home. I feel like I have done my work. Surely I do not need to stay to see that everyone finds a new land, makes a new home.

"What of the Good Men and Good Women?" I ask. "Can they not lead?"

"The Good Men and Women are responsible for the continuation of the Teachings of our faith and the spiritual health of the group. They cannot also be responsible for the day-to-day functions. They will need to be free to break off and go their own way, to carry the Teachings forth. Only a few will stay with the group to handle spiritual needs as you all settle into a new place."

I feel myself crushed. The Good Men and Women have more freedom than I do. They can leave as they please and I am left to tend to the daily needs and functions of the group. "But surely there are those older and wiser who can lead."

Father looks at me with concern. I don't think he expected my objections.

"Many of the people leaving are young and lack experience. There are only a few elders among you. The few Council members who will accompany you have their own tasks and will be responsible for establishing a new Council once you find a place to settle. They can help you make decisions, but it will be you who will lead the journey of our people, and your responsibility until you settle."

My body feels weighted down and as heavy as if I have bales of supplies and water casts strapped on my back. My knees begin to buckle.

Father stands and walks over to me. He places his hand on my shoulder and grips it tightly. "You can do this. You must do this. There is no other. You must trust in God and know that the light of Christ will be with you on this journey." He turns back to his desk and sits down, a sign that I have been dismissed.

As soon as I am out the door I begin to run, through the halls and up to the top of the Mont, to the walls where I can look out and see the mountains stretched before me. I can barely breathe. Trapped, I can no longer climb down the wall of the Mont, nor can I walk into its heart. All escape routes are cut off from me. I see the swallows soaring and hear their sounds. I see their carefree twists and turns and wish with all my heart that I could just fly away from this duty, this siege, and this war. I just want to live a life of peace, but I am caught in a vice grip that grows tighter around me.

At that moment I hear Uncle's voice. "I would do this for you if I could. I would take our people through the heart of the Mont to safety. But I am too old for such a task. The burden lies on you."

I hear the sweet song of the swallows as they fly away into the dusk. There is now only silence.

I close my eyes and wish I could disappear. My tears turn to stones in my heart. I feel Uncle's hand on my back. "You can do this," he says.

Do they not understand? I can do it, but I do not want to. As I hear those words in my head, I feel ashamed. Now, in the darkest days of my people, as so many have died and so many more will go to their deaths, I am thinking only of myself. I might be a man but I am acting like a child. To be a man means that the needs of others come before the needs of myself. I have changed from a colt who was free to run and play into a work horse, with reins around my neck tied to a wagon that will always be mine to bear.

This is what Uncle means. He and Father are old and are dying, so the burdens they have carried for many years must be passed on to those strong enough to carry them. There is nothing I can do but pick up my load and carry it willingly for the sake of my people.

I look up to see the swallows, but none remain. I wonder where they have gone and suddenly it dawns on me that they have gone to their nests, to their homes. In this moment I realize that when the swallows dance and spin there is a purpose. They dance to catch bugs in the air, to get food to feed their children. The swallows have never been entirely free; I only imagined them so. But yet, they still dance and sing as they work to care for others. Can I also fly with such grace and joy as I do my duty and fulfill the purpose given to me?

I feel myself lighten just a bit and the stones in my heart turn back into tears that run down my eyes. I look to Uncle and he wraps his arms around me one last time and pulls me close while I weep for the loss of my imagined life of freedom.

I will lead my people. I will do what I am asked to do for my community and faith. But I vow to myself that I will be like the swallows and be sure to lift myself above the burdens of such responsibility and be filled with the grace and light of Christ who did not succumb to the weight of the cross and the death of the body.

I look up to Uncle as I wipe my eyes. "I do not want the burden of this task but I will carry it. I will ask the Good Men and Women to lay their hands upon me to give me the wisdom to do what I have come here to do. You can tell Father that I accept this duty and that God and Christ will give me the strength to do it."

One hundred and fifteen of us leave the next day, through the crevice and into the heart of the Mont. In groups of 10, we walk the path and gather at the rocks in the valley some distance from the Mont's base. We camp that night in the safety of the rocks, with no fire or light. I do not want to take the chance of being seen while still so close to the Mont.

The next day we leave at dawn for the long journey before us to find a new home and continue our community and our faith.

The 25 Good Men and Women who accompany us carry far fewer of the Teachings than I had imagined. The Teachings they carry are so light they even have the ability to carry their own clothes and sleeping blankets. This relieves the burden on all others. I ponder this, and as evening falls on the first long day of our journey and we are setting up our camp, I have a chance to ask the Good Woman about it, the same Good Woman who encouraged the Council to accept my plan to leave the Mont.

"How are the burdens of our Teachings so light?" I ask.

She returns a sly smile. "We decided we did not need to carry any books that existed elsewhere, so all the philosophy and Biblical writings we left behind. We compiled the most important Teachings into a symbolic book that we will use to tell the story of our faith. It is a book of only 22 pages."

"Only 22 pages?" I ask, curious.

"Yes, each page is filled with the knowledge of our Teachings, but the story is told through drawings and symbols, not the writing of words. We think it will be easier to tell our story with pictures and parables. We condensed our Teachings down to their essence, an elixir of sorts. We call these 22 pages the Great Mystery."

"The Great Mystery," I mutter to myself, wondering what it means.

"Yes, the Great Mystery, though we are referring to it by the Latin name of Major Arcana. In our preparation to leave the Mont we made twenty-five copies. The Good Men and Women are each carrying a copy. Once we are far enough on this journey, we will each go our separate ways to spread the knowledge of our faith using the Major Arcana. Because the Great Mystery has only pictures and no words, we think that we are safer to share it, and that others of our faith will be safer to keep a copy. The Catholics will not expect a picture storybook, so if they search our homes, or us, they will not be able to accuse us of heresy. And, as you noted, it allows us to travel light and carry our own clothes and bedding, which we will need to be able to do once we leave on our own paths."

"I am interested in this Great Mystery," I say, my eyes alight with curiosity. "Will you share it with us?"

"That is our plan," the Good Woman replies with a large smile. "At the end of each day's journey when we settle for the night, we will share one page of the book with the entire company, beginning with the Fool. We will teach everyone the meanings of the symbols and the stories they tell. It is important for the Good Men and Women to gain experience using the symbols to tell the stories of our faith. We want to begin to share this with you as soon as possible, whenever you feel that the journey is settled enough for us to begin."

And so it starts. Every day I make the decisions of where to go, when to stop, and how to survive. Then I join my brothers and sisters around the glow of the fading fire to listen to the Good Men and Women tell the stories of our faith. Next to me is Justine, our hands lightly touching. The actions help me calm my mind and set my burdens down. Each night around that fire I become free in body, mind, and soul as I learn the symbols and stories of the Major Arcana. Each night I become filled with the light of Christ, the grace of God, and the love of Justine. Through this unwinding I find my way between responsibility and freedom, between duty and joy, and my heart is at peace.

Our path is long and takes many detours until we come to the end and find our place to begin a new community. We learn that 220 of our family and friends went willingly into the fire at Montsegur after the 30-day truce. Not one converted to Catholicism. All stood strong in their faith as they leapt into the flames, some carrying their children.

We weep together for our loss, and pray together for their reunion with Christ. But we also feel gratitude that our community and our teachings will continue with us.

Life Lessons from Montsegur

This was a life well lived in harmony and integration with Mind, Body, Soul, and Spirit. A main theme was letting go of the freedom of my childhood and taking on the responsibilities of an adult. And it did not come easily. I resisted maturity. I resisted responsibility. But I persisted, nonetheless. I am proud of who I was, my maturity, my willingness, my naivete that became wisdom. Willing. Able. Hopeful. Such great characteristics, and they all came together in this life. They are qualities that have continued. It is as if these characteristics were hard fought and I embraced them as my own.

I feel so fond of this young man. So earnest, so sincere. He is caught between the dreams of youth and the reality of age, between wanting to be free and taking on responsibility, between doing what he wants for himself and what needs to be done for the community. And he is caught at a time of war, when everything easy has been disrupted. Yet he holds his integrity, his sense of self, and his sense of obligation. He is poised at that cusp between child and man, and he holds the balance. This is the life where the lessons of my prior lives all come together.

I understand his resistance to take on the responsibility of leadership. All he wanted was freedom, to share a sweet life with Justine. But reality interfered and he put his personal desires aside to do what was necessary for his people.

This feels like a life where I cleaned up my karma. In the previous life I was a priest, a sinner, a murderer. Montsegur brought the possibilities of redemption and freedom of choice. I could have escaped the Mont on my own, or with Justine, and left the pressures of war. But I didn't even consider these options. I felt the desire to be free but never wanted to abandon my community or the constraints of family. My choice to set aside personal desire for the benefit of my people created a healing of my Soul and redemption of previous mistakes. I think one reason I chose correctly is that I had good parenting. Unlike in previous lives, I had a father who did not cast me off but who actually cared for me and gave me good advice. And in taking that advice, I rose to the occasion.

My relationship with Christianity in this life is mixed. I was still trapped by the church, not in a monastery but by Catholic troops. The difference is at Montsegur it was done in service and support of family.

A new karmic pattern emerged of taking responsibility in a way that is balanced and healthy. I accepted my role as leader and never tried to break off from the group. It settled on me, like a cloud on a mountain. It was always there, but never felt too heavy. Even after we stopped and created our own town, I still took a leadership role. People had come to expect it of me and I was used to carrying the burden.

I healed my Soul wounds in this lifetime, weaving together the lessons of prior lives to be a fully integrated, fully alive, and fully responsible human being. I was part of a family. I was part of the community. I had a good father who cared for me and gave me freedom and respect. I stood up and said I was not willing to be sacrificed.

The skills of using my breath to control my emotions were ones I gained in Atlantis and Egypt. Also my meditative walk in the labyrinthine tunnels to the Crystal in Atlantis was reflected in the underground path at the center of the Mont. This was another interior path that I knew by heart. I also developed the skill of speaking my truth, even when it was scary to do so. In taking on responsibility and leadership, I also learned the gift of love for another and the commitment of marriage. The connection that I had with Justine sustained me, even in the darkest and hardest times.

I look forward to my next life where I can stretch my wings and embrace more wisdom, confidence, and illumination. Montsegur was a life of integration, where I grew into the human I was meant to be. I had good support, took wise actions, and stood up for myself. I matured not only as the human Remy, but also as a Soul.

In my present life I do not want leadership; I do not want to make decisions for other people. As a Pisces I am the fish swimming on the boundaries, ready to dart off at any sign of danger. When I think of musicians and movie stars who have millions of social media followers, it seems overwhelming. A president? A physician? It all feels oppressive to me. I admire Captain Jean Luc Picard of the USS Enterprise, but I don't want to be him.

I take on responsibility in my work as a teacher and Astrologer where I share knowledge and give guidance. I love to teach religion and ritual and symbolism. That is when I feel happy. It is as if the peace I felt as we gathered around the fire to learn the symbols of our faith in the Major Arcana of the Tarot is the peace I feel when I discuss religion and symbolism. In this current life I completed my Master's thesis on the intersection between the symbols of the Major Arcana of the Tarot and Carl Jung's archetypal structure and process of Individuation. My love of symbol systems and understanding of the depth of knowledge that comes through them was born in Montsegur.

The Universal connection in this life is that in the broadest sense we all must make the transition from the freedom of childhood to the responsibility of being an adult. It helps if we have the proper parenting to ground us and a good family system to give us structure. But even with those things, the outside world can interfere. War, poverty, drugs, loss of jobs, political conflicts, and environmental disasters all challenge us in ways that are stressful and life threatening. There is also the memory of collective trauma. In Montsegur, as in Atlantis, a major destruction affected all people. These traumas are stored in the Soul's memory like post-traumatic stress disorder and can be hard to handle when triggered.

For you, the reader

Choices can be hard to make. In Montsegur, residents chose between escaping the Mont and leaping into the fires. What does this story bring up in you? Were you in Montsegur? Were you part of the Inquisition? Have you been in a trauma that impacted many people? What were the challenges and choices you faced and how did you meet them?

You grow from these experiences and there is no judgment, only lessons to be learned. Is there any place where you have been challenged by circumstances that seemed overwhelming? Have you had the support you needed? Are there any situations where you succeeded beyond what you thought was possible?

10

Astronomer:
Too Smart for My Own Good
Italy, c. 1350 CE

There are many ways to view the stars. My favorite is to slip out at night and lie in the meadow where the sky stretches across me, endless in its glory and light. *The Lord is my shepherd, I shall not want. He maketh me to lie down in green pastures; He leadeth me beside the still waters. He*

restoreth my soul. In the light of the starry sky, God is with me. I spend hours at night on my back, gazing at the stars. I can pick out most of the constellations, and name the twenty brightest stars of the sky. I repeat them over and over in my head, memorizing them in order of brightness – Sirius, Canopus, Rigel, Arcturus, Vega, and on and on. I am 7 years old.

My father takes me with him to the Observatory where he works. He must do so because I beg him until he gives in. My mother is quite frustrated with me, since I have no interest in household activities suitable for a girl, like embroidery or learning to sew. Instead I build miniature telescopes out of paper and my dolls become planets that I observe while they are sitting on the wall that surrounds our home. I have even named them after the planets: Venus is a lovely lady with silk skirts; Mars is the rascal bear I have outfitted in breeches and a vest; Jupiter is a lion with a crown on his head; and for Mercury I made wings; Saturn, I dipped in coal dust and he has a very bitter air about him; and the Moon, my favorite planet of all, is a stuffed cat that I covered in white buttons. I guess learning to sew has been somewhat beneficial to me. I am now 10.

My father's colleagues have tolerated me, since as a child they saw my curiosity as charming and cute. But as I grow older and am budding in my body and full of questions, they no longer see me as an invisible pest. My father tells me to stay in the background, quiet, until they are gone. Then he will show me the stars and answer my questions. I am 13.

I know Father loves me, or he would not take me with him to the Observatory and sometimes sneak out at night to join me in the meadow, pointing out the changing sky, since Mother would never approve. But I also know he is saddened that my elder brother Bernardo, his only son, has no interest in his Observatory work. Bernardo is only interested in hunting and fighting and drinking and women who are not respectable. Though my father is a scientist and his work provides us a means to live well, we are not wealthy, nor are we noble. So my brother must learn a trade or profession, because a daughter brings no status or money to a family unless she marries well. Since I have a very small dowry, it is unlikely I will be so fortunate.

It saddens me that, as a girl, I am not allowed to go to school. It is quite the irony that my brother, who has no interest in learning, is forced to attend school. We create a pact, my brother and I, that he will go to school during the day and I will do his lessons at night. After that he does very well in school. He even talks of becoming a doctor! I love the books he brings home and I read them all. The math is difficult but I manage to get him passing grades. I do not think our father knows what we are doing, though he sometimes helps me with the studies.

I wish our parents had money for a tutor for me. But there is none, nor would Mother approve, so I learn all I can by doing my brother's studies. Father will no longer take me to the Observatory with him when the other men are there, since they seem to now look at me in a way that Father does not like. But he takes me there on Sundays, when all the men are at church. We spend all day looking at sky maps and reading books on astronomy and science. When the sky darkens, we go to the telescopes and watch. I find all of my brightest stars and every planet that is visible. I trace the constellations and say hello to the Moon like she is an old friend. I am 15.

Sunday is my favorite day and I am happiest when I am with Father studying the skies and learning how the universe works. I want things to stay the same forever. I don't want to grow older. I don't want to be pretty. I don't want nice dresses and fancy clothes. I don't want anyone to notice me. I bind my breasts so that they do not bring attention. When forced to go to a festivity, I stay in the background and hope no one asks me to dance. My mother pushes me into social engagements. She dresses me up, like one of my dolls, and pulls my long dark hair to the top of my head with soft curls gently framing my face, which she paints with lipstick and rouge. When Mother leaves, I rub the rouge off my face, and I look down when I am introduced to a young man so he will not notice my bright and inquisitive eyes, so no one will notice that I am really quite beautiful. I am 17.

I know that I am of marriageable age and that my mother seeks to find me a good husband. But I dread that day and pretend it will never happen. I wait patiently for the Sun to set and night to fall, and then I sneak out of the house and lie in the meadow, watching the night sky as it sails over me. *Yea, though I walk through the valley of the shadow of death, I will fear no evil: for thou art with me; thy rod and thy staff, they comfort me.*

What I do not know is that my brother has been watching me. My brother the doctor, who cannot put two sentences together and make any sense. When I slip out of bed at night and go into the meadow, he sits at his window watching me. I do not know the thoughts that go through his head or the evil that lies in his heart. I do not know that he talks about me at the pub with his other drunken friends. I do not know that he describes me in terms that a brother should not use. I do not know that he tells them of my nights in the meadow as I lie beneath the stars.

It was the dark of the Moon, when the sky was so brilliant with stars but so quiet in light. I was lying on the soft grass in the meadow, picking out the stars in Virgo. I remember it well, seeing Virgo holding the sheath of grain in her arms. I was counting her stars, comparing them to the number of stars in Leo, which I could also see clearly. Side by side, Virgo and Leo, the Virgin and the Lion. Comparing their size, which is almost equal, and their lines, hers strong at the base and his strong at the spine. And one bright star each. I lay in the meadow and compared the size of Regulus, the main star in Leo, with Spica, the main star in Virgo. Full of quiet peace, alone with the sky as I had been these last 17 years.

That is when four hands grabbed me – two pushed my arms down to the earth and two held my legs wide, so that I could not move. I began to scream, but something was shoved in my mouth. It took me only a moment to realize that I was tasting flesh, salty and sour.

I would say it was over very fast, but it seemed a lifetime. A lifetime of having my safety destroyed. A lifetime of having my mouth and body polluted. A lifetime of having my sacred space turned into a hell – a sacrilege of my holy ground, both body and sky.

I wake in the early dawn to my father carrying me to the house. I feel the rise and fall of his steps, the silent heaving that comes with his weeping. I am carried like a baby who needs protecting, like a dead person who needs burying.

Next, I remember Father sitting on a chair beside the bed where I have been laid. I can hear him weeping, at times sobbing. I open my eyes and put my hand on his bowed head. I want to comfort him. I think he must be a fine man to care so deeply for his daughter. Then I drift back to sleep.

When I awake next, I see the face of my mother, who has cleansed me and put me in clean linen robes. I see my father next to her, a worried look on his face, his eyes cast down.

"Who did this?" she demands.

"I do not know," I answer. "It was dark and they came suddenly and unseen."

"Do you realize what this means? You are now useless to us as a marriage partner. Your worth was stolen last night. You are ruined."

I slowly realize what she means. The pain I feel in my loins means I am no longer a virgin. I have been taken by the lion. I am ruined. But fierceness arises in me. Anger rises in my soul and I do not think it is fair for me to be ruined. I did nothing wrong.

"Who was it?" Father asks. "Was it Bernardo?"

My brother. Was it my brother? Perhaps. I do not know. But it does not seem like a crazy question to ask, and I think that I have been unaware of the evil that has been stalking me.

Since I say nothing, my father assumes the worst. Why he would think such a thing I do not know. But it has truth that I can taste, steely and hard.

A week goes by and I do not leave my bed. No one knows of this tragedy, not even the servants, for gossip spreads quickly. Mother tends to me alone, which in itself should create speculation among the servants, since she normally does very little if she can avoid it.

The days pass and my wounds heal, and I am vaguely unaffected. Or at least I am not allowed to have any feelings about what has been done to me, for it is my mother who has been most sorely aggrieved. Her only daughter, her only chance at rising to a higher station, has been ruined.

For we all know that my brother is an idiot who will bring nothing to the family, even if he becomes a doctor.

Since I never had my eyes on young men or desired marriage, I do not regret that my marriage chances are ruined. But I do mourn the loss of my meadow and my freedom underneath the night sky. Father refuses to let me go there at night again, and as sad as that makes me, I do not try to go against his will. My heart is heavy and I have no spirit for it. I can only sit at the window and gaze at a small piece of the sky.

The rift between my mother and father increases by the day. The sweet man I have known all my life is now seething with rage, looking for revenge. Mother will not hear of it, for if Father finds revenge, that will mean that the town will know what happened to me, and she cannot bear the shame. I stand quietly outside their bedroom door and hear their harsh words. Mother wants to send me away to her sister, to either marry a foreigner or perhaps be a governess. She even mentions a life in the church as a possibility, locked away in a nunnery, cloistered in prayer. The thought of a life inside the church walls, away from the sky that I love, feels like a cruel death of suffocation. I toss in my bed at night in misery that such a life could be chosen for me. I wonder if I should run away but I do not know where I would go.

I stand outside their door and listen to them argue as often as I can. Father wants to throw Bernardo out of the house, for he is convinced that my brother is the cause of this despair to the family and ruin of me. Mother will not hear of it. "We have just lost our daughter, and now you want us to lose our son? What will people say? And who will care for us as we age and grow weaker through the years?" They only argue like this at night when all the servants are away. The weight of my loss begins to sink in. The pain in my groin moves up to my heart. I feel weighted down by doubt and the unknown. Nothing will ever be the same.

I go to bed and weep all night, but on this dawn when the Sun rises and falls across my face, I speak out loud: "Nothing will ever be the same. But nothing will ever be the same whether I was attacked or not. I have learned from the night sky that life is in constant motion. Everything changes and nothing in the heavens is where it was the day before. That is the beauty of it. The stars cannot stand still and the Moon is always shifting in brightness and position. If the Moon can sink into total darkness and become full again, then so can I."

That thought brings a lightness and peace to my heart. Perhaps I can be a governess. Or an assistant at the Observatory. I have as much knowledge as many of the men there, though I have had to keep that knowledge to myself. I may not be able to marry, but that was never important to me. I can still study and I can still watch the night sky. Maybe I can just stay here at home and study on my own as I did before. Maybe Father will get me a telescope! I must talk to him immediately. He has not spoken much to me since the attack. I think being near me brings him pain. But I cannot accept that my life has been broken forever, or that Bernardo stays in the house while I am forced to a convent.

For the first time since the attack, I call for a bath and put on new clothes. I go to the dining room where I find Mother and Father eating in silence. The room is large, the most formal of our house, with wooden walls and a richly colored rug beneath the table. They both look surprised to see me.

"Oh, you are feeling better, my dear," Mother says while scanning the room for servants close enough to hear. "That is very good. The medicines have been working." She gives me a weak smile and orders breakfast for me, then dismisses the servants. We all know that they are right behind the door, listening if they can, so I say nothing. Mother makes small talk until the servants have given up and we can hear them working in the next room.

I reach over and put my hand on my father's. He does not look at me, so I give it a squeeze. "Father, it is a New Moon and I would like us to go to the meadow tonight to see the stars. I have missed them while I have been limited to my room." He looks up, his eyes lidded and heavy. I can feel the grief in him and my heart is burdened. I hesitate, but I cannot let my parents decide my future without some discussion from me. For all I know they have already arranged a position as governess or will ship me off to my aunt, who lives in a bigger city where morals are not so highly valued. Both ideas were mentioned while I listened outside their door.

"I think I am too weak to go alone and the night air would refresh me." I pause, still holding his hand. He wants to pull away, to run from me. But I hold on and look him in the eye, imploring him to stay with me.

"It will do me good, and we can speak of the stars," I say, not leaving his gaze. I squeeze his hand ever so slightly and I think he understands that I want to speak to him alone, without my mother who cares nothing for my fate, only her own.

"I do not think—" Mother begins, before my father interrupts her.

"Yes, tonight after the dinner meal we will go and look at the stars. But not in the meadow. I know another place that will give us a better vista." And with that he gets up to leave.

My heart is pounding, but it feels like music. I take a deep breath and wait impatiently for night to fall.

Father and I sit in a small horse-drawn carriage, just the two of us. He has his hands on the reins and dusk is settling like a dark quilt across the land. I do not know where we are headed, nor do I ask. I am content to sit in silence next to him, listening to the constant thudding of the horse as she moves evenly along the road.

We do not go far and pull into an overlook near our house. It is a rocky outcropping that hangs over a large meadow. My heart starts to race and I want the freedom to run into the meadow. I want the freedom to run away from all of this. But Father shows no sign of getting out of the carriage, so we sit in silence and gaze at the sky as it darkens and the bright stars begin to show.

I see Jupiter in the west as he sinks toward the horizon. I think of the doll I made of Jupiter as a child, a teddy bear with a crown. The Astrologers say that Jupiter is the king of the planets and that he is a jovial king who will listen to my petition and bring me gifts. Jupiter is a bright light that shines on me, bringing me hope. I breathe deeply and calm my racing heart. I put my attention on the light of Jupiter and ask for his help to get out of the cage that I feel surrounding me. My body slowly relaxes and I begin my ritual of finding all the constellations that are visible and counting my brightest stars. I see Virgo and Leo, still high in the heavens, and remember that night only a month ago that changed my life forever. I wish I could make the sky move in reverse and turn back time. But I know that life only goes forward, and that I must move on. Since I have asked Father for this night, I decide that I must be the one to speak first.

"What is to happen to me? I hear you and Mother talking about where I must go, but I wonder why I must go anywhere. Can I not stay at home with you and live as I have always done?" My voice sounds stronger than I feel and that gives me courage.

Father will not look at me but instead stares straight ahead. I cannot bear to think I have lost him, my greatest ally. I reach for his hand, which feels warm. Still he says nothing.

"I have heard Mother say she wants me to go live with her sister, to either marry or be a governess. And I know that you blame Bernardo and push to have him leave the house."

Father turns to face me with a small smile on his face. "So you have been eavesdropping on your mother and me? I should have known you could not sleep through the night."

Then his face turns serious again. He takes both my hands in his and looks me straight in the eyes. "You have been wrongly violated. I do blame your brother for his witless ways. He swears he was not directly involved, though I am not sure I believe him. But I am your father and I should have protected you better. I should not have let you roam free in the nights, especially after you became of marriageable age. It is my fault you have been so harmed and I will never forgive myself." Tears shine in his eyes.

My first thought is to comfort him and tell him that what occurred to me is not his fault. But I say nothing. I realize that if Father feels blame then he might also feel obligated to help me.

"My failure to keep you safe is what your mother accuses me of again and again. My failure is why your mother says that she must be the one to make the decisions from now on, and that a position as a governess is well suited to you and you will be in a good home where you will be free from harm."

I hear the word *will* and realize that steps have already been made to place me. "Has a home been chosen?" I ask carefully.

"Not yet, but your mother is putting out inquiries. She wants you far from here, where no one will know where you went or why. So these inquiries take time."

"Why does it have to be out of town?"

"Your mother is ashamed of your ruin and does not want the town to know of it. She thinks it will hurt her status in society, which is most important to her. If you are gone then she can make up stories of your marriage to an important man and how you now live in wealth in a far-off country."

Shipped off in disgrace, in the quiet of the night, never to be heard from again. I would live only as a source for my mother's fantasy stories of my great success.

"And what do you think should be done?"

"I do not think you should be punished, for it is I who made the grave error of not ensuring your safety. I would be the one to leave, if only I could. The house feels like a tomb to me, and my duties, which I once took pride in, have turned to dust in my hands."

My heart leaps. "Father, you and I can leave and go to another town. We could go together."

"Ah, my child. If only I could. But I have to fulfill my obligations here. If I left my work at the Observatory there would be no money for our house or for your mother. I would be abandoning one part of my family to care for the other. And there is no guarantee I could find work elsewhere. As strangers to a new town we would not be easily accepted into society. No, I must stay here."

"Then I will stay here too!"

"Your mother will not allow it. She is afraid someone will find out what really happened and her life will be ruined."

Silence stretches between us. I ponder my options. I could ask Father to give me money to make my way alone, but based on his all-consuming guilt for not protecting me, I doubt he would be willing to set me off into the world to fare by myself. A governess would not be a bad job, since I do love to learn and would probably enjoy teaching. But there would be no guarantee where I would work, or the constitution of the family or the duties I might have. I could easily be told I would be a governess so I would leave willingly, but once I arrived I might be a servant. I would not put such a thing past my mother. I look at Jupiter, now lower near the horizon, and ask him again to help me, and to help my father, who is also suffering.

"Could I work at the Observatory?" I ask hopefully.

"Though you are as capable as any of the men, women are not considered equals in the world of science and you have no formal education to commend you even as an assistant."

"Maybe I could be a servant at the Observatory, and I could use the telescopes and books at night, like we have been doing."

Again, silence. Again, I look to Jupiter and ask for help.

"There is a slight possibility that you could be wed here, in this town."

"How would that be possible, since I am ruined for marriage?" I ask quietly.

"There is an elderly widower of quite advanced age who would be unlikely to seek any intimacy with you. He is a benefactor of the Observatory and has a large estate with several telescopes of his own. He might like a young wife to help him, and your ability to be an assistant in his research could be an asset. His studies of the Sun have left him without much eyesight, so you could write down his observations. He would be impressed that you read and write."

I feel my brows furrow and I try to understand this. A marriage to an elderly man, with the ability to work with the night sky? And I would not be sent to a strange town and could still be near Father.

"People may wonder that you would marry one so old, but often rich men take young wives. Without consummation, it would not be a real marriage, and you would be unlikely to have children or become a mother."

"But I could be his assistant and explore the stars. I would rather do that than become a wife and mother." I see Jupiter getting closer to the horizon where it will soon set and go out of sight. I feel pressed to make this decision while Jupiter can still help me. "Would you talk to him, Father? Will you find out if such a choice awaits me?"

He squeezes my hand and gives me a small smile. "I will go to him tomorrow," he says as Jupiter falls beneath the horizon. I take a deep breath and feel a bit of hope rise in my heart.

And so it comes to pass. We are married in a small ceremony on his estate. After the marriage, several of Father's associates at the Observatory give him the impression that they would have been glad to marry me if they had known I was available. Little did they know I was soiled and unworthy of them. Father tells me of their interest so I will know that once my husband, who is already frail, has died, that I might have some suitors if I choose to remarry.

But I am quite happy with the situation. Father comes each new Moon and we watch the stars together. Mother rarely visits, but she did not seem to be displeased with the match as my husband is a wealthy man and it did bring status to her.

He is more than three times my age and treats me more like a daughter than a wife. I have my own bedroom and an area of the house just for my purposes. I spend many hours alone and many nights in the gardens behind the house observing the stars. He has two telescopes and we spend much of our time gazing at the sky. I treat him well and he considers me quite a delightful companion. He is thrilled with my knowledge of the sky, and as the years go by, he depends on me more and more to make the observations he can no longer manage.

My favorite times in the marriage are when we work on research projects dealing with the phases of Venus and the motions of Mercury. We are a good team and he appreciates the help I give him as I peer through the telescope to calculate the movements of the planets. Since his handwriting is so poor, he dictates to me his opinion of the research and I write down his findings in papers that will be shared with the members of the Observatory.

At first, my husband goes to the Observatory to present the findings himself. As a major benefactor, he is held in great esteem and his research is considered as substantial a contribution as his money. My name is never added as a co-contributor though my husband lets me know that he values my input.

Each year his health declines until he is too frail to go out in public. I suggest to him that my father be the one to present his research to the esteemed body at the Observatory, and my husband agrees. There is a lovely ease between us, a collegiality, and my knowledge of the sky grows with each passing year.

But everything changes when my husband dictates to me a paper about the craters of the Moon that he wants to share with the men at the Observatory. I feel that much of it is incorrect and, to be honest, almost unintelligible. I show it to Father and he agrees with me. I try to get my husband to make some changes so that it would at least be accurate, but he refuses. It is as if he is not thinking clearly. I know he will be ridiculed if this paper were to be presented. I choose to rewrite it entirely so it is not only accurate but even breaks new ground in the understanding of the craters.

This is the first time I have written research from my own thoughts and in my own words. After this, all papers presented to the Observatory under my husband's name are actually my work. It is exciting for me to see my research presented to the scientists, even if I do not get credit for it. My husband seems to enjoy the extra attention when the work is shared and I am on fire with greater and greater understanding of the sky. So my father and I are collaborators of a sort. I spend hours researching and watching the night sky, writing my findings. And Father presents them as if they are my husband's.

My papers start to get some attention for their research and originality and my husband is invited to speak at a special gathering at the Observatory about "his" work. But my husband is unaware that I have been changing his papers or writing under his name. He is so feeble by this point that he would not have been able to complete a presentation before his peers anyway, so I hide the invitations and start reviewing his mail before it is given to him.

His lack of response to the invites only creates a flurry of more requests. I become anxious about this deception and begin to decline the requests based on illness or a bout of gout. Father knows what I have been doing and so I admit to him that I have been making excuses as to why all invitations have been declined.

One day Father arrives at our home, hurried and out of breath. "The trustees of the Observatory are on their way here to find out why your husband will not come share his work at the Science Academy. They say they will demand he come. This web of deception is closing and I fear you may be caught in its snares."

Panic rises in my chest and my heart begins to pound. I feel torn. Half of me wants to go to my husband, who was in his rooms, and confess all I have done. I don't know if he would hate me or protect me. To alter his words is bad enough, but secretly authoring papers under his name would likely seem a betrayal. Yet I know he cares for me and might protect me if I throw myself at his mercy and beg him. If only I had told him earlier or included him in the writing so he would have some idea of what I have done.

The other half of me wants to flee to my rooms. My writings are scattered about and it would be evident that I have been doing research. My notes are also at the telescopes, and drafts of my findings are in my study. I want to hide evidence of my work, of my own subterfuge. If there were no contrary evidence, I could claim my husband's senility had progressed so much that he didn't remember. I know this is a lie, and such a claim would cause my husband to question his sanity. To see research and papers he was supposed to have written but had no memory of would undermine his ability to trust his own mind, which is the part of himself he values most highly. To lie about him in this way feels wrong.

But I don't have time to take either of these actions since the trustees from the Observatory are being led into the drawing room where Father and I are in evident dismay.

"Good day," said the leader with a slight bow. He looks at my father and myself, his brows furrowed. "We have come to visit your husband for whom we have great concern. He is one of our most important benefactors and we feel we have been lax in our attention to him. We have not seen him at the Observatory nor visited him in over a year. We want to encourage him to reply to our invitations and share his recent research. Is he ill?" The trustee looks back and forth between me and Father.

Just as I am ready to reply that my husband is ill, our servant answers that the Master is in his rooms and she will see if he will accept the unexpected visit. With that she leaves the room, and as I watch after her, my heart sinks.

"Gentlemen, this is an unexpected honor," my husband replies. "Please have a seat and make yourselves comfortable while the servants prepare tea for your group."

I feel like running away, but I cannot leave Father to face this alone. With a brief touch of my hand to his, I say, "Thank you for the news of Mother and give her my joy at her good health. It was kind of you to visit and I look forward to hearing more from you next week." I look him in the eyes as I speak and I am sure he reads my desperate plea for him to leave, so he will not be caught up in my self-made deception.

But he does not leave me to face this alone. My greatest ally is still at my side, though I know he feels like his encouragement of my studies has again led me into danger.

I do not need to describe each step of the unraveling. I am not included in the meeting, but needless to say, my husband is shocked to hear his last few years have been so prolific. When presented with the papers, he is shaken and confused. He tells the trustees of my skills as observer and scribe and how valuable I have been to his work, but reveals that he has not written anything in several years, and does not know where the recent scholarship came from.

Perhaps, one of the men suggested, I had stolen his ideas and written them up for my own advantage. That must be it, all the men agreed; I was a thief. It was easier for them to believe that an ancient man at the end of his days had his work stolen, than that a woman in her prime could have created the work herself.

Father tries to defend me, saying that I expanded on my husband's ideas and wrote the works to give him honor. I had not stolen ideas, nor hoped to profit on my own. But the trustees are not convinced. My husband can barely see, and could certainly not pick out stars and cycles of the planets.

The trustees are concerned and suspicious. Only sorcery could explain my understanding of the skies and their turnings, for no woman would be capable of such knowledge on her own. What evil would cause me to do such a thing? Why would I publish under my husband's name and hide it from him? Why would I isolate him, keep him trapped in his own house, confined to his bed, and refuse to let others visit?

The more they talk, the more I am portrayed as a wife who steals her husband's ideas, and if I was stealing ideas, then what else was I doing that he did not know? Had I also stolen money? Was I keeping him isolated and in bed? What herbs had I given him to make him so weak? What lies did I tell him to keep him so alone? They paint a picture of a devious, deceptive lying wife. My love of the skies and my help for him in his research is twisted into treachery.

They do not ask me to defend myself or explain my actions. Father is left to speak for me, to share my love of the skies and the many years of learning from him at the Observatory. He tries to get the men to understand that my husband inspired the ideas I presented, but I had explored them on my own. The men could not believe that. Who was I working with? Whose deception was I spreading? What had been seen as creative breakthroughs when they were my husband's, were now turned into a desire to pollute the scientific community with lies and deception.

As my world unravels, I go to my room and look around. I cannot hide the evidence of my crimes, nor do I want to. It is my life's work. I am only 25 and I have explored the heavens and created so much. I know the men will soon come for me and that I have very little time, so I hide my work in the floorboards under the bed, where I have hidden my most valued objects. I guess that they might destroy all the research I have done and I want something to exist, even if no one ever sees it. I then sit in my chair and wait.

I do not wait long. They accuse me of sorcery, of bewitching my husband, of getting information from the devil to confuse the minds of the scientists with my false words. My husband is so shocked by all of this that his heart fails and he dies that night. I am then accused of killing him, even though he was in very advanced years. Only my father defends me.

They put me in a prison, a horrible dark place where they torture me to find out when I met the devil and the names of other witches. I don't know many people, so I name no one, but the pain is so great that I would have given any name to spare myself.

The Observatory doesn't want the extent of my crime acknowledged, since it would undermine their standing. For this reason, I am accused only of bewitching and killing my husband. Priests examine me, carefully, to see if I had sex with the devil. I am trapped underground, tortured in body and mind. I feel my connection to everything that gave me reason to live being cut, split and broken. My spirit fades and my hold on life unravels.

They say I will be burnt at the stake as a witch. But I don't really comprehend it since I am lying on the damp dark ground of my cell, trying to dissolve into the earth, to become a worm so I can crawl into a crack and disappear. I barely notice when they come to take me to the town square. It is dusk and the large pole in the center of the square is surrounded by sticks. A crowd yells at me, taunting me. I see Father at the edge of the crowd, tears flowing down his face, contorted with grief and anger.

All I want is silence, relief. Death seems like it will bring me those things. As they tie me to the pole, I look up and see Jupiter. For a moment I feel a faint stirring in my heart. I ask him to help me.

They light the fire. I hear the crackle of burning wood. The heat surrounds me. In panic, my eyes search out Father one last time. Through the rising smoke I see him separate from the leering crowd and leap into the flames to join me. He wraps his arms around me, as if he can protect me from the heat, as if his tears could stop the fire. My head falls into his arms and I weep. We cry together at all that we had hoped would be, all that we had learned, all the skies we had watched. The fire surrounds us, the heat and stench engulfing us. I look up at Jupiter one last time. *Thou preparest a table before me in the presence of mine enemies: thou anointest my head with oil; my cup runneth over. Surely goodness and mercy shall follow me all the days of my life and I will dwell in the house of the Lord forever.*

Life Lessons from the Astronomer

I understand why my father jumped in the fire. I would have done the same for him. How could he live in a world that did this to his daughter? How could he live in a world that was so misinformed and so cruel? Not to mention the reality that his work at the Observatory would definitely be finished. He would be a man shunned. His being with me in the end did bring me comfort, as did seeing Jupiter in the heavens. My father on earth and my father in heaven provided my center and point of balance. But still, him dying because of me broke my heart even more.

I was an Astronomer, not an Astrologer, as I am in this current life. An Astronomer gathers data by calculating the position and movement of the planets and stars in the celestial sphere. An Astrologer looks for meaning in that data. An Astrologer has a more personal connection to the heavens, mythologizes the planets and knows them intimately. Even though I was an Astronomer I still had a very personal relationship with the planets, which was different from my Mayan life where I observed the planets with more detachment. In this Italian life, I grew from child to adult, developing a relationship to the stars and planets, even creating versions of them as my dolls.

I didn't attend church or have a closeness to the Christian God. Instead I sent my prayers to Jupiter, who represented knowledge and wisdom. I was a passionate learner and loved doing research. If I had been content to just be a student I might have lived for many more years. But I wanted to share my findings in writing and publication. This is what got me killed. Publishing my work, even in someone else's name, was the reason for my destruction.

This Astronomer life brings up mixed emotions. In spite of the tragic end, much of it was good and I learned many lessons – my absolute love for the sky, for learning, for writing, and for research, and my love of my father. My determination, which is evident in many lifetimes, shows in my willingness after the rape to move onward to a life that had possibility for me. I did not accept my mother making choices for me, nor did I try to run away. Instead I took action so some of the decisions made would be my own. As long as I could see the night sky, life was acceptable. As long as my father was near, I would be happy.

I wonder how it would have turned out if I asked my husband for his consent to publish my own research. My sense is that he would have rejected it, in the same way it was rejected by the trustees at the Observatory. I really think that doing it secretly was the only possibility for me. Or else not to do it at all, and then perhaps I would have lived longer as a wealthy widow.

The karmic pattern of conflict and betrayal with my father finally came to an end in this life. Here there is only Love of the Father – my biological father, God the Father in the heavens, and Jupiter, Father of the planets. The love of my father and his love to me is really the heart of this entire life, which builds on the importance of the caring father I had in Montsegur.

The soul wound that my greatest gift is my greatest danger continues in this life. My love of the sky made it easy for me to be attacked at night. And my love of research and writing is what ultimately brought me to the attention of the men who accused me of being a witch. As a soul wound, there is a core belief for me that nothing good can come from being visible. This belief has been repeated in life after life, so it is no wonder that it is still strong in me and a clear example of how the bonds of karma can weave more strongly in each lifetime.

This soul wound is what I personally struggle with in my current life as Lilan. The backlash I received to making my research public as the Astronomer is still part of the unconscious pattern that challenges me today. For example, when I was in my 30s, with a Master's degree and license as Professional Counselor, there was an article written in a major newspaper about my using astrology in my counseling practice. The article was balanced, pretty positive, and accompanied by a photo of me at an Observatory. But the following day the newspaper printed a long response by the editor that was extremely negative, basically saying that I was a charlatan and my degrees were only a ploy to get people to trust me so that I could take advantage of them. My brother, who is a lawyer, felt that the editorial was so demeaning as to merit a lawsuit against the paper for libel. But I declined his willingness to start litigation. I was leaving town to pursue a Ph.D. and did not want a lawsuit to hold me back. But it did trigger my wound of being targeted because of my gifts and my need to stay hidden.

The skills I had as the Astronomer continued to build on my connection with nature that matured through many lifetimes and are present in my current life and central to how I have chosen to live.

In my next life I want to be a strong and powerful woman, not intimidated by the expectations or disapproval of others. I would like to take the determination, curiosity, and knowledge of the Astronomer and add a powerful dose of confidence and courage.

In this present life I am working to change the pattern of being invisible. Though still hesitant to put myself out in the world as a woman of strength, power, and wisdom, I have taken many steps forward. I have earned the educational status that I wanted as the Astronomer, with Master's and Doctoral degrees from major universities. I have done original research which I presented and published under my own name. I am visible with my monthly Moonletters I share online. Many of the challenges that stopped me as the Astronomer, living at a time when women did not receive education nor were seen as intellectual equals, have shifted in the 21st century. Writing this book to openly share my lifetimes and beliefs about reincarnation and the Soul has triggered some of the fear of being visible and putting my ideas out into the public. But I have be able to recognize these triggers and work through them, not an easy task, but a big step in changing my pattern of staying hidden.

In this present life I had a good father. I was born on his birthday and he was a solid man and caregiver. We were both Pisces and though he didn't actively pursue a spiritual life, he was committed to his church and sensitive to the importance of core values. He was proud of my intellectual abilities, and I was given all the same opportunities for education as my two older brothers. One year I made straight As and he framed my report card and hung it over his desk.

I think many women have a deep unconscious sense of disempowerment. For much of history, women have been pushed into roles based on cultural norms and have had their own authority dismissed. Many have an unconscious wound left over from the witch hunts. Over 700 years of the Inquisition led to many women experiencing multiple lifetimes where they were hunted down and killed for expressing their gifts as herbalists, midwives, or for their sexuality, confidence, and strength. Many of the women who were killed as witches were merely bossy and demanding. So it is easy to see why women doubt their strengths and hold back their opinions. I view the #MeToo movement as women joining together and taking back their power, remembering the importance of their gifts. This is a necessary action if we are to save the planet from the destruction caused largely by a male-dominated drive for power over others and greed. Since we have past lives as both male and female, many men can also have unconscious memories of abuse from the witch hunts and may be feeling these same issues.

Also there is a Universal aspect to my preference for a life of learning rather than life as a wife. I had a bright mind and loved the work of an Astronomer. I would have felt limited and constrained in the role of housewife. In earlier periods of history, marriage for women was mandatory and restrictive, and often a form of ownership. Presently, marriage for women in the USA and other countries is more empowering. Women have their own incomes and identities, have choice in whom they marry, and are increasingly in more equal partnerships with their mates. When I think of my marriage now, I realize the real benefits of marriage – which include safety, sense of home, connection, trust, friendship, physical touch, joy, and sharing. All of these are so good I wonder why I resisted so long. My marriage now actually gives me more freedom, not less. This is not true in all marriages or all countries in the 21st century, where women are still diminished, but there is a transformative arc in the education and liberation of women which is exciting to witness and be a part of.

For you, the reader

As you ponder this lifetime, consider what it triggers in you.

Are there cultural and familial expectations in your family and life that have held you back? Do you have patterns of self-doubt or a tendency to hide? Do you have a passion that is a great joy in your life? Do you have memories of trying to be capable and talented but something stood in your way?

Is there a history of abuse or a background of trauma that lingers? Is there a person in your life who feels like a helper and supporter of your dreams? Do you sense that you have been tortured or killed for being a witch?

11

The Herbalist: Wise Woman or Witch
France, c. 1450 CE

I am a wise woman, an herbalist. I live on the outskirts of a small town. I live alone and keep to myself. My house is a good size – one large room made of stone, with a central fireplace that keeps me warm in cold weather. There are beams across the ceiling where my herbs hang to dry. A rich herbal scent fills the room. My bed is in one corner and I have plenty of blankets and more than enough clothes. The other corner of the house belongs to my kitchen where I have many pots, kettles, and bottles for the herbal remedies my customers seek. I have some nice wool rugs that I roll out in the winter to keep the floor warm. I am content.

There are other wise women who live in the town. There are midwives, healers, spell-makers, and spell-breakers. I have met them all, for they usually come to my home at some point to ask about an illness they cannot cure. They come for my medicines, which I only sell to the wise women and healers. On rare occasions a townsperson will come to my door to purchase an herb, but I do not answer. It is best to not bring attention to myself.

The wise women come quite regularly so I know all the healers, not only from my town but from the neighboring villages as well. Sometimes healers meet while they are both at my home buying herbs. It seems as if they purposely arrive at the same time, as if they planned to meet to talk about who is sick and who is having a baby, and what woman is cheating on her husband and who needs a contraceptive herb to keep from becoming pregnant. Over the years the random meetings have developed into an established pattern, making my home the place where healers gather. Once I had ten healers from three different villages in my house at the same time! I don't like that many people in my home, but they bought so many herbs and remedies that my financial needs were met for most of the summer. So while I grumble and moan about such large numbers, I do not forbid it. They always buy when they come.

I can tell you many tales about the local midwives and healers, for I have heard them all. They sit around my fire, sipping my tea, and sharing the problems of a difficult birth, or how they have cured a fever that would not break. Some of the healers are married, some are single, some are young, and some are old, like me.

I think it is quite amazing that these healers don't have their own herbs. Not that I mind them buying mine, but how will they deliver cures when I am no longer here to provide for them? The young healers don't even understand the herbal properties or how an herb will work well with one flower but clash with another. And they surely wouldn't be able to find them in the woods, in bark, leaves, roots, berries, and even some of the rocks which provide lime and salt and minerals that make a tonic stronger. These new healers wouldn't be able to find poison ivy if it wrapped its vines around their legs. I am constantly shaking my head in amazement.

Even if they could find the herbs and berries and roots, they wouldn't know how to prepare them. Some herbs are best delivered naturally as a tea. Others do better steeped for a week and then drained. Some are made into tinctures and take only a teaspoon, while others are made into ointments and salves.

I am willing to share my knowledge if any would ask. But they really are not much interested. When I call them lazy, they reply that they are too busy to both heal the patients and prepare the medicine. So they count on me to provide the medicines they need. I guess I can understand that. I don't know how I would find time to see patients. Just the visits by the herbalists are distracting enough; townspeople would take up all my time.

Also, I want people in the villages to be healthy, but I don't like them well enough to actually work as a healer. I don't enjoy all their complaints or their tales that the medicines aren't helping, even though I know their gout hasn't cleared up because they are still drinking. A healer must have a way with people, and I am not so pleasant as to want to spend my time talking to strangers about their illnesses.

So it really works out well for me, and for the many women who buy my remedies. I make more money than I need, so I hide it in the back yard behind the house. I don't believe in bringing attention to myself with a bigger house or more cows or land. I have a warm blanket and plenty of firewood, and I hire someone to help with my vegetable garden from time to time. I am really quite content.

One day in the spring, just as the trees are starting to bud, there is a knock on my door. Marie, one of the healers who has been coming for years, and a young girl about 13 years of age are standing outside. This is unusual and I do not normally like unusual occurrences, so I slowly open the door, my face full of suspicion.

"Madam," begins Marie, pointing to the young girl. "This is my daughter Anna and she would like to apprentice with you," she finishes quickly.

Anna makes a small awkward curtsy. She has long strawberry blonde hair, with freckles across her nose, and large green eyes. She looks at me imploringly.

"I do not need an apprentice," I say, while starting to close the door.

"But please, Madam," Marie says. "She has been badgering me for months to come and ask you, and I have told her many times you would not want her. But she still insists. She has been helping me, but is much more interested in the herbs than the patients. I also need to buy some sleeping draft, so perhaps we could come in while I make my purchase. Anna most ardently wants to see your shop."

Marie was always one of the chatty ones and full of gossip. She is a good customer, and what harm would it do to let the child see my herbs? So I open the door and allow them to enter.

Upon crossing the threshold into my home I can see that Anna has become transported. Her eyes grow wide as she takes in all the herbs hanging from the rafters, the bottles and bottles of cures, the kitchen where I was cutting up roots, and the boiling water on the crackling fireplace, where I was ready to boil them. She walks as one entranced, leaning over the pot. "Ah, I love the smell of sassafras," she murmurs.

"Don't touch anything," I say harshly. "I must be sure my herbal remedies are clean, as well as fresh."

Anna does not seem to be put off by my unwelcoming attitude, which surprises me. Usually children think I am quite forbidding. "Have a seat," I say, pointing to several chairs near the fire, "and I will pour you some sassafras tea, sweetened with licorice."

I bring the cups of tea over to Marie and her daughter and sit near them. Marie prods her daughter and urges her to speak.

"I have spent hours in the woods and I know many of the common herbs and roots and where they can be found. I can help you collect your materials and I can go further out than you might want to go. I can be your eyes and legs and climb to the top of the mountain, and get the winter herbs as well."

As she speaks, I start to think how I have been slowing down lately, and how my range for collecting herbs has become smaller. I rarely go to the mountains anymore, and the cold of winter keeps me mostly indoors. It would be nice to have someone to collect for me, at least for the winter months.

My silence encourages her. She continues, "I can go with you into the woods and you can show me what herbs are what, and which I should collect. I can clean them for you and make them ready to use." She is a smart girl, for she knows this can be very time consuming. Picking off each leaf from a patch of thyme can take hours. But of course, in front of a nice fire, it is a pleasant way to spend my day.

"You can show me how to make the remedies. I will help you exactly as you say. I do not ask for anything but your knowledge."

"And why would I share my knowledge with you? What is in it for me?" I say with a harsher tone than I really feel.

Anna plunges in, "I will help in the vegetable garden, and bring in the water, and clean the house, and make the fire." She goes on quickly. "I will do all your chores."

I feel myself start to grin in spite of myself, and my heart lightens just a bit. "But then what would I do?" I ask. "There will be no need for me."

"Oh yes!" she cries. "You will make the remedies. Maybe with the extra time you can make more of them, for mother says sometimes you are out of the most popular ones. And you can invent new medicines. And," she says, pausing for effect, "I can write down your remedies and medicines so your knowledge will be passed on to other healers. For how will the healers be able to help their patients if your knowledge is lost?"

An herbal manual? I stand up and walk across the room so I can think. I had only considered such a thing a few times, but since I can neither read nor write, it was only a fantasy of an idea. But how wonderful it would be to create an herbal manual. That would mean I could record my knowledge for others to use when I am dead. I have always bemoaned the fact that the healers were not interested in learning about the herbs.

Now, here is a young girl who wants to learn, and who is smart and has ideas.

Marie does not know what to make of my silence and so to sweeten the pot she adds, "Anna will continue to live at our home, and just come when you want her. She will not be underfoot all the time, only when it suits you."

Still I say nothing. It is sounding very good; someone to help with all the chores and who can go further afield for herbs. In exchange I will let her watch me make my remedies and she can write down how they are made.

"I would offer you money," Marie says, "but I have so little, and my husband is not happy that we would lose Anna's work around the house. He has agreed to let her apprentice. But he would not want to lose money as well."

I turn to face them and see their worry. "I do not need money, but I could use the help. If Anna wants to apprentice with me, she can, but she must do everything I ask of her. She must be consistent and finish what she begins. I will not suffer a fool or a laggard."

With these words Anna jumps from her chair and hugs me. I am shocked, but the sweetness of her touch and the joy of her heart cause me to laugh, a very rare occurrence. "Now, now," I say, still smiling. "An herbal manual. That will be nice. We must find where to get paper and pens. Can you draw as well? It would be good to have a picture of the herbs and identify the parts that are used to cure." With that, Anna begins to skip and dance around the house. I have myself an apprentice, and I feel quite pleased.

Anna is a wonderful helper. Over the next several years she learns all there is to know about harvesting, preparing, and making medicines. She was right that with the extra time I am able to develop new recipes and tonics. I expand what I know and start making medicines in different potencies, instead of only one which has to be diluted correctly before use. This increases sales of the more popular tonics.

She turns out to be an excellent artist and loves spending her free time drawing the herbs and writing down the recipes. The handbook is half done and already gaining attention from the healers, who ask about it constantly and anxiously await the finished product.

All of this leads to even more healers coming to my home to buy their remedies. It seems that my stone house at the edge of town is not very private anymore. It becomes so busy, with healers coming and going and buying and gathering, that we never have time to do our work. So I limit the hours for purchasing herbs to two days only. This gives me and Anna more quiet time for preparations and work on the manual.

Instead of the healers' visits being spread throughout the week, this creates larger gatherings over the two days. It is wonderful to see the open sharing of knowledge between midwives and healers, even if sometimes their opinions differ on the correct course of treatment. They share ideas, come up with new treatments, and provide solace to each other if a patient dies. Sometimes I feel like the grandmother of an extended and rambunctious family.

But I do not complain. As I grow older, my own aches and pains encourage me to create a series of tonics and ointments for the aging body, which Anna tests on me with tender care. She always keeps the fire built and the house clean. I have even become better tempered and enjoy answering the questions of healers, suggesting just the right remedy to match the symptoms of their patients. I share some small part of the profits of the increased sales with Anna, which she gives to her family. Her father has quit complaining about her absence, now seeing the value of his daughter knowing the ways of herbs.

Over time, I notice a change in the conversations among the healers. It is less about which tonic to use for menstrual cramps and more stories of midwives in other towns being harassed, even arrested. At first, we all thought it was just gossip, the talk of an angry patient whose gout did not improve. And since all the tales came from villages outside of our region, we were not sure if any of it was even true. But the talk has become more frequent, with tales of women in other countries being accused of purposely injuring patients with their evil cures. One midwife was accused of killing a baby after it was born alive, and an herbalist was accused of poisoning the cow of her neighbor.

Anna's father is a sheepherder and every summer when lack of rain makes the grasses dry and the streams empty, he takes the sheep on the great route up into the mountains where they will be cool and have more plentiful food. He passes many towns on these annual trips, both coming and going, and when he returns that autumn, his stories are cause for concern.

The sun, low in the sky, is shining a golden light through the windows and around the chairs where Marie, Anna, and I sit in front of the fire. We warm ourselves with hot tea sweetened with honey. Marie shares, "My husband's stories have made me afraid. He said there were priests, dressed in black with their head shaved on the top, often covered in black hoods and cloaks. They looked like giant ravens and they swooped around towns asking questions of the village people, wanting to know who was going to church and who still worshipped the old gods. If people were not going to church, these black raven priests would make them go to confession to explain why they had not attended. The number of people in the churches increased, for they were afraid that if they did not go, they would be taken in and questioned."

Marie fidgets in her chair and looks around, as if someone might be hiding, listening to her tales. Seeing nothing, she begins again. "He saw this in several towns. It seems that once the priests have frightened people to go to church, so there are plenty of tithes, they then move on to another town and start all over again. He said that from the time he passed through the mountains in the early summer to when he returned again in the late autumn, there were twice as many priests in twice as many towns. The taverns were silent and villagers did not venture out on the streets."

Her voice becomes a whisper. "In one town the priests chased out a midwife. They said she had sinned against God for giving her patient herbs to lessen her pain, and that a woman's pain in childbirth was the punishment for the sin of Eve. No one knew where the midwife went and they never saw her again. Her house was found burnt to the ground."

A chill grows in my heart. It is hard to believe the stories. A midwife's house burned to the ground! How could it be? I feel as if a rope is slowly but surely being tightened, and will soon strangle us all.

"I want to tell the other healers," Marie says with concern. "They need to know." I nod in dazed agreement.

The next day when healers come to buy remedies, Marie shares what her husband has seen and heard. At first there is stunned silence, which is soon shattered by frantic words of concern.

The women become afraid. In their fear, they find comfort together, so they start coming to my house more frequently and at random times during the week. They talk in low anxious voices while drinking tea in front of my fire. It seems as if the healers are trading in fear.

I do not want my home to be a place of refuge for the fearful, so I shut my doors except on the two purchasing days, turning the women away. But they come anyway and walk in the woods together around my house. On the two open days, my house is not big enough to hold them all, so some move into the barn to comfort one another. They hope that surely such raven priests would not be allowed to come to our villages. The healers drink more tea than they buy my remedies, a fact that does not please me.

Later that week, Anna asks, "What will happen to our herbal manual if we are captured and killed?"

Such a question takes me aback. I know there is fear in the air and real problems in other regions, but nothing has happened to any of the villages of the healers who gather in my home.

"Where did you get such an idea? The priests are forcing people to pray and go to church. But they are not killing healers!" Yet, as I say those words, I feel cold.

Anna looks up from the herbs she is cutting. "Myrtle said that they are killing healers and midwives in other regions. It is only a matter of time until they come here. What are we to do? If we die, our manual will never be finished."

She says this very matter of fact, and I am surprised at how little fear she has. "You sound like you are more concerned about the manual than your own life."

She pauses and turns to look at me. "You do not seem afraid."

"That is because I do not believe it. The healers are too necessary to life in the villages. The priests do very little for a person. They try to save the soul, but we save the body. They will not kill the healers."

Anna looks at me, her eyes narrowed, a bit annoyed. "The priests do not care anything for the body. They do not care whether we live or die. They do not care if the whole village dies."

"Except that no one will show up with money to tithe," I say with a grin, returning to my chopping.

"You must take this seriously. Don't you understand? You are at risk."

"Me? Why would I be at risk?" I stop, the knife poised above the herbs now forgotten. "I am not a healer, or a midwife."

Again Anna stares at me, shaking her head. "You provide all the medicines. Without you, what would the healers use? And all the healers meet here. Myrtle says it will look as if you are their leader. She thinks they will come here first."

I pause. I have no patients, I do not sell to anyone in town, I know very few people. Why would they come to me? "Myrtle is a busybody," is all I can think to say. I had never viewed myself like this before. I live alone on the outskirts of town. I bother no one. But now I am in danger? A leader? I step away from the table and shake my head to clear it from such nonsense.

"I cannot believe this. This is ridiculous." I shake my head yet again. "I am not a religious person, and it is true that I do not go to church; but I do not practice the old ways either. Will they arrest me for gardening? Ha!" I sit down in front of the fire.

Anna follows me and I can see her concern. "You must leave," she says.

"Leave?" I am shocked. "Why? And where would I go? What of Myrtle and Claire and Margaret and the others? What would become of them?"

"Many of them are quitting. Margaret is refusing to take patients. She is afraid. But then her patients complain they are getting sicker because she won't see them, and so now she is blamed for their illness. The attitude about healers is changing among the townspeople."

"Then let God take care of the townspeople, and lift them to heaven when they all die," I say.

Anna gasps. "This is serious. We must consider what to do, now, before we have no options left."

I finally understand. I want to be able to choose my destiny, not have it chosen for me. "Well, I have a feeling that you have an idea," I say with a grin.

Anna comes and sits next to me by the fire. She takes a deep breath, as if to gather her nerve. "Yes, I do have an idea. For the first time ever, Mother is going with Father when he moves the sheep to the mountains in the spring. Instead of coming back here in the autumn, they will take the sheep into Italy. We have been told that many Italian towns refuse to let the black raven priests in. Father has agreed that you and I can go with them."

I am silent for only a moment. "Leave? My home? It is all I have known. And what of the other healers who cannot leave. It seems as if I would be abandoning them. Where would they go?"

Anna answers, "It would be best for the healers to disperse now, until the priests have passed through our villages. If you are not here, then the healers will have no place to gather. It would be best for everyone for us to go."

I stand quickly. This is really more than I can take in. I feel numb. "It seems you have given this a lot of thought."

"Mother and I, and Myrtle, and some of the others have been trying to figure it out the best we can. The raven priests are not far away. It is possible that they will be here before the sheep are ready to be moved, and that would not be good. But we are hoping the priests will stay put over the winter, for they like their comforts, or so I have heard. Hopefully they will not arrive until spring. It is the best plan we have."

I stand motionless, staring at the rafters, counting the bunches of rosemary I have tied to them. They are nearly dry enough to crush and bottle. I cannot leave the rosemary behind. As if from a distance I hear Anna continue. "Over this winter we can finish our herbal manual and pack as many cures and tonics as we can. We can spend this winter preparing for our departure and leave as soon as the trees bud, taking our medicines and manual with us."

There is a sensation in my heart that I have never experienced before. It is a cold chill, as if my chest were bare and made of stone. I suddenly realize that the feeling is hatred. I hate the priests, I hate that they are running off the healers. I hate the townspeople for allowing it to occur. I hate Myrtle for spreading all this gossip. I hate that Marie and her husband are going to take Anna away. I suddenly hate everything. I feel completely undone. If a priest showed up right now I would probably kill him if I could.

Suddenly an idea comes to my mind, sent by my hating heart. I could kill the priests. I could easily do it with the herbs that I have stored in a secret place. I rarely provide a killing herb, and only then if the patient is too sick or too old to recover. It is gentler for a healer to kill with an herb than to allow suffering. I could kill the priests, make them afraid to ever come to our region again.

"Why do not the townspeople stand up to the priests?" I ask quietly. "Why don't they just make the priests leave? There are more villagers than priests. The villagers have weapons and the priests do not."

"In some towns the villagers do stand up to the priests," Anna replies. "But the priests threaten to excommunicate the townspeople to suffer in eternal hell. That frightens people, so they give in. I have heard in one town a healer refused to be afraid and would not go to church as the priests demanded, and she helped a prostitute through a difficult birth after the priests told her to let the woman die in pain for her sin. It is said that the priests took the midwife and set her on fire. I find that hard to believe, but that is the story I was told."

I am shocked to hear such a tale. It is clear I would get no help if I did stand up to the priests. "Well, it is close to winter and there is not much we can do now. By spring, who knows what the situation will be? But for now, your idea of finishing the manual and preparing the herbs makes sense. Let us put our hands to those tasks."

So we spend the winter doing just that. Some days stretch out while others fly by. Anna and I finish our herbal manual. It is so beautiful, with over 100 herbs, roots, berries, and bark. It covers symptoms of the most common ailments and has over 200 recipes for cures, explaining how to make a tonic, a tincture, a tea, and a salve. We find a metal box and place our manual inside to protect it from fire and flood. Anna insists we hide it, so we place it in my secret hiding spot in the back of the house.

Spring comes and the trees begin to bud. We have packed many herbs into traveling bags. Anna's father gathers his sheep and preparations are nearly complete for the journey to the mountains, and then on to Italy. He is leaving earlier than usual this year, to be sure to get out of town before the priests start to travel again. We have heard that they wintered in a town in the next region.

I still don't know if I will go, but I know Anna needs to leave. I am an old woman. I might not even be able to make the journey to the mountains, much less to Italy. My days as an herbalist are nearly over. But Anna is young, and smart. She must take the herbs and our manual.

"You could start a school in Italy," I say one day while we are crushing herbs and soaking them for tinctures.

"Me?" Anna replies, surprised. "You are the one to start a school, and I will be your assistant."

"And not my student?" I laugh, as she blushes. "Yes, you are no longer my apprentice. You know most of what I know and are smart enough to figure out the rest. When the fear of the black ravens has ended and life is back to normal, you can begin a school in Italy."

I suddenly feel very sad. Tears come to my eyes and I put my hand on hers.

"You will not come with us?" she asks.

"I am too old to make the journey. And I do not want to leave my home. If times get hard here, the other healers will need a place of comfort and peace. I want to stay to help them."

"But you might die," she says slowly, looking me in the eyes.

I pat her hand again. "I will die whether the black robes come or not. But I will not die running away. I will die right here, where I was born, doing what I was born to do."

"You think I am a coward for leaving?" she asks, eyes cast downward.

"No, I think you are wise. The black robes will not remain here for long. This threat will pass. But we need to know that the healing ways will be remembered. Your idea for the manual is what you were born to do. Now you must protect that manual, and start a school to teach new healers, since the old ones are too frightened to work. You will make the journey that I would make if I were your age. You will make the journey for me."

Just then the door bursts open and Marie enters, her face in anguish.

"Mother, what is the matter?" cries Anna.

"I have just heard that the black robes are in the next village." She pants to catch her breath. "There are ten of them, and they are demanding that the midwives and healers be brought forth to stand trial as witches who are in league with the devil."

I can hardly believe my ears. "Witches? But there are no witches here. There is no one in our village who will even do a love charm."

"The black robes say healers are in league with the devil, and that they are witches and that witches must die. They are questioning five healers, asking who else is a witch. I hear there is torture."

"My God!" I exclaim. "What can we do?"

"We must leave now, immediately. Hopefully it is not too late." Marie looks from her daughter to me. "They will probably stay in that village for a few days to hold a trial. Then they will come here. Your father is preparing the sheep. We leave at nightfall."

"I have decided to stay," I reply. "But everything is ready for Anna." I point to the two bags already packed.

"You cannot stay," says Marie. "Your name was mentioned by one of the healers. She said everything she had was from you, that you supplied her with the medicine to ease the childbirth."

I am silent, stunned.

"I do not think she meant to say it, but I was told she was tortured. The black robes are coming here. We must leave!" Marie is pacing in a panic.

"I have decided I will not leave my home. But Anna must get our herbal manual to Italy, and when things settle down, she will start a school. Marie, you get these two bags of herbal remedies loaded on the mules. Anna and I will get the manual ready to travel. She will be with you within an hour."

Marie hesitates. "Mother, it is so," Anna tells her. "I will be there to take this journey with you. Take these herbs and wait for me. I will be there by dusk." Marie gathers the two bags laden with herbs and begins the walk to her home.

Anna and I are alone in the silence. "It is much worse than I thought," I say, "and you were right. I am glad we spent the winter in preparation. Let us get the manual and start you on your way."

I retrieve a well-used traveling bag, one that won't bring much attention, and we go out to the back of the house where the manual is hidden. I open the lid of the box to look at it one last time. The paper is so soft and textured; the ink drawings and writing are works of art. I feel tears again in my eyes. I turn to Anna and take her hands in mine. "You have given me a great gift. With this manual you have honored my work and my knowledge." I hand the box to her.

"Madam, you have given me a great gift," she says as she accepts it. "You have taught me the way of herbs and healing. I will take your knowledge and share it with all who will learn."

"There is one more thing," I say, as she places the box within the old traveling bag. I pull out a sack from my hiding place and hand it to her. Anna opens it and when she sees the many silver coins inside, she is struck dumb. "I have saved this money my whole life," I tell her. "There is almost a fortune here. I want you to take it, but keep it quiet. Let your mother know, but no one else. Find a place to hide it well as you make your journey. Give some to your father and say it is from me, but keep the bulk of it for when you arrive in Italy. There should be enough to have the manual copied and to start a school."

Anna grabs me and wraps me in her arms. She has grown to be a tall and strong young woman. She will do well. I feel proud of her and what I have shared with her.

"I will always love you," she says, "and I will never forget you. I will name the school after you, and your name will be on the manual."

I laugh. "Put both our names on the manual, but leave mine off the school!"

I walk with Anna to her home to help carry the bags and to be sure she gets there safely. I wait there until after sunset, watching them pack the mules. My heart is both heavy at the loss of Anna and also light that she has been wise to foresee what I was too blind to acknowledge. I walk home in the dark and sit by the dying embers of the fire for the entire night, thinking.

At dawn I begin to cook. I make cinnamon rolls, sweet and tasty, hard to resist. I make sassafras tea, sweetened with licorice and honey. I put all these things in a basket along with some herbal tinctures. I change to traveling clothes and cover myself with a hooded cape. I leave my house at midday. I take my time walking to the nearby village where the black raven priests are staying. I arrive at dusk and find out the name of the inn where the priests are boarding. I stay at that inn too. And I watch the ravens at the tavern as they have their dinner. Other than the priests, the tavern is empty. People are afraid.

The next morning I get up very early, even before the innkeepers. I go down to the tavern before dawn, to the table where the priests had their dinner the night before. I ponder my next moves.

Clear and decided, I set the table for breakfast with freshly washed glasses and plates for ten. I put the sassafras tea in each glass and a tasty cinnamon bun on each plate. Satisfied with my work, I leave the inn, crossing the dusty road and waiting outside, seated on a rock partly hidden by the spreading limbs of an old oak.

As everyone begins to stir with the dawn, I know the innkeeper will think that his staff has been told to prepare the breakfast table for the priests; the priests will think this is the breakfast the innkeeper provided. I like to think of it as the last supper.

I am an herbalist, dedicated to healing. But I know that sometimes, albeit rarely, the best thing to do is use the killing herbs. A rabid dog cannot be healed and the dog's life must be ended. I think of these black-robed raven priests as a plague on our land. They bring torture and death wherever they go. They kill women who help other women give birth and women who cure the sick. These black ravens do not understand the ways of nature, for if they did, they would realize that the physical body is important too, and that a life is worth trying to save. They would know that all things go through the cycle of life and death, and that now is the time for their death.

I know the killing herbs I baked into the cinnamon rolls and blended with the sassafras tea will take nearly an hour to cause their demise. I couldn't make the potency too strong or one priest might die and the others would wonder what had happened, and avoid the food.

All ten of the black robes are dead by mid-day.

At first the townspeople are shocked, afraid they will get punished for this murder. But then those with cooler minds realize that since all the priests died, no one is alive to report their deaths. The priests could have just traveled on to another village, or gone back to the main church. The townspeople bury them at the far end of the church graveyard with proper prayers, since they are superstitious folk who worry about ghosts if the priests are not given the correct funerals. Within a week's time it is as if it never happened. No one speaks a word.

I go back home and say nothing. The days are quiet at first, but slowly the women begin to return to buy their herbs and to share stories of the ravens that have flown away, never to be seen again.

Life Lessons from the Herbalist

This lifetime was healing for my Soul, where my Soul found peace and rest. There was no taking on a huge responsibility as I had in Montsegur or trying to become something I was not, as the Astronomer. I integrated the lessons from previous lives and found a way to harmonize them, right from the very beginning. I lived a simple life that I enjoyed, and when trouble came, I was eventually able to see the truth of the situation and take the necessary action.

I was a healer, which has been a major theme in my Soul's evolutionary path. In this life as the wise woman herbalist, I also had an apothecary. I did not want to deal with the troubles of patients or be at anyone's beck and call. But I liked providing the healing herbs, being alone in my house, preparing the herbs, making tinctures and mixing brews. Hours, days, weeks, and even months would blend into each other as I fell into the love of natural healing. I mastered mindfulness, a modern term but a timeless concept. I watched nature change each season and was aware of the herbs, berries, roots, and bark that needed to be harvested in each time of the year and phase of the Moon. My connection to the natural world was amazing.

The theme of not bringing any attention to myself is also repeated in this life, as seen in the desire to live on the edge of town and be left alone. However, the desire for privacy was balanced, in that I was not isolated or withdrawn as in previous lives, and I was closely connected to my community.

The karmic pattern of wanting to make my own decisions and not having my life decided for me by others was an achieved goal of Montsegur and an attempted goal as Astronomer. As the Herbalist I became stronger in this karmic pattern of making choices for myself and taking responsibility for my actions. I had the strength and confidence of the Mayan and Shaman, but it was balanced now. I did not run away from the threat. Like the young man in Montsegur, I stood my ground and took action. I did kill but it was not in hatred, revenge, greed, or power. I killed because the monks were a plague that needed to be eradicated. I was not afraid and had no guilt.

Soul wounds were healed in this life. The goal of reincarnation is not to reach perfection or live a stress-free life without mistakes. The murders I committed do not weigh on my Soul. I understand the murder of the novice priest was a result of repression. I learned from that experience and understood the dangers. The murder of the ten raven priests was necessary to protect the healers, and I was strong enough to make the decision to do it. Knowledge and lessons are what is important for the evolving Soul, not punishment or blame.

This life also shows how Allies and Adversaries show up in various lifetimes to bring support. In Atlantis, it was young Emna who followed me around. In Egypt, it was my granddaughter and the young princess I healed. In Montsegur, it was my uncle and father as well as my wife Justine who were my companions and Allies. In this life as the herbalist, it is Anna, my apprentice. The Adversary is the group of Inquisitors. My heart felt the chill, a sign repeated in many lifetimes of danger.

This Herbalist life illustrates how the skills we develop in other lifetimes can be active in future lives. I have always been drawn to herbs and natural healing. When I lived in New York City I took herbal classes and learned to make tinctures. I remember one day I had a horrible bladder infection that moved to my urinary tract. There was blood in my urine and I was very ill. I walked to the nearest hospital, planning to get pharmaceuticals to heal the infection. But I couldn't make myself go into the hospital. I sat on the front steps, in pain, but immobile. I went home, looked up herbal remedies and treated myself. In three days I was well.

I have books on herbs, some which could be considered herbal manuals, with beautiful drawings of herbs and their necessary parts. I became curious after this memory of creating an herbal manual and so did research and found that the earliest illustrated manual was printed in Italy. According to Wikipedia: "The *Herbarium Apuleii Platonici* depicts 131 plants with their synonymy and instructions for their use in medicines and was first published in 1481 at Monte Cassino near Rome by Johannes Philippus de Lignamine, a Sicilian courtier and physician to Pope Sixtus IV. This was the first printed work on plants with numerous illustrations and is generally termed the first printed illustrated herbal. The history of the work has been lost with the passage of time, leading to endless speculation on the identity of the author." It is pleasurable to think that this might have been Anna with our manual.

For my next incarnation, I want to expand on this life by gaining even more self-confidence and freedom of action. I enjoyed researching both astronomy and herbs and documenting the results of my work to educate others. I hope the life that follows this one will be my strongest yet, my most balanced. I want to be confident, unafraid, have great wisdom, and take my place in the community.

I feel very fond of this life as the Herbalist. She seems to be the most similar to who I am now. In this present incarnation, when I was in my 20s, my idea of a perfect life was to be an old woman in the woods whom people sought out for her cures. I grew up in West Virginia, and in addition to our home, my family has acreage up a hollow with old log cabins in various states of disrepair. One cabin was located way back in the woods, along a small trail that bordered a creek. I would fantasize about that cabin, imagining myself there as the old witch in the woods. Visitors would seek my advice and request my healing ways. A main part of this fantasy is that it would not be easy to find me. Only those people dedicated and persistent enough would discover the path to my log home, where I would be waiting, with a fire blazing, ready to dole out sage advice and healing herbs to those who were worthy.

This idea of an ideal life as a wise herbal elder in the woods of West Virginia lasted for many years. It never entered my mind that I might be lonely, or get old and have a hard time living alone in the woods. My fantasy came directly from this life as an herbalist on the edge of town. I can see why I would be drawn to live this life again if I got the chance. It was a good life, a pleasant life, a life of being helpful, a life of inquiry, and research, alchemy, community, and teaching. What was not to like about that life? Yes, I was not married, nor did I have children. But I was never alone.

On a universal level, we have both male and female lifetimes, depending on what will provide the best experience to learn the lessons we need. Most of my previous lifetimes have been in the male gender. There are many contributing factors as to why we choose to reincarnate as a particular gender, and they include geographical, cultural, and historical context. It makes sense to me that I would be born male in earlier lifetimes because historically, males had more power, choice of action, and range of experiences. But over the centuries, women gained status, power, education, and authority with greater opportunity for action. Integrating the male and female perspective is part of the understanding gained in reincarnation.

For you, the reader

Is there a fantasy that you have about how you want to live your life? Or an adventure you want to take, or a skill you want to master? These dreams and wishes could be resonances of past lives where you were happy or succeeded.

Have you had an experience where you needed to stand up for yourself, your family, or your community? What were the major issues at stake? Have you ever taken an action that was difficult, but necessary?

12

The Soul's Journey: An Overview

The Crossing

I stand naked at the river's edge.
I look both ways but there is no one to be seen.
I put my toe in first, then my foot.
Silently I enter the cool water
Like glass.
I walk through.
Up to my neck I feel the cool,
The mud in my toes, smooth on my feet.
With each step I seek the other side,
Slowly, not fast, but deliberately,
Step by step I cut through the glass,
Until I reach the other side
And emerge
Full clothed
To begin again.

The lessons I gained from these eight lives is that the purpose of Soul evolution through reincarnation isn't to become more spiritual; it is to become more human. Or more accurately, the goal is to fully integrate the human and the divine, to become a celestial human where we are fully of the earth and fully of the heavens.

We arrive into physical form as a spirit-filled Soul whose evolutionary journey has to do with becoming human. As Soul we are here to experience and understand the human lessons of limitation, focus, purpose, love, compassion, health, healing, fear, loss, and connection, to name a few. As human, we are here to discover our sacred celestial nature and to align our Body, Mind, Soul, and Spirit to become more conscious. What developed in each of these eight lives are various insights and skills that hopefully I learned to weave together into a masterful whole and use with wisdom.

Atlantis

In Atlantis, I gained interpersonal skills such as integrity, courage, and sensitivity to those around me. Those are skills worth living and dying for. I was a highly trained and specialized energy worker. But that was all I did. I spent my time alone (except when in training or work), had no relations, no family or friends, no hobbies or passions. My life was limited. My evolutionary growth in that life was not spiritual, but rather physical and practical. The real growth was in seeking the truth for myself. My growth was making friends with a little girl and learning about what went on beyond my sheltered existence.

Living in Atlantis, a city so mythic that people doubt its existence, did not make me an enlightened person. I did know how to sense energy and then to direct it, and that is an important skill, both then and now. But it is not as if I started at the top of the evolutionary heap and everything went down from there. In Atlantis everything took place in my head, not my heart or body. I don't ever remember being touched or hugged.

A major theme for this Atlantis incarnation was to learn what it means to be human and act with individual authority. I was a fully developed, even somewhat evolved Soul before I came into a physical human body. I came from someplace else. Maybe another planet, maybe another dimension. But it was my first life on Earth, so I didn't know a lot about humans and how they functioned. I certainly didn't know about evil, or love, or honor. I did know obedience and loyalty, because those were the things that I was taught in Atlantis.

My skill level with energy work and astral travel was highly tuned because I came in with those skills. There were a lot of off-worlders in Atlantis at that time. We were to embed the human species with higher genetics and more fine-tuned brain function – like a grafting of two species in order to raise the humans to a higher level of consciousness that would allow them to go beyond subsistence living. We were concentrated in a few places on Earth's surface, like Atlantis, Egypt, Mesopotamia, India, and Mexico. Many major deities, for example Isis and Osiris in Egypt and the Greek gods and goddesses, were off-worlders.

I was neither male nor female, in any way that I would understand as a category that would define me. I was tall, thin, pale, white-haired, almost albino, in that I had blue eyes. I was definitely not like the average human in Atlantis. As a Chosen, I was brought in as a young child to work in the energy fields and be part of the higher levels of consciousness to which humanity was striving. But as in most cases of reincarnation, I didn't remember any of my mission once I arrived in Atlantis. That is the paradox about the Soul and birth and rebirth. You may know everything before you arrive, have it all planned, even to the soul friends you will meet. But once you come into the density of the Earth, you forget it all. It is covered over. You have a sense, a hint that there is more to you. You long for the sense of the totality of who you are. You feel limited and not fully useful in your job, life, and relationships because you remember on some level that there is more. Once the Soul enters the dense material and energetic field of planet Earth, it forgets its true essence and becomes a bit lost. It can take time to uncover this essence of the Soul and to wake up to the core truth.

I slowly awoke, and through my dreams and visions I became aware that something was wrong in Atlantis. But I was told by my teacher, Dem Majer, not to believe my insights and instead to trust him. I was betrayed by him, who used me for his own selfish plans. It was my gift, as one of the 12 who worked with the Crystal, that Dem Majer wanted. Once I realized his intent, I did everything I could to stop the destruction of

Atlantis, even trying to destroy what was most dear to me – my heart and shield. But I discovered too late the truth around me, and failed in my efforts, a failure that created self-doubt and distrust. This was my first soul wound, of the belief that my greatest gift would lead to my undoing. This soul wound has been mine in all lifetimes, even this current incarnation. It is the wound I hope to heal by writing this book and sharing these stories.

Egypt

In Egypt, as the healer, I built on my energy-sensing skills that were so developed in Atlantis, and added a longing for personal relationships. I brought with me a disdain for elite authorities and a distrust of those who were arrogant or authoritarian. I wanted personal freedom and engagement in the natural world, a world that in Atlantis I had only seen in meditation. I found freedom and nature in the quiet desert. In Egypt I had integrity, compassion, and courage. My evolution from Atlantis to Egypt was remarkable as I sought to understand the natural world and to live in community, very different from my isolated life in Atlantis.

But when I died, killed by Ben Mal, I felt a fool. I had been too humble, too quiet, not courageous enough to take action. I did strategize a way to save my family and village, and for that I am grateful. But I might have been able to save myself as well if I had spoken up earlier and gained the friendship and trust of the queen and princess. I was so busy lying low that I missed the chance to better control my destiny. Once again it was my gift, of natural healing this time, that became the reason for my death.

Maya

As the young Mayan warrior, I came back with the sole purpose of gaining courage and confidence. I was going to be strong and brave, not weak and in the shadows. I would be in the center of life, and people would respond to me, respect me, even fear me. All of this would be done to help my community, my family, my people. I would hone myself like a finely pointed arrow, an effective force of power. But all that was for nothing. The skills I thought were necessary to develop were turned against me. The excellence I strived for ended with a sacrifice I did not choose. I felt betrayed and used, again.

Amazon

I understand completely why, as the Shaman, I regressed and became a self-righteous, arrogant manipulator. It is as if all the good I developed as the Mayan went sour, curdled, sickening me and turning into cynicism. I was still powerful, even more so. I had all the energy-sensing skills of Atlantis, the relationship to the natural world of Egypt, combined with confidence and power developed as a Mayan warrior. But I was brought low by greed and pride.

Priest

The next life was a lesson in humility, which I greatly needed after Amazon. I was a proud, strong young man brought unwillingly into service to God. My aim as the Priest was to be humble, to serve, and be close to nature. I pushed down personal desires, my need for love and lust for life. I went in the opposite direction from the Shaman, going from a man in control and manipulating others, to becoming a man cast off and under the domination of those around me. I was obviously easy to manipulate, as even Sybil controlled me.

The Priest was a life of finding balance – between humility and power, service and self, ego and others, love and hate, lust and prayer, heaven and earth. All of my raw power was repressed as I tried to be what others expected of me. But my inner needs could not be contained, and when they erupted, I was turned inside out. By the end of my life I found a way to bring my power and desires into balance. I figured out how to care for myself, have a family, and be of service to others as an herbalist. But it meant staying hidden. This is the life where I perfected the belief that it is best to lie low and remain unseen.

Montsegur

As the young man and Cathar, I was still working on balance between self and others and between a life of personal love and public prayer. I accomplished it in large part due to the lessons of the Mayan life, where I was also a young man entering adulthood. Because of my reluctant Mayan sacrificial death, I was unwilling to sacrifice myself again at Montsegur. I insisted on having a choice and on giving others that same consideration.

This is the life where I matured as a Soul, understanding the importance of caring for myself and others. A large part of my success was thanks to family, especially my father and uncle who listened and helped me find my way. I took on the mantle of responsibility, yet I also had love, intimacy, comfort, and community. However, the amount of responsibility I was given was too much for my liking. I desired freedom, and leading a refugee community was not what I wanted. But in spite of my hesitation, I did it.

Italy

I was reborn next as a young female Astronomer. I had enjoyed freedom and empowerment in Montsegur but didn't want as much responsibility or visibility. I loved learning and the quiet peace that comes from research and study. I had a good father, who loved and cared for me, and that was a central pillar in my life. I was passionate about my investigation of the sky and was so happy to do research and share my knowledge. But this was at a time in history when women were not considered intellectual equals. Female power and intelligence were associated with evil and witchcraft. It was necessary to hide my research, to not be fully seen for who I was. After that life I was exhausted. I wanted to be a woman again, but I needed a life that was not so challenged.

Herbalist

In my next life as the Herbalist I brought the knowledge and willingness to contribute to community, but without the heavy load of being a leader. I lived on the edge of town, worked hard, and gave a lot, but had no desire to be in charge. Yet when the time came, I stepped up and did what needed to be done. My previous life experiences around the threat of persecution led me to take action to rid my community of the traveling raven priests. Once I became convinced of their threat, I took it seriously and did not hesitate to act. The powerful female part of me woke up as the Herbalist, and I wanted more knowledge and independence as a female, to let my wings unfurl and fly.

Current Life

In this current life as Lilan, I am repeating the parameters of the Herbalist life but at a time when women are gaining more power, where I can become educated and independent. I have incorporated many of the skills learned in previous lives. I am an energy sensor, healer, community collaborator, rebel, priestess, teacher, and astronomer/astrologer. I have close family and good friends. And I have the freedom to act. It seems as if I have all the qualities I have been developing except for courage and confidence. I wonder why it feels like courage and confidence are lacking in me. Is it because I gained them in my Mayan life and they led to my death? Is it because they corrupted me in the Shaman life and so I distrust them?

On the other hand, courage and confidence served me well in Montsegur and as the Herbalist, so they can serve me well now. This is the Soul wound I need to heal, the karmic pattern I want to change. This is part of my present purpose… to find confidence and act with courage.

13

Body, Mind, Soul, & Spirit

The Four Elements of Life

Our lives are made from a combination of four components: Body, Mind, Soul, and Spirit. In many ancient traditions these are known as the elements of Earth, Air, Water, and Fire. This elemental description of life on planet earth is foundational to many religious and philosophical systems, dating back millennia. Also called the Four Directions, Four Winds, or Four Humors, the integration, harmony, and balance of these four elements create and maintain life on our planet. Medicine in ancient Greece and Rome included balancing these four elements. Astrology describes the four elements as essential building blocks of the Cosmos, and Asian religions see them as the structure of life. So it makes sense that our journey from lifetime to lifetime is also defined by these four elements, each associated with one of the four components of life – Earth is our Body, Air is our Mind, Water is our Soul, and Fire is our Spirit.

These four components need to work in synthesis for our lives to function at full capacity. Using an automobile as an analogy, our Body is the limousine, the vehicle that gets us around in this life. Our Mind is the driver who controls the car. Our Soul is the passenger who sits in the back seat and directs the driver where to go. And Spirit is the energetic fuel that keeps the car in operation.

Let's see in more depth how these four parts work together to guide us through the process of birth, death, and rebirth.

BODY

The very foundation of our experience in life is our Body which works on the material plane and is only good for one lifetime. The Body is of the element Earth. Its tools are the five senses of touch, smell, sight, taste, and hearing, which it uses to gather information about its surroundings. When we are born into this physical world, our Body is brand new, a crying baby taking its first breath. Our life cycle is like other life forms on this planet; we begin life with a burst of energy, we grow, mature, age, and die. Death is what occurs when the physical life is over and the Body ceases to function. Our bodies, no longer filled with radiant life force, break down and decay.

After the death of that Body, we have a rebirth into a new Body, a new incarnation. It's like getting a new car each time the old one is beyond repair. Similar to how a car is a tool that gets you around, your Body is the vehicle for your earthly experience. Your time on earth might be easier if your Body vehicle is strong and healthy and born in an environment that encourages growth. But sometimes the Body has challenges and limitations. So the physical circumstances of each new birth, including race, gender, ethnicity, and health of the body, as well as country, culture, ecology, urban/rural environment,

> *Body, Mind, Soul, and Spirit need to work in synthesis for our lives to function at full capacity.*

home, family, and wealth, set the foundation for the experiences of any particular incarnation.

Once incarnated, there are many aspects of the Body we cannot control, like race, for example. There are, however, many aspects we *can* control. We can change our location, size, weight, and appearance. And we can take care of our health to give our Body vehicle the best chance to run well. Even if our Body is not a deluxe vehicle and has to deal with limitations, there are still the Mind and Soul and Spirit to compensate. Think of Ray Charles and Stevie Wonder. Blind, that never stopped them from successful and creative lives as musicians. Nobel prize-winning physicist Stephen Hawking was physically incapacitated, but his Mind was clear and brilliant. So the Body does not define what we can accomplish in this life, but it does create limiting circumstances. Sometimes those limits force innovation. For example, if Stephen Hawking had been a robust man, he may never have had time to develop his Mind and make his contributions to science.

> *The Body does not define what we can accomplish in this life, but it does create limiting circumstances.*

MIND

The Mind uses the left hemisphere of the brain, which includes the tools of intellect, logic, linear thinking, analysis, discernment, judgment, and strategy. The Mind is vast and is associated with the element Air; like Air, it is invisible. We can see the effect of air as the wind moves the trees, and we can see the effect of the Mind when thoughts and intentions turn into actions.

Our Mind uses the brain to express itself, but it is not defined by, nor limited to, the brain. Our brain is like the physical computer while our Mind is the personal software. In many ways the Mind constructs our reality, building it out of our thoughts. We tend to see what we believe, and this is why understanding and having control over the Mind are so important. The Mind can stir up the Body in the way air can stir up a storm and create chaos. The Mind can also be calm like a spring breeze that brings comfort and joy. The ability to develop control of the Mind is important because if the Mind is limited, unfocused, or undisciplined, the physical environment will be disrupted. If the Mind is trained, the ability to direct, focus, and manifest visions can be a great asset in navigating the world.

The Mind, like the Body, is incarnated into a single life. At the Body's death, the physical brain ceases to function and therefore the facts and data on the computer of that Mind are erased. But the Mind does not die in the same way the Body dies. The Body is made of the Earth element, and when it dies and decays, it turns into ashes and dust. But the Mind is connected to the Air element, and when the Mind dies, its thoughts, ideas, and accomplishments scatter in the wind, like dandelion seeds that can take root and grow in the future. If the Mind is filled with higher uplifting thoughts, like love and kindness, then when it is disbursed at death, those higher molecules go out into the air and raise the mass level of consciousness. Lower thoughts like hate, greed, and envy carry a lower vibration. The level of consciousness of a person matters because any increase in a person's individual consciousness raises the mass consciousness, even after that person dies.

> *If the Mind is trained, the ability to direct, focus, and manifest visions can be a great asset.*

Associated with the Mind is what we call the Ego. Ego is tied to the singular identity of the current life and the details of day-to-day existence. The Ego typically runs the show and is who we think we are. It is the part that responds to Me, Myself, and I. The Ego programs and operates the computer of the Mind and directs where the Mind puts its intention and focus. The Ego inputs the destination in the vehicle's GPS (global positioning system) and implements the route with its hands on the wheel and its foot on the gas. The Ego, like the Mind, uses the tools of the left hemisphere to gather and process information.

Ego is focused on the here and now, and its central job is managing the safe continuation of this current life. The Ego has no interest in past lives, the evolution of the Soul, or spiritual consciousness. All those broad concepts take attention from its central task, which is survival. Once we begin to see our life, humanity, the earth and Cosmos as interconnected and unified, then our Ego, with its separated sense of identity, is threatened. *So, as we seek to expand in our Soul and Spirit and comprehend ourselves as more than a Body, the Ego resists and pushes the attention of the Mind to the daily task of living.* For this reason, it is necessary to understand the role of Ego in spiritual awakening, and how the Ego will do what it can to obstruct this awareness. The Ego is hard-wired to protect this singular current life identity. That is its job. There is no moral issue involved. Ego seeks to extend the current life and keep you safe, even if it keeps you small and isolated. The Ego is for one lifetime only, and ends with the demise of the brain and dispersal of the Mind.

By its very nature, the Mind is active and always processing. It is easily distracted. It chatters about the past or worries about things that will never happen. The Mind, when managed by the Ego, pulls you away from the present, and takes you away from your Presence. Ego and Mind work together to set the agenda, each day, hour, and minute, with thought.

> *Ego seeks to extend the current life and keep you safe, even if it keeps you small and isolated.*

Thought is an abstract concept that creates the building blocks of the world we construct around us, like Lego bricks that alone have little substance, but when put together build reality. For this reason it is necessary to be aware of the thoughts that are creating the reality around you. One needs to learn to quiet and focus the Mind, otherwise it will stay in its distracted state. If you stay lost in the active chatter of the Mind – which Buddhists call monkey mind – then the single building blocks of thought never join together to create anything of substance. It is important to understand and align with your Mind. Meditation can remove the veil of illusion and show the nature of the Mind and the role of the Ego.

The ability to focus is needed for the Mind to create something of substance. Focus is like a camera zooming in on a specific idea or object, giving it the intention and attention of your Mind. The Mind can also zoom out and use a wider focus to ponder more complex questions or to engage an idea.

I want to be clear on the distinction between brain, Mind, and Ego. The brain is a physical part of the human Body. The Mind is mental, our operating system with ideas, thoughts, and left-brain logic. The Mind is sometimes called the conscious left brain, since we have ready access to it, and to distinguish it from the unconscious right brain that is associated with Soul. The Ego is the programmer of the Mind and manager of the current physical body.

SOUL

In the same way that the driver of a limousine needs a passenger to set the intention and direct the journey, each Mind needs a director to set the intention of the Body vehicle. That director is the Soul. When we reflect on directors we often think of movies, and just as a film is the vision and responsibility of the director, our life is the vision and responsibility of our Soul. Our Soul is our very essence. It is our Soul that is taking this adventure. It is our Soul doing the great work.

Our Soul is eternal. Since it is not physical, it does not age and die like the Body. While the Body changes with each rebirth regarding its sex, size, health, and abilities, the Soul has a coherent existence. Our Soul has continuity. Our Soul is the same Soul, life after life. Our Soul is on a journey of wisdom, evolution, and illumination, and remembers the experiences and memories of all its prior lifetimes.

With each rebirth, the Soul gets a new Body and a new Mind. It downloads and stores its past life memories in the unconscious right hemisphere of the brain which operates symbolically using imagination, intuition, dreams, images, and sensations. These memories are not in the intellectual conscious left hemisphere, so our Mind and Ego have no knowledge of the existence of these prior lifetimes. Young imaginative children, before their intellect becomes dominant, can have dreams or

> *Our Soul is the same Soul, life after life, and remembers the experiences of all its prior lifetimes.*

memories of other lifetimes. There is excellent research by Dr. Ian Stevenson and Dr. Jim Tucker of the University of Virginia School of Medicine who used scientific methods to empirically investigate children's memories of past lives. But if reincarnation is not part of the child's culture, then past life memories can be dismissed or ignored by parents, so by age seven or so, children tend to no longer remember previous existences. Children become socialized as they are caught up in the expectations of school, religious upbringing, and cultural norms. Memories of Soul from previous lifetimes, that we had at a young age, are forgotten. Later on, we forget about Soul altogether. Once a person has forgotten about their Soul, it takes intention to encourage and awaken Soul memory.

It is as if the Soul is in the back seat of the limousine, separated by a glass window from Mind, which is in the front seat driving. Soul is trying to get Mind's attention by banging on the window, to then give some guidance and direction, to let Mind know where it needs to go. But Mind is not paying attention, and is either talking to a different passenger or on the phone, engaged in technology and social media. Soul sits in the back seat but has lost its ability to be heard. Soul does not get to say where it wants to go, or what it wants to do or accomplish in the life journey that Mind is now taking, programmed by Ego. Eventually with no connection to Mind and Body, Soul seems distant and disengaged.

> *Once a person has forgotten about their Soul, it takes intention to encourage and awaken Soul memory.*

For your Soul to be fully functioning in this current life, your Body and Mind both need to have awareness of it. You need to understand the Soul's reincarnation cycle and its purpose for your life. The Soul needs to be heard. This is what Consciousness is about – an awareness, both mental and emotional, of the Soul.

The Soul tries to get your attention in a variety of ways, including dreams, movies, books, music, signs of nature, synchronicity, chance encounters, prayer, meditation, nature, past life memories, and *déjà vu*. Many people are asleep to their Soul; they think they are only a Body and Mind and forget about the bigger and deeper part of life, which becomes a distant voice.

To know your Soul's history you need to be open to the depths of your intuitive unconscious right brain and bring prior lives up and out into the light of conscious intellect. In doing so, you bridge the right and left hemispheres of the brain, sharing with the Mind these past memories held in the unconscious, and giving Mind a larger perspective of life. These are important steps in the development of Consciousness. *Consciousness is a state that occurs when Soul and Mind are aligned in harmony and Mind is no longer managed by Ego, but rather directed by Soul and radiant with Spirit.*

Soul is associated with the element Water. The Body is like a sponge and the Soul is the water that is absorbed and permeates the entire system, physical and mental. Like water, it binds with the Body in the same way that rivers, lakes, and oceans are connected to earth. The Soul and the Body are interwoven and embedded. The Soul isn't intellectual like the Mind, but communicates through vibration and resonance, symbols, imagination, and feeling. It is the part of us that is intuitive, linked to the unconscious, with hidden depths and deep compassion. The Soul uses the physical heart to express its feelings and emotions, thus the Soul is often identified with the heart, but it is neither defined by nor limited to the heart.

> *Your Soul needs to be returned to its position as the director, conductor, and navigator of this life journey.*

The Soul learns and grows in each of its incarnations, and holds emotional memory from all of its previous lifetimes in the right unconscious hemisphere of the brain. Your Soul needs to be returned to its position as the director, conductor, and navigator of this life journey. This is the central reason I am writing this book. Our Souls are not being heard, and the Body vehicle and Mind/Ego driver are in control of this current life. We must awaken to the existence of our Soul so that we can participate in the journey that really matters.

SPIRIT

Spirit is the energy, spark of lifeforce, and divinity in you. It is the Divine, no matter what name you give: whether God, Goddess, Allah, Shiva, Christ, Universe, Source, or other. Hindus say there are over 1000 names for the Divine. Spirit is the core of all faiths and a powerful and everlasting force that religions have tried for millennia to explain.

Spirit means "breath" and is the invisible source of everything alive. Religion means "to bind" and provides structure for this invisible spiritual essence of life. Religion is not the essence itself but is instead the container for the essence, like a bottle that holds perfume. There is much that is good in organized religions. They can provide a community of shared values and a framework for spiritual beliefs, as well as comfort in the present and hope for the future.

Spirit also exists outside of organized religions and is the Sacred, ethical source that permeates many belief systems, philosophies, and indigenous spiritual traditions. Spirit provides a moral and ethical center to help guide people toward right action.

There is a spiritual/sacred/magical world. Choose your word – metaphysical, multidimensional, quantum, fairy, shamanic. It doesn't matter since they all seek to explain an invisible world. I was going to write "unknown world," but it used to be known. People are forgetting about other species and races, never mind other dimensions. I want to remind us that this sacred world exists, and it is real, and it can be experienced outside of religious boundaries.

> *This sacred world exists, and it is real, and it can be experienced outside of religious boundaries.*

Religion has an important role in helping us understand the presence of Spirit in our lives. But in recent times and for a variety of reasons, interest in religion is declining. The proportion of Americans who consider themselves members of a church, synagogue, or mosque has dropped below 50 percent, and in the UK, more than 70 percent of those under age 30 are religiously unaffiliated. The data may suggest that religion and belief in the sacred are becoming obsolete. But people are not abandoning religion; they are reinventing it to suit their own lifestyles, becoming "spiritual but not religious." Spirit will always exist. But when religion no longer provides the doctrines, rituals, and structures we need to find new ways to provide it so we do not forget about this sacred world.

Spirit is the element Fire. It is the spark that gives us life. Spirit is the fire of energy and fuel for living. You can feel Spirit in your flow of power, unconditional love, enthusiasm, and joy. The word *enthusiasm* means "filled with Spirit." When you are connected to Spirit you feel the energy within you. When you are not connected to Spirit you might feel like you have no passion or purpose. We are alive because of Spirit. When the Body ceases to function, either due to illness or sudden injury, and is no longer animated by Spirit, the Body dies.

But Spirit never dies. Spirit exists in all things, not just humans. Spirit is the divine life energy in all creatures on earth and can be sensed in even the smallest bird, deepest ocean, or tallest mountain. The existence and recognition of Spirit in nature, called Animism, is a reason certain places are considered sacred sites and can be powerful centers of energy.

Your Soul is your very own connection to the Sacred and spiritual source of all things. The ancient Hawaiian mysticism *Kahuna* explains that our link to Spirit is made through the unconscious/right brain, the same right brain through which the Soul communicates. This is because our Spirit speaks the same symbolic language as the Soul. This language of symbolism is found in ritual, prayer, signs of nature, synchronicities, the realm of the unconscious, dreams, shamanic journey, and other types of trance such as dance or drumming, and symbol systems such as Astrology and Tarot. Soul can speak to Spirit, and Spirit can speak to Soul. Creating a relationship to your Soul gives you a more direct relationship to the spiritual world which you might refer to as your High Self, Wise Self, Guardian Angel, or Ancestral Spirit.

How Body, Mind, Soul, and Spirit Work Together

Spirit is the teacher, Soul is the student, your current Body and Mind are the schoolroom, and life provides the lessons.

The Soul is the evolutionary student who is reborn to experience and grow through multiple lifetimes. The Soul sees each lifetime from its own personal and unique perspective. In other words, the Soul may be immortal, but it is not necessarily wise. It is like the student who begins in kindergarten and, through time and effort, progresses from elementary to middle school and on to college. Sometimes it seems easy, sometimes difficult, sometimes like starting all over; some despair, some hope. But the Soul has a *telos*, an end purpose, which is to evolve in awareness and wisdom, and to illuminate the life journey of the human it currently is. The more times a Soul is reincarnated, the more life lessons it experiences, the more growth is possible, the more it evolves and gains awareness and an increase in consciousness. It is your Spirit that provides the higher, more divine and sacred connection to existence. It is Spirit that fuels the desire for expansion and growth and brings the magic of life. So engaging Spirit's energy, perspective, and sacred sense into each lifetime through a Soul connection enriches that lifetime tremendously.

The aim is to have the four aspects of Body, Mind, Soul, and Spirit aligned and harmoniously acting as one unit. Soul is the unconscious right brain, intuition, love, and compassion. Mind is the conscious left brain, the logical, decisive, discerning, code maker, and code breaker. When Soul and Mind are working together in the Body, joined by Spirit, they create increased Consciousness. Consciousness is experienced as a more expansive Mind, a more energetic Body, a more loving and wise Soul, and a closer connection to Spirit. Consciousness is Illumination, the light of awareness that brings clarity to our thoughts, actions, relationships, psychology, and all of life. Mind and Body are your humanity. Soul and Spirit are your divinity. When all four work together you are a Celestial Human, one who is connected to both heaven and earth. This is the *telos* of the Soul. It is the goal to which our Soul aspires.

> *Mind and Body are your humanity. Soul and Spirit are your divinity.*

The Purpose of Reincarnation

In each new lifetime you have a Body vehicle. Soul is sitting in the back seat ready to direct the journey, Mind and Ego are working the computer system, ready to drive, and Spirit is filling the tank with energy and life force. The question then becomes: *Why am I here?* This is one of the most basic and profound things asked in philosophy and religion as well as each morning when waking from a night's sleep. *Why am I here? What am I to do? What difference do I make?*

Who we are as human beings, and the meaning of our current lifetime, is far bigger in scope than our limited awareness and expectations. You might wonder if this were true, why aren't you aware of it? This is because you were born as a tiny baby with limited mental and physical functions. As a squalling infant, dependent on those around you, you learned the expectations of your family, village, and culture in the same way you learned how to walk. It was all just taken for granted, step by step, as you grew to be the person your culture expects, even demands, you to be. If you go outside the perimeters of your culture, you could be shunned, or worse, killed. So you learned very early how you were supposed to act. Even the language of the culture determined your limitation. For how could you yearn for something that has no word to describe it, or understand a concept that has no articulation?

There is a word in the English language that describes this programming well – *socialization*. It is a process of conditioning that occurs as we move from home, to school, to house of worship, to job. We learn and follow the rules each step of the way. If our family members are farmers, we will likely be a farmer; if our family is Catholic, we will likely be Catholic. If our family goes to college, we will likely go to college. If we are born poor in the desert of Africa, we will likely die poor in the desert of Africa.

If we only see the world from the smaller perspective of the mouse, we will never see further than what is right before us.

If this is starting to sound bleak, as if there is no escape from the fate of our births, it is not true. There is escape, but it comes through an increase in knowledge and Consciousness, which comes with knowing the Soul.

As we grow in Consciousness, it is as if our perspective expands from that of an earth-bound mouse, focusing on the small details of life, to a free-flying hawk who sees the larger reality. Both perspectives are necessary and good. A small mouse sees only what is right in front of it, as day to day it works for the most basic needs like food and shelter. The mouse's perspective is essential and necessary as we build the foundations of life on earth.

But we can also have a broader outlook, like a hawk, where our perspective is higher and our vision is wider. Being able to see further with the eyes of a hawk brings new awareness and understanding of the broader circumstances of life, which helps us decide what to do and how to do it. Expanding our vision and our point of view will be beneficial in understanding life. Yet it does not guarantee that all choices will go well. Nor does it guarantee enlightenment. Nonetheless, if we only see the world from the smaller perspective of the mouse, we will never see further than what is right before us.

Some people don't want to see further; they don't want to expand their options. They want to keep their reality small because they find the larger world and broader ideas threatening. There are good reasons for wanting to keep life simple. It is a survival technique, even a necessary breather after a previous lifetime that left the Soul exhausted. I have witnessed this myself. For example, in this current life I call myself a Seeker, and I am curious, educated, experienced; I have lived in many different environments, and explored many countries around the world. But what I learned from my past-life memories is that I have had other lifetimes where I wanted nothing more than to rise with the Sun and search the desert for healing herbs. And I did that every day in perfect contentment.

Each lifetime is different and each has its purpose.

The point is: Each lifetime is different and each has its purpose. When we realize this, when we expand to take in the whole trajectory of our Soul over many lifetimes, we can learn to appreciate the life we are currently living and find a way to embrace it. Many of our lifetimes are a simple existence, where the entire focus might be to love one single person, or to understand the cycles of the seasons by working with the land. But when we expand our vision and see our life as a single chapter – and not an entire book – we can relax into and appreciate that the simple pleasure of a less complex life is a choice, not a limitation.

Reincarnation also expands the sense of what it means to love. When seen from the perspective of any single lifetime, love feels personal. I love my house, children, and husband, and when the Body dies (either mine or theirs), then the things I love are taken from me. It is difficult to grow in love if we believe it is only attached to a single lifetime. Personal love is beautiful and we learn much from it, but it can also turn into jealousy, hate, greed, and lust. We are wounded, if only because personal love ends at death. In reincarnation we discover that the important people in this life may be part of our Soul group and that we have experienced many lives together, supporting and loving each other over many rebirths. It is a love that lasts lifetimes and we may well see our loved ones again after death.

There is also universal love that extends from lifetime to lifetime – love for humanity, animals, nature, environment, water, peace, health, the sacred, service, compassionate action, and justice. This broad and interconnected love is known as oneness, the interconnectedness of all things. Part of what the Soul is learning in its journey from lifetime to lifetime is a love that includes much more than an individual person at any particular place and time.

In addition to personal and universal love, there is also self-love. By expanding our sense of self to include the Soul, we gain a larger perspective and greater compassion on our life journey. It is unfortunate, but often as we grow up we learn to be very self-critical, to the point that our Mind and Ego tell us negative things about ourselves, like we are not any good, have no talent, or can't do anything right. These messages often start in childhood as a result of our upbringing and are repeated

In reincarnation we discover a love that lasts lifetimes.

countless times through our lifetimes. When a message or belief recurs consistently, it turns the neural pathways in the brain into a superhighway where these thoughts navigate easily and quickly until they become habitual. We need to learn to identify the negative messages we give ourselves and replace them with feelings and messages of love and compassion.

The concept of reincarnation demonstrates that all of life is interconnected. What we do today influences our future lifetimes through cause and effect, known as karma. Karma impacts our future lifetimes on this planet. For example, if we pollute the rivers today, we might think we will not be here to experience the effects of that action, but in fact we will be here in another lifetime in another Body to experience the consequences of that act. And in reverse, if we clean the rivers or we protest the destruction of wildlife, that action has consequences, one of which is an increase in Consciousness. As Consciousness increases in the individual, it carries forward to the next life so that the individual is reborn with greater awareness.

Opening to the possibility of reincarnation expands our notion of love, time, and space, and gives our Souls plenty of opportunity to learn and evolve. We live beyond this current time. We live beyond this current physical space. What we learn continues to grow beyond our death, so learning has no endpoint. We cannot say, "Oh, I am 80 years old and can no longer use this knowledge, so why bother to learn or do anything new?" Whatever we do in this life continues into the next... like planting seeds now that will grow in future lives. Emotional issues also continue forward as patterns into future incarnations, so healing destructive emotions, like envy or hate, even in the final hours of the Body's physical existence, has value.

Whatever we do in this life continues into the next... like planting seeds now that will grow in future lives.

You are off on a grand adventure. Of experiences and learning. Of loving and sacrificing. Of joy and suffering. The journey is not pre-destined, the map is not set, and the decision of what roads to take and what places await you is not fixed. You have full power over your decisions, based on a combination of your Soul's memory, the state of your Body, the clarity of your Mind, your connection to Spirit, and your level of Consciousness. The more awareness you bring to the journey, the more important and meaningful your trip. Every life adventure has ups and downs, successes and failures. But as long as you start the process and are willing to learn from experience, you grow and evolve.

14

Living an Illuminated Life: The Power and Purpose of Knowing Your Soul's Past Lives

I hope for you that reading my Soul's journey has made you curious about your own Soul and your own journey. I hope you discovered that you are much bigger than you realize, with a much longer trajectory and more extensive history. But now, what is the next step? How do you draw upon this knowledge to guide you in making choices in this life? How can knowing about your past lives affect your present purpose?

People often ask how knowing the Soul and its past lives can change you. From knowing my Soul's journey, I realize that the goal of a reincarnation isn't spiritual perfection or Enlightenment. I previously thought that if I worked the spiritual path long enough that eventually I would get that flash of awareness called Enlightenment. I would wake up and immediately see the world differently, be all-knowing and wise, calm and compassionate, an Enlightened Being. I knew of Enlightened Beings, like the Dalai Lama, so I knew Enlightenment was possible and considered it a reasonable goal. Well, I waited and waited and waited, and it still hasn't happened. I have had moments, even days of awe, bliss, total spiritual surrender, and connection to all things. Then the next day I would be just the same Lilan as the days before, with a bit more Spirit in my tank, but still dealing with the everyday issues that we all have.

I finally understood that Enlightenment is possible, but not probable. Even though we have a celestial Soul and divine Spirit, we are, after all, Human, and that comes with certain emotional, physical, and mental tendencies, and perfection is not among them. This is why so many spiritually-oriented people struggle. We desire the perfection of a spiritual Source, and long to live in its radiance and share it with a world that desperately needs it. Yet it always seems a bit out of reach. Instead of the light of Enlightenment and the bliss of sacred Source, we feel the challenges of just trying to make ends meet, taking care of the people we love, and finding a way to help heal the world even just a little.

I realized that rather than being Enlightened, I am Illuminated. In creating a relationship with my Soul, I did become radiant with the power of Spirit and warmed by my interior source. Just not all the time. Being Illuminated is like having a dimmer switch on a light. The light is not just on or off; it has many variations. It can be just a little bit on, fully on, or somewhere in between. And it constantly changes. I realize that I am always connected to the light of divinity, but sometimes I shine brightly and other times I am in the dark.

One way to understand this is to think of Enlightenment as the Sun, a constant fiery source of life that is always shining brightly, like Spirit. Illumination, however, is the Moon. The Moon has no light of its own but acts as a mirror to reflect the light of the Sun-Spirit. The amount of light reflected changes daily based on the Moon's relationship to the Sun. The New Moon reflects just a sliver of light, the waxing crescent becomes even brighter, the waxing first quarter Moon shines even more, and the Full Moon is exquisite in its radiance. Then the Full Moon begins to wane and lose its glorious light, becoming finally the dark of the Moon, those days just before a New Moon when it is invisible and unseen.

We are like the Moon. We sometimes shine so brightly that we are like the Full Moon. Other times our light is unseen, like the dark of the Moon, which could be due to illness, sadness, overwork, family troubles, or the death of a loved one. Most times we are somewhere in between – a quarter Moon, where our light is clearly visible, bringing insight and awareness to daily living and touching those in our lives.

Once you understand yourself as Illuminated, you can accept that your essential light is always there, like the Sun's, but that sometimes you are mirroring that light fully and sometimes you are in the dark. All these phases are beautiful, even necessary, as we learn our lessons and grow in Consciousness.

Loving yourself in all your phases, from the radiant to the dark, is part of the gift of knowing your Soul. You understand that you are living this lifetime to learn and evolve, and that includes some successes and some failures, some bright days and some dark ones. Embracing the constantly changing phases of your life is what occurs when you are Illuminated. When you see yourself more clearly, you learn that the gift of Illumination is to appreciate life each and every day, where your own radiance waxes and wanes like the Moon, never the same, but always present and in perfect rhythm.

As the Moon changes all the time, so do you. You have moments of clarity, moments of enlightenment, and those moments can stretch into hours, days, months, even years. But when the light gets dim again, it is all right. Know that even though you are now in the dark and can't see clearly, you once did, and you will again. Remember, you are awake, you are Illuminated. You have Illuminated your life journey.

A benefit of Illumination is that it takes the pressure off. The focus becomes more on how you live each day. It takes into consideration that we humans struggle with insecurities, including how to feed ourselves and our family and how to find love. We are imperfect; it's our very nature. Illumination builds imperfection into the mix. Some days you are on, some days you are off, some days you are shining lightly, some days you are shining brightly. It's a dimmer switch for the Soul.

You can learn to cultivate Illumination by paying attention to the circumstances when the dimmer switch turns bright and clear or becomes dark and murky. Maybe it was bright when you were in nature, running at dawn, in meditation, playing with your dog, waking up in a dream, or dancing. And maybe it was dark when you were paying the bills, lonely, or fighting with your children. Whatever it is, you start to notice so that you can develop a life journey which has more Illumination.

With Illumination you can enjoy whatever level of brightness you currently inhabit. There is a Mindfulness about accepting yourself as you are, and not comparing yourself to an ideal that seems unattainable. When I arrive at the pearly gates and God wants to know how I did in this lifetime, I can tell her that I averaged 75 watts and feel good about it.

In addition to Illumination, knowing the past lives of your Soul can create a multi-dimensional depth in you where nothing is on the surface. Your decisions and actions have complexity, like a multi-layered cake with a lot of ingredients. It might not be anything anyone else sees, but you can feel it. Most people are oblivious to the multiple dimensions in their lives, but you begin to sense bigger issues at play – the issues of your Soul evolution, of the world's trajectory, of the challenges of history, of the spiritual nature of the world, and the intersection between sacred and profane.

Knowing your Soul can deepen your appreciation of the simple things in life and living fully in the present moment. Often after a past life of conflict or despair one needs a life that is restful, where things are less complicated and Soul gets a chance to recuperate. Perhaps an entire life aims to teach a single lesson, for example, living every day searching for herbs in the woods. Those resting lives are necessary in our overall evolution and need to be honored for the lessons they give.

You can become better able to sense your triggers. A trigger occurs when something in your current life stirs up an unresolved emotion or karmic pattern from a past life (or past experience in the current life) that is still active in your Soul. When triggered, it is easy to overreact because you are responding with the same unresolved emotion of the past. Being aware of triggers from the past can keep you from overreacting in the present.

Likewise, you can become more aware of projection, which occurs when feelings of an unresolved emotion is projected on someone else. For example, if the pattern of being betrayed gets triggered, it will likely be projected onto the person or event that triggered it. So a simple event like a friend forgetting to meet for dinner gets blown out of proportion to the point where it feels like the person is unreliable and can't be trusted.

You can become better able to let go of old emotional blocks or misconceptions. For instance, my belief that I was responsible for the fall of Atlantis led me to carry a sense of unworthiness through many lifetimes. Now when thoughts of unworthiness or guilt arise, I can acknowledge that I have been triggered and that a soul wound has been reopened. This leads to more self-compassion and can redirect your attention to being more present in the here and now.

You may see an increase in Consciousness that occurs as you become aware of your integrated self, which combines Body, Mind, Spirit, and Soul. It leads to more faith in the Universe and greater trust of inner guidance.

You may also see a more objective appreciation for your Body, which is the vehicle for the Soul and the circumstances of this life. For me, being born healthy in the United States to a solid and stable family is a real gift to be acknowledged each day with gratitude. An objective appreciation can also bring you greater patience and compassion for the challenges of this particular life, which can be unpredictable. At some point you may have been a different gender, race, and physical ability, so it makes you more understanding and accepting of people who may be different.

Remembering your past lives also brings a clear understanding that this life is short and that it ends in death. The manner of your death makes a difference in the next incarnation, and recalling that can reduce the fear of death and bring more awareness to the dying process. This does not mean that I do not have sadness at the thought that this life will end. This has been a very good life and I will miss it. But each physical life ends eventually, and there is an acceptance in that truth and more appreciation of each day.

You can gain the ability to talk to Soul and let it guide you in many ways. You may also begin to sense Soul in others, including nature beings like trees and birds. Since it is through Soul that one aligns to the wisdom of Spirit, you can strengthen your spiritual connection and realize that you live in a sacred magical world.

You can become aware that what your Soul might need is different from what your Mind or Body needs. For example, maybe Mind wants to spend the weekend engaged at an academic conference, while Soul wants to be in silence near water. You might be able to compromise by going to a conference that is at a peaceful place close to water.

You can recognize the people who are probably Allies and part of your Soul Pod, who are in your life so you can assist each other. You also learn to recognize those who could be Adversaries. If I have dealings with an Adversary, I work to clear up the negative karma between us and set us both free, so I never have to meet that person in another lifetime.

You can tap into the gifts and mastery that you have developed in other lives and use them with confidence. For example, I am an Astrologer in this life, which is fed by my skills as a sky watcher in previous lifetimes.

In learning of your Soul's past lives and gaining insight into its evolutionary journey, you can become aware of your longer history and the important lessons learned so you can better recognize your present purpose in this lifetime. Each of our Souls has a unique purpose for this Body at this time and place. This purpose becomes clearer the more you know and align to your Soul.

You may realize that you are a Celestial Human, both of the earth and of the heavens. The purpose of the Soul's evolutionary journey is to become Human. Human Beings are among the most complex, sophisticated life forms on planet earth. Yet the irony is that as Souls are learning to be Human, Humans are separating from their natural humanity and becoming robots of technology. It is said that on average, Humans spend only 9 minutes a day in nature compared to 9 hours a day on technology. These are challenging times. This very beautiful planet, teeming with diversity of life and our only home in the wide galaxy, is in danger. If we think of ourselves only as earthly humans, then our vision has blinders on it and our focus goes no further than our limited physical reality. But by expanding the notion of who we are – that we are Celestial Humans, part star-being and part terrestrial, living on a small planet that is hurtling through space – then we can take our roles and actions more seriously.

I believe that it is absolutely necessary for there to be an increase in Consciousness in order for us humans to make the changes necessary to protect our world. We need to raise our awareness to include our Souls, knowing that we are bigger than this single Body, larger than this single life. By raising our individual Consciousness to include the Soul, we raise the Consciousness of the world. In this context, connection to one's Soul could be the act that saves humanity from its own destruction. We need harmony in the world, and it begins through harmony within ourselves.

I understand that I am a physical Body, that has a Mind/Ego, is filled with Soul, and is energized by Spirit. I realize how important it is to keep these four aspects in alignment and to live each day in connection. Below I share a practice of Alignment.

Alignment of Body, Mind, Soul, and Spirit

As shared earlier, we are a combination of four parts: Body, Mind, Soul, and Spirit. To live a Soulful and Magical life it is necessary to keep these four parts interconnected and working together. One way to do that is by daily Alignment. I will share a practice that is short and simple. You can create Alignment based on your own inspiration and beliefs.

You can do your Alignment while standing, sitting, or lying down. It is good to experiment to see what posture feels strongest to you. A good way to remember to align is to connect it to something you already do. For example, I align after my morning yoga. Since I end my yoga session laying down, that is my most frequent position. Maybe you do a meditation, so you can align in crossed leg posture, or you might choose to sit against a tree after your evening walk. Let's begin.

Settle into your posture by taking a few deep breaths. Breathe in through your nose, deep into your belly, and let your breath sigh out of your mouth until you feel settled and calm.

Using your breath to focus your intention, take a deep breath, and as you breathe out, say either out loud or inwardly while focusing on your Body: *I am my Body, the physical vehicle for this Earth journey. I am grateful for this Body.*

Take a second breath, and as you breathe out, focus on your head and say: *I am my Mind, which is invisible like the wind, but connects to my brain through the thoughts and ideas that create my life. I am grateful for this Mind.*

Take a third breath, and as you breathe out, focus on your heart and say: *I am my Soul, which permeates my entire Body with love and emotion. I am grateful for this Soul.*

Take a fourth breath, and as you breathe out, focus on the heavens above you vertically and say: *I am Spirit, the energetic force of Life which connects me to the sacred in all things. I am grateful for Spirit.*

Take a fifth breath, and as you breathe out, imagine the radiating space circling you horizontally say: *I connect to the World in which I live as fully aligned in Body, Mind, Soul, and Spirit. I engage in the world as balanced and in harmony.*

Stay in this interconnected and aligned space, breathing deeply for as long as you like. If you want, you can add a particular intention for the day, for example: "In my job interview, I feel my presence fully and express with confidence." Or "My creative projects are filled with Spirit and easily radiate into the world."

Use this process as the basis for whatever meaningful and imaginative Alignment you create. Breath is an essential part of connecting and focus, but you might also do your Alignment in your garden with your hands in the earth, or at night as you go to bed. Do what feels right to you.

You can choose to be Illuminated… to love the dimmer switch and enjoy all the levels of light and the always changing world around you. Some days you are off, and some days you are on, but you are always connected to the radiance of Spirit and Soul.

Illuminate!

Wake up to the realization that

You are not just the bee, you are the hive.

You are not just a fish, you are the sea.

You are not just a tree, you are the forest.

You are not just the Sun, you are the Moon.

You are not just the planet, you are the Solar System.

You are not just the Body, you are the Soul.

You don't live just once, you live many times.

Thank you for sharing this journey with me. I hope it brightens and expands your reality.

Other Books by Lilan Laishley

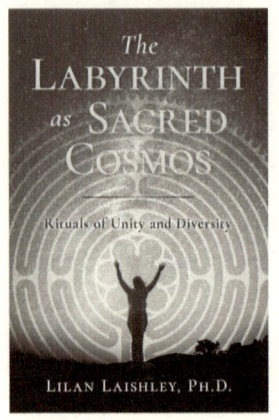

Join the millions who have been captivated by the mystery and beauty of this 4000-year-old geometric form. As we walk, pray, meditate, and participate in rituals on the labyrinth's winding circular path, it guides us with certainty into the center. Labyrinths bring together people from a broad variety of spiritual pursuits, providing an excellent window through which to view the growing trend of religious diversity. With wonderful images of labyrinths from around the world, we uncover the labyrinth's ancient history and contemporary uses to discover the importance of ritual as a means to engaging with a Sacred Cosmos.

www.ingramcontent.com/pod-product-compliance
Lightning Source LLC
Chambersburg PA
CBHW060557080526
44585CB00013B/601